Chickamauga, Andersonville, Fort Sumter
and Guard Duty at Home

ALSO BY ROBERT P. BROADWATER

The Battle of Perryville, 1862:
Culmination of the Failed Kentucky Campaign
(McFarland, 2005)

Chickamauga, Andersonville, Fort Sumter and Guard Duty at Home

Four Civil War Diaries by Pennsylvania Soldiers

Edited by ROBERT P. BROADWATER

McFarland & Company, Inc., Publishers
Jefferson, North Carolina, and London

Library of Congress Cataloguing-in-Publication Data

Chickamauga, Andersonville, Fort Sumter and guard duty at home :
   four Civil War diaries by Pennsylvania soldiers / edited by
   Robert P. Broadwater.
         p.   cm.
   Includes bibliographical references and index.

   ISBN 0-7864-2221-1 (softcover : 50# alkaline paper)

      1. United States— History — Civil War, 1861–1865 —
Personal narratives.   2. Pennsylvania — History — Civil War,
1861–1865 — Personal narratives.   3. Soldiers— Pennsylvania —
Diaries.   4. Soldiers— United States— Diaries.
5. United States— History — Civil War, 1861–1865 — Campaigns.
6. United States— History — Civil War, 1861–1865 — Regimental
histories.   7. Pennsylvania — History — Civil War, 1861–1865 —
Regimental histories.   8. United States. Army — Military life —
History —19th century.   9. United States— History — Civil War,
1861–1865 — Social aspects.   I. Broadwater, Robert P., 1958–
   E464.C4   2006
   973.7'4480922 — dc22   2005031452

British Library cataloguing data are available

On the cover: *top* Union troops at Hilton Head; *bottom* Union
troops in the trenches at Petersburg (*U.S. Army War College*)

Manufactured in the United States of America

McFarland & Company, Inc., Publishers
   Box 611, Jefferson, North Carolina 28640
      www.mcfarlandpub.com

To my parents,
Paul and Carolyn Broadwater,
with love, gratitude, and respect

Acknowledgments

I would like to gratefully acknowledge the kind assistance of the following people in helping to make possible the writing of this book: The research staff of the National Archives, the staff of the Huntingdon County Courthouse, the staff of the Somerset County Courthouse, the staff of the Indiana County Courthouse, the staff of the Blair County Geneological Society, and the staff of the Inter-Library Loan Department of the Altoona Public Library.

Special thanks to Mary Cherry Brunner, without whose material assistance the creation of this book would not have been possible. Her kindness has been warmly received and is greatly appreciated.

Special thanks also to Jamie Truitt and the Indiana County Historical Society for kind assistance in helping me track down which of the several William Duncans was the one who belonged to the Second Pennsylvania Militia Battalion.

Table of Contents

Preface

While it is true that all soldiers who fought in the Civil War, North and South, shared a comrade's bond as those who had together experienced danger, privations, and hardships, it is also true that no two experiences were exactly alike. The differences arise even among soldiers who fought in the same battles. The average private in the ranks sees only the part of a battle that is taking place in his immediate front and has no conception of what is transpiring on other portions of the field. For example, Union and Confederate troops who fought on Culp's Hill have very different reminiscences than those who struggled in the Wheat Field and Peach Orchard, even though they were all veterans of Gettysburg. It is the purpose of this work to show the nature of these differences by following the war experiences of four southern Pennsylvania men who joined different regiments in the Union Army. All four were patriotic, anxious to do their duty for their country, and anxious to uphold the cause in which they believed. Each man fulfilled his obligation to honor, but the paths their services took contrasted with one another to such an extent that they all could well have been serving in different wars. Through their diaries, we can follow their army careers and view, through their eyes, the particular portion of the war in which they fought.

All four men were from the same general area, south-central Pennsylvania, but only two were enlisted in Pennsylvania regiments. One served with the western army, fought in every major engagement that took place in that theater, and attained the rank of lieutenant. Another enlisted in a ninety-day militia unit and spent his entire term of service doing guard duty, never firing his musket in action. A third acted in the role of the modern-day marines as he took part in the combined army/navy operations at Charleston, South Carolina. The fourth served with the Army of the Potomac. He had already served a three-year enlistment with an infantry regiment and had enlisted for another tour of duty with the cavalry when he was captured and spent the remainder of his war service at Andersonville Prison.

Lieutenant William Glisan observed in a diary entry that although the fighting had been costly and the price was high, he believed that the course the army was taking was "the right road to glory." In truth, the service performed by every soldier in the war was the right road to glory. It was all an important part of an overall campaign, and each man performed his own particular service and fought his own individual war. They shared convictions, hardships and boredom — and the Pennsylvanians shared in the final victory, but they each had memories that were shared only by the comrades in their own units and by the enemies they faced, not by one another.

This book will follow these four men through their experience of war. The reader will see that for all soldiers, army life was typified by long periods of camp boredom broken by short periods of terror and strife. Whether he served in Maryland or in South Carolina, the average soldier was constantly looking to improve his harsh lot and to increase his creature comforts. Clothes, food, and shelter were a constant concern to Civil War soldiers and, in this, all four men shared a soldier's lot as they sought to provide for their basic needs as best they could. As with soldiers on both sides, all four were homesick for the families they left behind, and news from home served as a link to the civilian lives they had forfeited. A letter from a friend or family member was a treasure to be read over and over again, the thoughts and salutations of loved ones providing both comfort and resolve.

Readers will follow William R. Glisan and John M. Kelly as they face the perils of battle and come face to face with the foe in armed combat. They will also read of Will Duncan and his comrades, who performed guard duty along two major lines of communication and supply, while disease took a toll of human life almost equal to that of a battlefield. Last, readers will be introduced to the horrors of Andersonville Prison, through the diary of George Schmittle. Andersonville was a place where starvation, sickness, and exposure were enemies more to be feared than any encountered on a battlefield.

A sense of duty motivated each of these men, young and old, and each performed his duty honorably, in a manner that brought credit not only to themselves but to the generation of which they were a part. In each case, this sense of duty was satisfied in clearly individual ways, but it was satisfied for all, nonetheless.

Wars are fought by armies, but armies are made up of individual men. In the following pages, readers will learn of the private war each of these four men fought. We will see it through their eyes, as they recorded the experience in diaries and journals. It is a personal glimpse at the Civil War that readers can't get in any other way, tagging along with these four soldiers who were all on the right road to glory, though different roads all.

I hope that readers will enjoy *Chickamauga, Andersonville, Fort Sumter and Guard Duty at Home* and that it may give them a fuller understanding of what it meant to be a soldier in the Civil War. Although this book deals with four Union volunteers, the same correlations could be made for soldiers fighting for the Confederacy. Indeed, garrison troops in Charleston would have more in common with John Kelly and the members of the Thirty-ninth Illinois than those Union troops had with the members of the Second Pennsylvania Militia. Confederates who faced the Sixth Ohio at Chickamauga and Chattanooga shared a closer bond of brotherhood with them than Glisan or his comrades shared with George Schmittle or the other members of the Thirteenth Pennsylvania Cavalry who were captured and sent to Andersonville. One reason the old vets made such a point to visit their former foes at battlefield reunions was that other than the comrades in their own unit, the enemies they faced were the only ones who could truly understand their own personal memories of the war. As such, they often shared more in common with their former enemies than they did with other members of their own army. In many ways, the reminiscences of enemies on a battlefield are two parts of a whole. No comrades in a soldier's own army can relate to those memories, only the soldier who experienced them and the foe he faced.

As much as possible, the diaries and reminiscences have been reproduced here in their original forms. Spelling errors are included as written. The use or nonuse of capitalization in the entries is also true to the original texts. Where given names are misspelled, they have been noted, and the correct names given. Every effort has also been made to present these recollections to the reader in a format that is as close to reading the actual diaries as possible. Commentary has been inserted in *italics* to give the reader a better grasp of the overall situation in battles and campaigns and to provide background information for many of the soldiers' entries. However, the inclusion of such commentary appears only when necessary, to provide needed information or to give flow to the writings, so that the reader may, as much as possible, evaluate the experiences of these men from their own words and writing.

A capsule regimental history as well as a company roster for the company that each of the men served in has been included at the end of each section. Wherever possible, individual notations have been made for the men contained in the rosters. They have been reproduced, as originally written, which accounts for the somewhat loose nature of the alphabetizing. It was a common practice in the nineteenth century to group names together according to the first letter of the last name, but that was usually as far as putting things in alphabetical order went.

One

Lieutenant William R. Glisan,
Sixth Ohio Volunteer Infantry

The Sixth Ohio Infantry was one of the early war regiments that answered President Lincoln's first call for seventy-five thousand volunteers to put down the rebellion. The regiment had its roots in a prewar militia unit known as the Guthrie Guards, and the Guards were combined with other volunteer companies and mustered into Federal service as the Sixth Ohio Volunteer Infantry on April 29, 1861, just a little more than two weeks after the firing on Fort Sumter.[1]

The regiment was sent east as soon as it was mustered and became part of General George B. McClellan's army that was operating in the mountainous region of western Virginia. It took part in the battles of Rich Mountain, Carrick's Ford, and Carnifex Ferry before being transferred back to the west in December of 1861. From that time till the end of the war, the regiment took part in every major engagement of the Western Theater. By the time Lieutenant Glisan started keeping the journal that follows, the Sixth Ohio had already taken part in the battle of Shiloh, the Corinth Campaign, Perryville, Stones River and the Allatoona Campaign. It was already a bloodied, veteran regiment with more than two years of service by the time Lieutenant Glisan's diary entries begin, just before the battle of Chickamauga.

William Glisan was a twenty-four-year-old farmer from Somerset County, Pennsylvania. He was described as being 5 feet 6 inches tall, having a light complexion, and having dark hair and eyes. Glisan enlisted in Company D, Sixth Ohio, for three years of service, at Camp Harrison, Ohio, on June 17, 1861. He was promoted to sergeant in December of that same year and received a commission as second lieutenant in April of 1863,

serving first with his own company before being detached to assume com-
mand of Company A. He was already a proven veteran, having survived
the engagements at Shiloh, Corinth, Perryville, and Stones River, before
he began keeping the diary that follows.²

AUGUST 15TH 1863:
    From the 5th to this date we were laying in camp. Nothing occurred
outside of the Regular Routine of Camp life worthy of note.

SUNDAY AUG. 16TH 1863:
    Left camp at Manchester at 9 A.M. and rushed out on the war path
again takeing the Altamont Road. About noon we was visited by one of
the most terriffic thunder storms I ever witnessed. Marched fourteen miles
and camped on Hickory Creek in a beautiful valley.

MONDAY 17TH 1863:
    I did not sleep much last night. Our train did not get up so I had no
blankets. I had to make my bed on the wet ground with no covering but
my shelter tent. Marched at 9 A.M. Moved fourteen miles and camped on
Rock River, day very warm, men fell out of the ranks by scores.

TUESDAY AUG. 18TH:
    Sleep better last night. I had a good soft bed made of two rails.
Marched at 6½ A.M. Country mountainous. Day extremely warm. Made
seven miles and camped at 3 P.M. on the top of the mountain. Our train
is still behind. If it don't get up tonight we will have to stop eating. Our
rations have run out. Officer of the picket tonight.

    A Confederate raid on the Union wagon train had destroyed several
    hundred wagons loaded with provisions for the army. The raiders, mem-
    bers of General Nathan Bedford Forrest's cavalry, had also damaged the
    railroad between Stevenson and Nashville, creating a severe supply prob-
    lem in Rosecrans's army. Under these circumstances, it was questioned if
    the army could be properly supplied before the fall rains made the moun-
    tainous roads impassable.³

WEDNESDAY AUG. 19TH 1863:
    Took my picket in at 3 A.M. Got our breakfast and marched at 5 A.M.
We were all day crossing one chain of the Cumberland. It beat all the hills
that I ever saw. Day very warm. Marched twenty miles and camped in
Sequatchee Valley on the Sequatchee River two miles east of Dunlap. Our
Regt. temporarily assigned to Gen. Hazen's Brigade.

THURSDAY AUG. 20TH:
   Reveille at 3 A.M. Marched at 5 A.M. This 9 A.M. we were resting on top of the principal chain of the Cumberland. Col. Wilder's Brigade of mounted infantry is passing. It is a fine Brigade. Took up our line of March again at 1 P.M. Marched until 7 P.M. and camped at the foot of the mountian at Poe's Tavern the mountain was eighteen miles across. We are within fourteen miles of Chat[tanooga]. We captured a picket-post of fifteen [men], four wagons, and twenty four mules and over one hundred head of cattle. They were at the tavern when we came in.

   The mountains that Glisan referred to were Waldron's Ridge, part of the eastern range of the Cumberland Mountains. Poe's Tavern was located at an important crossroad in the valley of the Tennessee River, and the occupation of this point by a portion of Rosecrans's army confused Bragg as to the nature of the Federal commander's intentions. Bragg was led to believe that Rosecrans was going to cross the Tennessee River and try to bag the forces of General Simon B. Buckner that were then retreating from a failed attack on Ambrose E. Burnside's Union Army in east Tennessee. Bragg's incorrect assumption concerning the objective of the Union Army was set straight the following day when Wilder's artillery began shelling the city of Chattanooga.[4]

FRIDAY AUG. 21ST:
   In camp all day the 9th Ind[iana] Regt. went out on a reconnaissance with Col. Wilder's Brig. Went as far as the river. Shelled the Rebs across the river a while and returned to camp at 8 P.M.

   Wilder's Brigade was shelling the Confederates in Chattanooga with a battery of mountain howitzers. Although it caused a great deal of commotion in the city, the shelling did little harm to the Confederate Army.[5]

SATURDAY AUG. 22ND 1863:
   Still in camp. There was a great many citizens come in today to see the Yanks.

   East Tennessee was known to be a bastion for supporters of the Union in the South. The Lincoln Administration had long coveted military control of the area, as it was felt that substantial support, both in manpower and means, could be gathered from the area. Many of the citizens of east Tennessee welcomed the Union soldiers as liberators, not as invaders.

SUNDAY 23RD:

Camp full of young ladies. Some of them come ten miles. They seem to be perfectly happy since we got in here.

MONDAY AUG. 24TH:

There was a great many citizens in camp today with peaches and apples to trade for coffee. Some of them say they haven't had any coffee for eighteen months.

TUESDAY AUG. 25TH:

Got a pass and went out into the mountains about nine miles to forage. Got a chicken, some peaches, some tomatoes, and some butter, and returned to camp late in the evening after having had any amount of fun talking to the mountain Pinks. They are all in for the union to a man.

"Mountain Pinks" was a contemporary slang term that was used interchangeably with hillbillies.

WEDNESDAY AUG. 26TH 1863:

Officer of the Picket about one mile out of camp. All quiet along our lines.

THURSDAY AUG 27TH:

Relieved from Picket at 9 A.M. and come into camp. No news.

FRIDAY AUG. 28TH:

Drilling. Resumed Dress parade at 6 P.M. Capt. Bense returned from Cincinnati where he has been on furlough.

SATURDAY AUG. 29TH 1863:

Still in camp and blessed with plenty of fine society from the mountains.

SUNDAY AUG. 30TH:

Brig[ade] reviewed by Gen. Hazen at 3 P.M. There was not less than three hundred men, women, and children in camp to see it. It was a big thing on ice for them. Gen. [Hazen] has given officers permission and we are to have a dance at his Head Quarters on next Tuesday he [the General] furnishing all the nic nacks. The Girls are highly delighted with the idea and they will all come. I have my pardener picked out. I am going to furnish her with a pair of Gov sevens to dance in.

The "Government sevens" Glisan is referring to are a pair of size seven shoes.

MONDAY AUG. 31ST 1863:

Officer of the Brigade guard, Lieut. Antrem, has gone out to invite in the Society for the dance.

TUESDAY SEPT. 1ST 1863:

Days that are brightest are soonest to fade and thus faded all our bright prospects of the coming pleasures of the dance. Relieved from guard at 6 A.M. and joined the Regt. which had marching orders during the night. Marched at 8 A.M. for Dunlap to join our old Brig. My Co. and Co. H train guard. Had a hard time getting our train up the mountain. Day very warm. Reached Dunlap at 7 P.M. our Brig. had left distance twenty miles.

WEDNESDAY SEPT. 2N 1863:

Reveille at half past three. Marched at 5 A.M. Moved down the Sequatchee valley towards Jasper. Day very warm and the roads terrible dusty. Made eighteen miles and camped for the night in a field by the Road Side.

THURSDAY SEPT. 3RD:

Marched at 5 A.M. Passed through Jasper at 8 A.M. a small county town of no importance. From Jasper we took the Battle Creek Road. Reached the Tenn[essee] River at 12 m[idday] and where we joined our Brig. and went into camp for the remainder of the day Marched twelve miles. Gen. Branan's Div. is crossing the river now.

As can be seen from Glisan's entries, the troops began their marches very early in the day, before the sun was fully up, and concluded those marches at or around midday. This was done in an effort to try to protect the men from the effects of a punishing heat wave that the area was experiencing. Straggling was a common occurrence under such conditions, and the officers were not only being humane in taking such measures. They were also trying to ensure that they could keep their men well in hand and not be caught by the Confederates, reduced in numbers, or exhausted in physical stamina by the sun.

FRIDAY SEPT. 4TH 1863:

Regt. formed at 1 A.M. moved down to the mouth of Battle Creek where we crossed the river on rafts made of logs. Our Regt. was across at 4 A.M. We moved up into the woods. Stacked arms, got our breakfast, laid down and sleep until the Remainder of the Brig. got across which was accomplished at 3 P.M. We then formed, marched eight miles, and camped for the night at Shell mound.

SATURDAY SEPT 5TH:

Remained in camp until 2 P.M. waiting for our train drawing rations.

We formed, marched until 11 P.M. and camped in a cornfield by the road-side. Distance ten miles.

SUNDAY SEPT. 6TH 1863:

Reveille at 5 A.M. Marched at 7 A.M. Moved seven miles and camped. I have heard several wires [rumors]. Some say the Rebs have left Chat[tanooga] and some say they will fight. We will know in a few days for we are getting into close quarters but as yet, everything is quiet in front.

Glisan reports all as being quiet in front, but the Confederates had been found to occupy a strong position on Lookout Mountain, and General Charles Woods's Division had been sent along the railroad from Whiteside Station to develop the position of the enemy and report its strength. The Sixth Ohio was being held in reserve to support this movement should it become necessary.[6]

MONDAY SEPT. 7TH:

In camp all day. Wrote two letters— one to Emmie and one to Miss Annie Anderson. Some of the boys say they heard some skirmishing on the mountain while they were out foraging but I have heard nothing myself.

TUESDAY SEPT. 8TH 1863:

Reveille at 2 A.M., marched at 3 A.M. Took the Trendon Valley Road, advanced five miles, formed line of Battle. Sent out reconnoitering party to feel for the enemy which returned at 6 P.M. haveing found no enemy. Heard heavy cannonading all day but it was very distant.

WEDNESDAY SEPT. 9TH:

Three Regts. left the Brigade at 3 A.M. to Reconnoiter. An order has just come to be ready to move at a moment's notice that Chat[tanooga] is evacuated and our Corps is to pursue the enemy. Moved at 8 A.M. Passed Chat[tanooga] one mile to the right at 2 P.M., had a fine view of the town and its defenses as we crossed Lookout Mountain. Camp for the night at Rossville on the Ga. state line. Our advance had a skirmish with their rear guard just before we went into camp. Day very warm. Marched fourteen miles.

By this point of the campaign, Rosecrans had already accomplished his objective. Chattanooga was in Federal hands. The city held the key to control of much of east Tennessee and could be used as a jumping off point for Federal incursions into the heart of the Confederacy. Rosecrans was receiving reports that General Braxton Bragg's Confederate Army was in full retreat, and he sensed an opportunity to cripple the fleeing foe while they were disorganized and in flight. If Bragg's army could be seriously damaged, it might even open the door for a campaign against Atlanta, Georgia. Rosecrans hurried his corps forward in pursuit of the Confederates, hoping to catch them before they eluded him. However, Braxton Bragg was not retreating. He was consolidating his army at Lafayette, Georgia, preparing to fight the decisive battle of the campaign. The Confederate Army had been reinforced by the addition of Lieutenant General James Longstreet's Corps from the Army of Northern Virginia, and with this new force, Bragg was ready to make a stand. He had given up Chattanooga without a fight, but he now planned to make the struggle for the possession of the city across the state line, in Georgia.[7]

THURSDAY SEPT 10TH:

Moved at 8 A.M. taking the Reingold [Ringgold] Pike. Our advance was skirmishing all day. Marched twelve miles and camped one and a half miles from Gregsvill [Greggsville] About the time we got settled down the assembly was blown. Our Regt. was formed and sent out to Reconnoiter as far as town. Found the Rebs and had some skirmishing. Took fifteen prisoners. Night closing in. We returned. the boys found a wine cellar in town and by the time we got to camp they were nearly all drunk.

FRIDAY SEPT 11TH:

Marched at 6 A.M. Our Regt. in the advance and my co. advanced as skirmishers. Arriveing within one mile of Reingold [Ringgold] a small county town we made a junction with Wilder's brig. who was then shelling the Rebs Rear. We passed through town one mile and went into camp. Wilder is still driving them. My co. at picket tonight.

SATURDAY SEPT. 12TH 1863:

Joined the Regt. at 6 A.M. Returned to town took the Road leading to Rome. Our advance had heavy skirmishing all day. Col. Wilder had seven men killed and twelve wounded. Marched ten miles and camped near Gordons Mill.

General Crittenden's Corps, of which the Sixth Ohio was a part, was in a most precarious situation as it made its camp near Gordon's Mills, toward the head of McLemore's Cove. Bragg's Confederate Army was but a few miles south of Crittenden's position, massed and ready to take the offensive to reclaim Chattanooga. Crittenden was in the advance of the Union Army, and his corps had outdistanced the other two corps, leaving him, for an anxious period of time, isolated and alone in front of Bragg. The Union

Fourteenth Corps was some eighteen miles away, while the Twentieth Corps would have to travel more than forty miles to reach Crittenden's position. Although the lead elements of Crittenden's forces were reporting brushes with strong elements of the Confederate Army, it was still generally thought by the Union high command that Bragg had retreated further south, toward or past Lafayette, Georgia.[8]

SEPT. 13TH:

Skirmishing commenced at 5 A.M. Formed line of Battle where we remained all day. Gen Vancleave's [Van Cleve's] Div. moved out in front at 8 A.M. and after some heavy skirmishing in which artillery was freely used Succeeded in drieving them back. We had two officers and several men wounded. One officer killed.

Rosecrans was now aware that Bragg's army was in front of him in force. His own army was badly scattered over several different lines of march, and he was desperately trying to consolidate his forces before a general engagement was fought. Bragg was well aware of the situation with the Union Army. For one of the few times in the war, the Confederates enjoyed a numerical superiority to their foe, which was only magnified by the scattered condition of Rosecrans's army. Bragg was trying to bring on the general engagement that Rosecrans feared, but his plans were being miscarried by subordinate officers. On several occasions, the Confederate commander ordered that attacks be made upon the isolated Union corps, but each time the orders failed to be carried out.[9]

MONDAY SEPT. 14TH 1863:

Marched at 5 A.M. from Gordons Mill. We moved in a north western direction. Struck the Chat[tanooga] Valley Road and moved South towards Fayettevill[e]. Marched twelve miles and went into camp. One of my men got his arm broke.

TUESDAY SEPT. 15TH:

Marched at 5 A.M. Returned to Gordons Mill and then moved South and Camped on the Chicamauga River after Resting. I took thirty men and went out forageing. Run into the Rebel Pickets. They fired on us but hurt no one. Got some chickens and some bacon. Found it under a niger hut. Marched fourteen miles.

WEDNESDAY SEPT. 16TH 1863:

Our Regt. and the 36th Ind[iana] went out on a Reconnaisaince at 1 P.M. Run into the Enemys Pickets one mile from camp. After some heavy skirmishing we drove them back two miles and got two wagon loads of potatoes that they had dug for their own use. My friend Lenheart was wounded. Returned to camp at dark.

THURSDAY SEPT. 17TH:

Rebs attact our pickets at 4 A.M. Their Cav[alry] charged into Gen. Hazen's lines but the Brigade was up Standing at Arms so they gobbled about one half that come in. Moved five miles to the left. Got into camp at 10 P.M.

FRIDAY SEPT. 18TH 1863:

Formed a camp in the forenoon and moved at 2 P.M. Changed our position three miles to the left and Relieved Gen. Vancleaves [Van Cleve's] Div. which had been skirmishing all day. Our Regt. was sent to the front. My Company with Cos. A and F was sent out as skirmishers. Skirmished until dark and then formed a picket line. Had one man killed and one wounded.

The skirmishing was with General Nathan Bedford Forrest's cavalry and General W.H.T. Walker's corps of infantry. The Confederates were attempting to seize control of the Chickamauga Creek crossings, but Wilder's men held them stubbornly. Wilder's troopers were all armed with Spencer seven-shot repeating rifles, and the superior firepower these weapons afforded to the cavalrymen had caused them to be nicknamed the "Lightning Brigade."[10]

SATURDAY SEPT. 19TH:

Relieved from picket at 1 A.M. Joined our Brig. and moved off to the left. Arrived at Gordons mill at daylight. Stopped one hour for breakfast then moved two miles farther to the left to support Gen. Baird's Div. which was then engaged. Our Brig. went into the fight at 10 A.M. By this time the fighting had become general all along our lines and continued with unabateing fury dureing the remainder of the day. About 4 P.M. they broke through our left center but we got support and drove them back and at dark we held our old position. The Battle was fierce and terrible in the extreem. The men fought with a Bravery and determination seldom if ever equaled. I had one man killed and eight wounded in my company.

The battle began at 10 A.M. and was furiously fought through the morning, with charges and counter-charges taking place on both sides and neither side gaining any clear advantage in the bloody melee. Then, just before 11 A.M., General Rosecrans ordered a change in his lines. The aide who delivered the order misstated it, resulting in the creation of a huge gap in the Federal line of battle. General James Longstreet was pushing his corps forward to the attack just as this hole was created, and his forces caught the Union troops unprepared to meet his assault. Longstreet's corps exploited this breach and cut the Union Army in two, creating great panic among the Union soldiers on the right wing of the army, many of them retreating toward Chattanooga. Major General George H. Thomas was in command of the left wing of the army, and with the disintegration of the right, he prepared his wing to meet the whole force of the Rebel army. Thomas assumed a strong position around Snodgrass Hill and repulsed repeated attacks by the Confederates throughout the day. The fighting was some of the most fearful that was seen in the war. Thomas's resolute stand, aided by the timely arrival on the field of Major General Gordon Granger's Division, which had been in reserve, prevented a serious defeat from becoming a complete disaster and earned for him the nickname "The Rock of Chickamauga." The Sixth Ohio took part in the stand made by Thomas on the field that day, as units that had not been routed by Longstreet's attack made their way to the left and joined with Thomas's line.[11]

SUNDAY SEPT. 20, 1863:

Sleep or rather laid on the Battle field last night for we could not sleep as it was very cold and I had no blankets. At day light I with the rest of my Battle worn comrades arose but my limbs were so benumbed from the cold that I was hardly able to stand up. After eating a hard cracker and supping a little coffee which one of my men made for me (for I had none of my own) we were ordered to fall in and our Brigade was moved off to the extreem left of our line and put in position. About 9 A.M. the enemy made their appearance in our front moveing in solid column. Our skir-mishers were soon driven in. Our lines then rose up and poured volley after volley in to their advanceing columns while our batterys were belch-ing forth their showers of leaden hail and strewing the ground with their dead and wounded. (The scene at this time was grand and terrible) But on they come hooping and yelling like a sort of wild devils. But our boys had got used to their yelling and didn't scare worth a cent. Finding it impossible to break our lines in front they gave back and moved around and come in on our flank. This movement beat us and forced us back. We made a change of front fell back to our Barricade and let them come out in to an open field where they were met by another column and we opened on their flank. It was more than they bargained for and they had to get back but more than half of them had layed down their arms. But as fast as we drove them back they were strengthened by fresh columns and

Snodgrass Hill, where General Thomas made his valiant stand during the battle of Chickamauga. Lieutenant Glisan and the Sixth Ohio saw some of the most bitter fighting of the war while fighting in this area. Picture dates to the turn of the century (Military Photographic Archives, U.S. Army War College, Carlisle, Pa. Hereafter referred to as U.S. Army War College).

would renew the attack. They made charge after charge on our left but was as often driven back by 12 m[id day]. Our entire lines were engaged and then followed one of the most desperate and bloody struggles the world ever saw. We stayed on the field untill darkness put a stop to the work of Death. We were then ordered to leave the field. We fell back four miles to Rossvill[e] where we went into camp for the night. In this day's fight I lost one man killed and seven wounded. This is the first time the army of the Cumberland ever had to leave the battlefield. We are repulsed but not whipped nor never can be.

The brigade to which the Sixth Ohio belonged lost 517 men killed, wounded, and missing during the two days of fighting, with the Sixth accounting for 110 of that number. The Union Army sustained 15,851 casualties in the battle, while the Confederates suffered 17,804, making Chickamauga the bloodiest battle to be fought in the Western Theater.[12]

Although the battlefield encompassed an area of some fifteen square miles, the Confederates lost half of all the casualties they sustained in the two-day struggle in a 900-yard-long stretch of ground in front of General

*Thomas's position at the Horseshoe. Some of the most desperate fighting
ever to take place on the American continent took place here.*[13]

MONDAY SEPT. 21ST 1863:

Arose at daylight got our breakfast moved out one mile in front and
formed our line of battle. Our position is on a high hill where we have a
splendid view for miles around. We can see the clouds of dust riseing from
the enemy's advancing columns. Their advance attact our outpost at 11
A.M. We have had some heavy skirmishing and some heavy artillery dueling to day but all is quiet at this 5 P.M. God only knows what will be the
result. The men are in good spirits and seem hopeful they that we can hurt
them a little while they hurts us a good deal but we have had no rest for a
week night nor day and we are about worn out. I have been temporarily
assigned to the command of Company B. I have a distressing headache
this evening but I hope it will be better by morning.

*Although there was indeed some skirmishing and artillery fire between
the two armies, the Federals did not need to worry about the battle being
resumed this day. The Confederates had won the field, but their army had
been heavily bled in doing so. Colonel William Oates was much surprised
when the only orders he received from General Bragg on the 21st "was to
furnish details to gather up the arms scattered over the field." The only
real threat to the Federal Army on the 21st came from General Nathan
Bedford Forrest, whose cavalry was mounting the pursuit.*[14]

TUESDAY SEPT. 22N:

Left our position on the hill at 10 ocl. last night and fell back four
miles. We were moveing all night. At day light we formed our lines and
went to throwing up rifle pits. The enemy has been feeling us with their
artillery but made no general attack.

*General Rosecrans had determined to fortify Chattanooga, and he pulled
his army back into the city and put it to work throwing up breastworks to
resist the Rebel attack he was sure would come. The works were completed
in short order, but by the night of the 22nd, the Confederates had taken
up positions on the high ground on Missionary Ridge and Lookout Mountain that ringed the Union position. These heights gave them a commanding position from which they could harrass the Union forces, but they spent
their first day by simply throwing a few inaccurately aimed artillery shots
at the town.*[15]

WEDNESDAY SEPT. 23RD 1863:

The Enemy are in heavy force in our front but they don't seem very lively. We are strengthening our position while our artillery is feeling around trying to discover their battery's but they keep quiet. The Boys are in fine Spirits and say they would smile to see them but[t] against us here.

THURSDAY SEPT. 24TH:

I was woke up at 2 A.M. and sent out with my Company in front to build fires so we could see the movements of the enemy. They made an advance at daylight. Our batterys opened on them and drove them back. Our Regt. was relieved from the front at 8 A.M. and sent back on the Reserve. They have made but little demonstration in front today. Our artillery has been shelling them all day but got no reply.

FRIDAY SEPT. 25TH:

The enemy attat our picket 10 P.M. last night for about one hour. The fireing was terriffic they drove our pickets back within one hundred yards of our works but our batterys soon drove them back. Regt. moved out in our works at 8 A.M. All quiet except some artillery dueling.

Bragg's Confederates engaged in numerous small-scale assaults against the Union line in an effort to determine its position and strength. It was soon decided that the Federal works were too formidable to carry by storm, and the Southerners set to work strengthening their own works upon the ridges that surrounded the town. If Bragg could not drive the Yankees out of Chattanooga, he would lay siege to the place and starve them out.

SATURDAY SEPT. 26TH 1863:

Very cold last night. Rebs attact our pickets at daylight after about one hour's skirmishing they were driven back. I was struck on the foot with a spent ball. Gen. Palmer was slightly wounded. Relieved from the front at 8 A.M. and went back on the Reserve.

SUNDAY SEPT. 27TH:

Formed our camp this afternooon. This afternoon I went into town. In times of peace it contained about three thousand inhab., but now it is one of the most deserted places I ever saw. All quiet in front not a gun fired today.

MONDAY SEPT. 28TH 1863:

The enemy tryed to drive in our pickets last night but they were driven back. Regt. sent out to work on the entrenchments at 10 A.M. Bragg sent in a flag of truce this morning for us to send after our wounded. Relieved from the trenches at 4 P.M. and came into camp.

The offer of a truce was accepted by Rosecrans, and some two hundred ambulances were sent through the Confederate lines to Rebel hospitals at Crawfish Springs to bring back the Union soldiers who had been wounded at Chickamauga and left behind in the care of the enemy. Between six hundred and seven hundred wounded were brought back, many of them in terrible condition. Among their number was Captain Tinker of the Sixth Ohio, whom everyone in the regiment had supposed to have been killed in the battle.[16]

TUESDAY SEPT. 29TH:

Officer of the picket. Our pickets are within speaking distance of each other. We exchanged papers with them today and made an agreement not to fire on each other unless they go to advance. So we had a very quiet day.

Informal truces, such as this, were a common practice among soldiers in the opposing armies, especially between the veteran troops. Officers did their best to prevent these unapproved cease-fires, but the men would often resume them as soon as there was not an officer around.

WEDNESDAY SEPT. 30 1863:

Relieved from picket at 9 A.M. and come into camp. Made out some reports. Got a letter from Emmie and answered it. All quiet in front. I think it will rain tonight.

THURSDAY OCT. 1ST 1863:

Rained last night and has been raining all day. About one half our camp is overflowed. This is the first rain we have had since the 16th of Aug. It is very cold and disagreeable. Planted some thirty two pound seige guns in one of our forts. All quiet in front.

By the end of September, the work on the entrenchments in Chattanooga had progressed to a point where the men began to feel secure that Bragg would not commit his army to a frontal assault against them. The works had been made sufficiently strong that it was now possible to pull some regiments back from the line to allow them a rest period, the first since the battle at Chickamauga.[17]

FRIDAY OCT. 2ND 1863:

Working on the breastworks with my Company. All quiet. The Enemy were moveing heavy columns along our front.

SATURDAY OCT. 3RD:

Have been engaged all day makeing out our quarterly reports. Every thing quiet.

The First Ohio Light Artillery gathered around a cannon in one of the defensive works built in Chattanooga, Tennessee, after the retreat of Rosecrans's army to that place following the battle of Chickamauga (U.S. Army War College).

SUNDAY OCT. 4TH:

Had a sermon preached to us to day. The first that has been preached in this Regt. since it has been in the service. I was pleased to see our Regt. show the speaker so much courtesy. Dress parade at 5 P.M. Wrote two letters. All quiet along our lines.

MONDAY OCT. 5TH 1863:

Very cold last night. The air is still very chilly. The enemy has been shelling us all day. They light them inside our works but they do very little damage. Our guns reply occassionally but only from one or two batterys. They are feeling around to find out the position of our guns. Dress parade at 5 P.M. While on parade a 32 pd shell passed over my Company and lit about one hundred yards in the rear. We all made a very graceful bow and wished it a pleasant visit.

Unable to dislodge the Federals with an attack on the Union lines, Bragg contented himself with harassing the enemy through an intermittent bombardment. The shelling did little real damage to the Northerners, however, and as can be seen by Glisan's remarks did not even disturb the troops to any appreciable degree.

TUESDAY OCT. 6TH 1863:

Rebs threw a few shells into our Camp last night. Was out in front with a detail of men from the Regt. working on the fortifications. One shot fired at 5 P.M. by the Rebs.

WEDNESDAY OCT. 7TH:

Still engaged at our company reports. The Reb Cavalry tryed to charge into the rear of our pickets this afternoon but they were sent back a hooping.

THURSDAY OCT. 8TH:

Very cold last night. If this is what they call the Sunny South, I have enough of it. Wrote a letter to Miss Annie Anderson.

FRIDAY OCT. 9TH 1863:

Still busy at our reports. The days are pleasant but the nights are very cold. Gen. Crittendon relieved of his command. We are now under the command of Gen. Granger in the 4th Army Corps. Had some pretty heavy artillery dueling today. Most of the Rebel Shells fell inside of their own pickets.

Major General Thomas Crittenden, along with Generals Alexander McCook and James Negley, was censured by General Rosecrans for his conduct during the battle of Chickamauga. He was relieved of his command and, although he was later absolved of any misconduct in the campaign, his military career was tainted and he resigned his commission in December of 1864.[18]

Crittenden's corps was eliminated when the Twentieth and Twenty-first Corps were consolidated to form the Fourth Corps under the command of Major General Gordon Granger. Granger was well known to the men of the Sixth Ohio. He had been the officer who had mustered in the regiment for three months of service before they eventually signed on for three years. In fact, the Sixth had considered offering him the colonelcy of the regiment when they reorganized as a three-year unit. Now, he was to be their corps commander.[19]

SATURDAY OCT. 10TH:

Our Regt. transferred to Gen. Hazen's Brigade and Gen. Wood's Division. Gen. Crittendon takes his fare well of his troop. He said they could rob him of his good name but his old corps never.

SUNDAY OCT. 11TH 1863:

Our Brig. was reviewed by Gen. Hazen at 4 P.M. Out in front at our breast works in full view of the Rebel Camp. I was expecting every minute to see a shell light in amongts us but I was very agreeably disappointed.

MONDAY OCT. 12TH:

Light skirmishing all along our line this morning and some artillery fireing this afternoon.

TUESDAY OCT. 13TH:
Raining all day. Held an election for Gov. I was elected for one of the clerks. There was but one vote cast for old Vol. in the Regt.

WEDNESDAY OCT. 14TH 1863:
Rained all last night and it is very wet and disagreeable today. Regimental officer of the day. Rec'd a letter from Annie Anderson and wrote one to Father.

THURSDAY OCT. 15:
Still raining and it is very cold. Relieved from duty at 8 A.M. Saw three deserters come in to day. the confederacy chaps are hard up for grub. We are on half rations.

Major General William B. Hazen, Glisan's brigade commander at Chickamauga (U.S. Army War College).

Although Bragg's army had the Federals surrounded and cut off from their source of supplies, conditions in his own army were little better. Problems of supply bedeviled the Confederacy during the entire course of the war, while Union troops generally were provided with an abundance of food, clothing, and materiel. Chattanooga had long been considered to be one of the three most important places in the Confederacy for the Union Army to seize, following Richmond and Vicksburg. With the surrender of Vicksburg in July of 1863, the Confederacy had been cut in two, east and west, by the Mississippi River, which was now entirely in Union hands. If the Union could hold on to Chattanooga, they would be in a position to further divide the eastern half of the Confederacy by launching a campaign against the heart of the deep South in Georgia. Furthermore, east Tennessee, including Chattanooga, was home to a large segment of Union sympathizers, and the Lincoln Administration desperately wanted to bring this region back into the fold of the national government.[20]

FRIDAY OCT. 16TH:
Have been writing all day. Saw two more deserters come in today. Weather cloudy. I think we will have more rain.

SATURDAY OCT. 17TH 1863:

Officer of the fatigue detail. Day pleasant. All quiet until about 4 P.M. when one of our batterys opened on the Rebs and shelled them until dark. They did not reply. Lieut. Col. Christopher returned to Regt. from Cincinnati where he has been on recruiting service since the 16th of Aug. Nary a recruit did he get.

SUNDAY OCT. 18:

Officer of the grand guard. Rained on me all day. All quiet along the line. One deserter come into my line just after dark. He says that Bragg's army only gets one meal a day.

On October 18, General Rosecrans was relieved of command of the army and General George H. Thomas was given the position. He would be in charge pending the arrival in the city of General Ulysses S. Grant, who would assume overall command of the Union forces being marshaled there to break the Confederate seige.[21]

MONDAY OCT. 19TH 1863:

Cleared off last night and got very cold. Was relieved from picket at 9 A.M. and come into camp. Saw two more deserters pass through camp today.

TUESDAY OCT. 20TH:

There was some considerable moveing around in the army today. They have been consolidating Brigades and divisions and they were moveing into their new positions. Our Regt. cleaned up a camp for us to go into tomorrow. Was in town this afternoon. Wrote a letter to Father this afternoon. Some Art. Fireing on the Right this 6 P.M.

WEDNESDAY OCT. 21ST 1863:

Regimental Officer of the day. Regt. moved camp. Rained most all day which made it very disagreeable for the men to work at their tents. It has stopped raining at this 6 p.m. and has turned quite cold. Men on quarter rations. All quiet in front.

Both armies were running desperately low on food. The besiegers were facing the same hardships in that area as were the besieged.

THURSDAY OCT. 22ND:

Relieved at 8 A.M. Day pleasant. Men busy firing up their tents. Three more deserters come in through our lines. All quiet until 5 P.M. when the guns of Fort Wood were opened and shelled the Rebs till dark.

FRIDAY OCT. 23RD 1863:

The guns in Fort Wood were shelling the Rebs all night last night. It has been raining all day and it is very cold and disagreeable. I have had the blues all day. That's what's the matter with the Infant.

SATURDAY OCT. 24TH:

Day very cold and disagreeable. All quiet in front. Gen. Palmer's Division leaves tonight — destination unknown. Received a letter from Emmie and answered it.

General Grant had arrived in Chattanooga to assume command on the previous day. His first order of business was feeding and supplying the army. A line of supply and communication must be opened from the city to the outside world. General John Palmer was now in command of the Fourteenth Corps, but his old division was being repositioned to set in motion a chain of events that would lead to the opening of this supply line. Members of the Sixth Ohio would play a key role in the drama that was to unfold.[22]

An amusing story is told of how Grant was given the command at Chattanooga. He had been ordered to Louisville, Kentucky, where he was to have a secret conference with an emissary from the War Department. His train was halted at a switch point along the way, and Secretary of War Edwin Stanton boarded. Stanton spotted a distinguished looking bearded man sitting in the car and immediately approached him. He extended his hand, proclaiming that he would know General Grant anywhere from his pictures. Stanton was greatly embarrassed to find out that the hand he was shaking belonged to a doctor, not the famous commander, who was the small unimpressive-looking man sitting in another part of the car.[23]

SUNDAY OCT. 25TH:

Officer of the grand guard. Sent out at 5 A.M. Day cloudy and cold. Everything quiet.

MONDAY OCT. 26TH 1863:

Sleep but little last night. There was some canonadeing on the right of our line about midnight. Was relieved from picket at 6 A.M. and come into camp. Rations very scarce. These are the roughest times this army ever experienced. Assigned to command of Co. A. Spent the most of the day in takeing an invoice of the company property. Day pleasant with no rations nor no prospect of any. Almost starved and there isn't a bit of bread in the house. At 12 m[idday] we got an order to [form]... Seven detachments ... composed of twenty men and one commissioned officer in each detachment. The men and officers selected were of those who had distinguished them selves on the Battle field for their Bravery. Accordingly seven officers were selected and ordered to go through the Regt. and pick out their number of men from the different Companies. I was put in command of the Second detachment after selecting our men and organizing our detachments which was not accomplished until 9 P.M. We stacked arms and at this 10 P.M. we are laying in Readiness to march at a moment's notice. The regts. in the Brig. Rec'd orders. Something terrible is about to happen I suppose.

TUESDAY OCT. 27TH 1863:

The several detachments of the Brigade numbering in all about Eleven hundred and fifty men was formed at 1 A.M. and moved about one mile to the River where we were embarked in Pontoons twenty four men and one officer in each pontoon. This was the first intimation we had of what was to be done. And I must say that the prospects was not very flattering. At 3 A.M. the men were all loaded in the Boats and we shuved out from the shore heading down stream, moveing cautiously. We succeeded in Running past the Rebel Batterys on Lookout Mountain and all their pickets on the river unobserved and landed seven miles below Chat[tanooga]. The first boat had struck the shore before the picket discovered us. We landed as soon as possible and moved forward to gain a position. My detachment with several others was thrown forward as skirmishers. We did not move far until we ran into the enemy lines and the ball opened the fight. Lasted about one hour when we succeeded in driving them from their position. They fell back about one half mile where they planted a battery and shelled us for about three hours with but little effect when they fell back towards the mountain. They left about twenty dead on the field. Our loss was two killed and about ten wounded. We were reinforced by two Brigades dureing the day from across the river. We have gained a strong position and thrown up barricades. So I think we will be able to hold our position. The Pioneers have thrown a pontoon bridge across the river and we will [throw] some artillery across tonight and I hope we will get some rations for I have not had a mouthful of bread for forty eight hours.

Grant's plan to open up a line of supply was being put into operation. General Joseph Hooker, with two corps of reinforcements from the Army of the Potomac, was at Bridgeport, Tennessee, marching east toward Chattanooga. Grant directed that the force Glisan mentions above seize and hold Brown's Ferry and construct a bridge at that point so that Hooker's troops, and supplies from Nashville could be brought into the city. The action began at 3:00 A.M. on the morning of the 26, and by 7:00 A.M., all of the

expeditionary force had crossed the river in pontoon boats and was dig-
ging in on the opposite shore, while a detail set to work constructing a pon-
toon bridge across the river. The bridge was completed by 10:00 A.M. On
October 28, General Oliver O. Howard's corps of Hooker's army arrived
at Brown's Ferry, and the Confederate siege of Chattanooga became a siege
in name only. The Union forces now had an open link to the outside world
and the balance of power in the campaign had shifted to the North.[24]

WEDNESDAY OCT. 28TH 1863:

Sleep but very little last [night] as I had no blankets and it was very
cold. Got some rations this morning. Had a big breakfast so I felt a good
deal better. Got out Batterys across the river. Drawed them up the mountain by hand and put them in position. So if the Rebs want to shell us now
we can return the compliment. I was on duty this afternoon in command
of a fatigue party. There has been a heavy artillery duel going on all day
between one of our batterys on the other side of the river and a rebel battery on Lookout Mountain. Hooker made a junction with us at 6 P.M.

THURSDAY OCT. 29TH 1863:

The enemy attacked one of Gen. Hooker's Divisions at one ocl. this
morning and a fierce fight ensued which lasted three hours and a half. It
was about two miles to the right of us but from our position we could
plainly see the flash from the muskets and artillery. It was a grand sight.
Our troops drove them back and took possession of their rifle pits. Our
loss was pretty heavy but I have heard nothing definite of the result. The
Rebels Batterys on Lookout have been shelling Hooker's forces all day but
without much effect. Gen. Grant visited us on the heights this afternoon.

The action that Glisan describes was an attack by General Longstreet's
corps on the division of General John Geary in an attempt to close off the
supply route the Federals had opened. Geary was outnumbered and hard
pressed, but he stubbornly held his ground. Hooker ordered General
Howard, then at Brown's Ferry, to march to Geary's assistance, but it was
three hours until those reinforcements arrived, and Geary was forced to
fight it out alone till then. An interesting incident occurred when the team-
sters of Hooker's wagon train deserted their wagons during the battle. The
mules, frightened by the roar of the firing, broke free from their fastenings
and ran directly toward the Confederate position. In the inky darkness,
the Confederates mistook the stampede of the mules to be a cavalry charge
and retreated from their position. By 4:00 A.M., the fighting had ceased.
This was the only serious attempt the Confederates made to close off the

supply route at Brown's Ferry that the Union troops had nicknamed the "cracker line."[25]

FRIDAY OCT. 30TH 1863:

Still on Brown's Ferry heights. It has been raining all day. We have no tents which [makes] our posision a very uncomfortable one. The steamboat from Chat[tanooga] ran the blockade last night. She was discovered by the Rebs about one mile above this point. They fired about fifty shots at her but done no damage except cutting a small steam pipe which was repaired at this point. She went down to Bridge Port twenty miles below this point after rations and I hope she will soon get back. Things generally quiet but few shots fired from either side.

SATURDAY OCT. 31ST 1863:

Had a terrible rain storm last night. It stopped raining about day light and this afternoon the clouds broke away and the old day god deigned to smile upon us once more. Had regimental muster and Inspection at 2 P.M. The rebel battery on Lookout Mt. has been fireing some this afternoon at one of our Bat. on the north side of the river. We can see them plain from this point. Some of their shells explode over our camp at Chat[tanooga]. I think it is a 32 prd. They are fireing now. I am looking for one over this way before long.

SUNDAY NOV. 1ST 1863:

This has been a beautiful day. I am sitting on a log on top of a bluff about five hundred feet high. The Tennessee [River] is rolling along on its winding way far below me while the Rebels Batterys on Lookout are belching forth their leaden messengers which fall far away in the valley and while my ears are saluted by the deep thundering tone of the cannon my mind wanders back to my dear friends who are far away. I wonder what they are doing or where they are while I am writing this. I hope they are all well and happy. I would like to be with some of them to night.

MONDAY NOV. 2ND 1863:

Left the heights this morning and moved down into the valley. The Rebel Battery on lookout has been fireing all day down into the valley at our twins but with no effect. Day cloudy with appearances of rain. Out of rations. Am hungry and I am in rather a bad humor.

This was the low point of the siege for the Union defenders of Chattanooga. They had opened a supply route at Brown's Ferry, but as yet the anticipated rations had not arrived. The troops were hungry but not disheartened. They knew that food was on the way as well as reinforcements, and they steeled themselves to hold on until both were at hand.

TUESDAY NOV. 3RD:

Regt. went upon the heights at 9 ocl. last night. Remained there until daylight this morning and then came down into the valley to our Bivouacks.

WEDNESDAY NOV. 4TH 1863:

Officer of the picket. Left camp at 7 A.M. with my detail, got lost in the fog and after traveling around about five miles I found the post about two miles from camp in a mountain gorge on the river the most god forsaken looking place I ever saw. All quiet on our front. At this 6 P.M. I am sitting on the River bank watching some wild ducks. They don't seem to care whether the world goes on or not. So they have the Tennessee to swim in. They would feel funny. Their foot would slip and let them in over their heads.

THURSDAY NOV. 5TH 1863:

I was relieved from picket at 8 A.M. and come into our bivouac camp. At 2 P.M. Regt and Brig. got orders and returned to our camp at Chat[tanooga] which we reached at 5 P.M. makeing a march of five miles. We had got orders this morning to move our camp and the most of the tents had been taken down when we got here but fortunately mine was left standing. It appears like home to get under my tent again after being exposed to the storm and rain for the last ten or twelve days without any shelter. It has been raining all day. The Rebs are trying to advance their lines.

FRIDAY NOV. SIXTH 1863:

Regimental officer of the day. The Boys have been engaged all day in firing up their tents again. I had a chimney built to my tent and just got it done when we rec'd orders that we should stop fixing up camp as we move again in the morning. That's the way it goes, the Rebs have been shelling all day from Lookout. Got a mail this morning. I rec'd five letters and answered too.

SATURDAY NOV. 7TH:

Relieved from duty at 8 A.M. Moved our camp ¼ of a mile into Fort Palmer. The Rebs have been wasteing some more powder today from Lookout.

SUNDAY NOV. 8TH 1863:

I had to go to church today but I put it off and worked the most of the day fixing up my Shanty. Had Co. Inspection at 4 P.M., day clear but the air is quite cold. There has been some fireing from Lookout and a few shots from Fort Wood.

MONDAY NOV. 9TH:

Finished my Shebang and made out my pay rolls. The Pay Master is in camp and thinks we will be blessed with some green backs in a day or two which will be a good thing. Day clear and very cold. which is bad on the natives.

TUESDAY NOV. 10TH 1863:

Company and Regt. on picket. It has been unusually quiet today but three shots fired. Day clear and cold.

WEDNESDAY NOV. 11TH:

Very cold last night. I thought I would freeze. Company G Regt. was relieved at 6 A.M. and came into camp. Was payed four months pay by Maj. Diver. I rec'd 411.24. I have my money now but don't know what to do with it. Every thing quiet. Wrote a letter to Miss Annie Anderson, Phila.

THURSDAY NOV. 12TH:

Some very heavy Art. dueling on our right. Wrote two letters, one to Emmie.

FRIDAY NOV. 13TH 1863:

There was some fireing along the picket line last night but I learned that there was one hundred and thirty five deserters come into our lines and the Rebs were fireing on them. Bully for the rebs. I wish they would all come in. There were two men shot today. Their crime was desertion. I did not go to the place of execution but I witnessed it from our camp. It was a hard thing but I suppose that it was just. Day pleasant with prospects of rain. Wrote a letter to Miss Anderson.

The grueling campaign was taking its toll on the men of both sides. Shortages of rations, the constant exposure to the elements, and the strain of the almost constant picket and artillery fire caused men's nerves to break. With the route at Brown's Ferry now open and the promise of the supplies that would be able to reach Chattanooga, the spirit of the Union men was somewhat more optimistic than that of their Confederate counterparts. Even so, supplies had not yet reached the city in any appreciable amounts, and the numbers of Confederate deserters who were coming into the Union lines only served to increase the food shortage problem that already existed.

SATURDAY NOV. 14TH 1863:

Had a heavy Art. duel this forenoon between the Rebel Bat. on

Lookout and our Bat. on Machison [Moccasin] point. Day made up of rain and sunshine. Nothing going on in camp but gambling. How strange it is that men are so thoughtless as to squander their hard earned money when so many of them have friends at home that need it and are almost starving for want of it.

SUNDAY NOV. 15TH:

Brig. was reviewed by Gen. Hazen at 11 A.M. Two men drummed through the Brig. with a play card [placcard] coward and the other Deserter, heavy cannonadeing on the right.

MONDAY NOV. 16TH 1863:

Regimental officer of the day. Heavy fireing from Lookout. Day cloudy and cold. Wrote a letter to father. Enclosed him a draft for two hundred and seventy five dollars. Number on the draft 331.

TUESDAY 17TH 1863:

Relieved from guard duty at 8 A.M. Some heavy artillery fireing up the River at daylight this morning. The Rebs trying to shell Gen. McCooks camp but were soon silenced. Resumed drill orders to drill three hours a day. Day pleasant. Rec'd a letter from Brother Sam.

WEDNESDAY NOV. 18TH 1863:

Company and Regt. on Picket. Day pleasant at this 2 P.M. I am out on the vidette line looking at the jonney Rebs. They are about two hundred yards from us and they are as thick as hops in Kent. Two of their officers are riding along their lines. I think they are generals. They have mounted orderlies with them. I would like to take a shot at them. Advanced our picket line on the right. This morning about ¾ up a mile had a brisk fight for about one hour. But few shots fired from lookout today. A Reb Band is playing the Bony blue flag at this 6 P.M.

THURSDAY NOV. 19TH 1863:

Had a very quiet night. Five hundred Rebs come over in one squad and give themselves up without fireing a shot. Relieved from picket at 6 A.M. and returned to camp. Battalion drill at 2 P.M. Weather cloudy. Rec'd a letter from Miss Carrie C. Johnson.

FRIDAY NOV. 20TH:

Regimental officer of the day. Our batterys on Machison [Moccasin] point have been shelling the Rebs some today. Orders to issue 100 rds of cartridges to the men and two days cooked rations. I think there will be war. Raining some this evening.

General William T. Sherman had arrived in Chattanooga with his Army of the Tennessee, and Grant was now ready to undertake offensive operations against Bragg's army. It had been decided that a direct assault against the Confederate position on Missionary Ridge would be extremely hazardous. The Rebels were so firmly entrenched in their position that Grant was not sure that their lines could be carried from the front, and the cost of attempting to do so would certainly be staggering. He therefore decided to try to position Sherman's army to flank Missionary Ridge. The Army of the Cumberland was to make a demonstration in front of the Confederate position, while Sherman's army made the main assault from the northeast against the right flank of the Confederate line. General Hooker's army was given the assignment of threatening Lookout Mountain to hold the Confederates there in place and prevent them from sending reinforcements to Missionary Ridge. The attack was to have taken place on the 21, but Sherman was having difficulty getting his men into position, so the order was suspended until Sherman's forces could get into position.[26]

SATURDAY NOV. 21ST 1863:

Rained all night and has been raining most all day. Our orders to move was countermanded on account of one of our corps not being in position. Was relieved this morning by Lt. Lewis. Wrote a letter to Cuz [cousin]... Our Battery on Machison [Moccasin] point has been shelling the Rebs some today.

SUNDAY NOV. 22ND:

Cleared off last night and this has been a most beautiful day. Fort Wood has been shelling the rebs all day. They threw about 60 shells. The enemy has been moveing large columns of troops along our front to their left. A great many of our shells light in their ranks. I suppose from all indications that this is the Eve of Battle with us. It is a sad thing to muse upon the prospects of a coming Battle. How many poor fellows are alive tonight that in the event of a battle will sleep in death tomorrow night. What would be the anxiety of our friends at home if they knew what our chances are of a battle on the morrow. I for one am glad they are ignorant. But come what may we can only put our trust in God. Howard's corps has just stacked arms in our rear at this 7 P.M.

MONDAY NOV. 23RD 1863:

At 1 P.M. the assembly was blown. Our line of battle formed as soon as our skirmishers were thrown out. The forward was sounded and our lines put in motion. The right acting as a pivot, the first gun was fired at ten minutes of two. We drove in their pickets, charged and took their first line of rifle pits which we are in possession of at this 6 P.M. While the shells from their batterys on Mission[ary] Ridge is makeing it very unhealthy around these posts. The loss in our Brigade is about one hundred killed and wounded, took over two hundred pris.[oners], several of their dead in our possession.

The Sixth Ohio was part of a reconnaissance that General Grant had ordered to probe the Confederate line. The commanding general feared that the Confederates were trying to withdraw from Chattanooga before he could launch his grand assault against them. The reconnaissance was directed against a spot known as Orchard Knob and was in full view of the Rebels on Missionary Ridge, who looked on admiringly as two divisions of Union infantry formed, thinking that they were preparing for a review by their officers. It was not until the blue-clad lines swept forward and engaged the Confederates at Orchard Knob that the onlookers realized that an attack was under way. The Confederate rifle pits were captured, and General Thomas ordered the attacking column to entrench and hold the ground. The reconnaissance had proved Grant's fears to be unfounded. The Confederates were not withdrawing from Chattanooga.[27]

TUESDAY NOV. 24TH 1863:

Threw up some rifle pits last night. Hooker attacked the enemy on Lookout at 9 A.M. The battle has been rageing all day and still continues at this 6 P.M. Our forces have gained the top of Lookout and if the rebs don't lookout some of them will get hurt. It has been raining some and the fog is so thick at times that we can't see any thing but the flash of the guns. Go in Boys, I wish you well. We remained in our new position. All quiet in our front with the exceptions of some artillery dueling. Regt. on picket to night. I think we have got old Bragg on the right road to glory.

The opposing lines at Missionary Ridge were largely inactive on the 24, with only an occasional shot from the skirmishers to break the calm. The action of that day had shifted to Lookout Mountain, where General Joe Hooker's troops were trying to force General Carter Stevenson's Confederates off the summit. Although Hooker enjoyed an advantage of almost ten-to-one in troops, the Confederates were in a strong position, and the steep sides of the mountain made it difficult for the Union attackers to get at them. The day was quite hazy with many low-hanging clouds, making it difficult for onlookers to follow Hooker's progress. Despite the difficulty of the terrain, Hooker's men advanced steadily, which could be ascertained only by the sounds of musketry from his line of battle going up the mountain. By

2:00 P.M. the clouds had settled in so heavily that Hooker was forced to temporarily suspend his advance due to a lack of visibility. Once the fog had subsided sufficiently, he pushed his lines forward again, and by 4:00 P.M. he was able to communicate to Grant that the Confederates had been driven off and he was in possession of the summit. The Confederate artillery from Lookout Mountain would no longer pose a threat to the Union Army when it advanced against Missionary Ridge. The fight for Lookout Mountain was dubbed "The Battle Above the Clouds," because of the fog and haze that had prevented it from being observed by those in the valley below.[28]

WEDNESDAY NOV. 25TH 1863:

The fighting continued until 11 P.M. Gen. Sherman attact their right flank at 8 A.M. At 10 A.M. our picket line was deployed and sent forward to reconnoiter some breast works in open front. We moved forward driveing their skirmishers before us. We had no support and when we got within about two hundred yards of their works at the foot of Mission[ary] Ridge they provided such a rakeing fire into us that the Gen. had the recall sounded and we fell back. In this little affair we lost our major killed and sixteen men wounded. The Regt. was relieved from picket at 1 P.M. and 2 P.M. the signal was sounded for the entire line to charge the enemy's position. We had about one mile to reach the top of Mission[ary] Ridge one fourth of which was nearly perpendicular. The fire from the enemy's Bat. was terrible when we reached the foot of the hill the infantry opened on us and then followed one of the most grand and terrible struggles the world ever saw. Such courage I never witnessed not a man faltered, we reached their works drove them out at the point of the Bayonet and planted our colors on their works at 4 P.M. We captured their artillery which I moved with my Co. and turned it on their flying columns. At this 6 P.M. we have driven them from every position captured seventy five pieces of art. and several thousand prisoners. Our Brig. [Gen. Hazen] took 18 pieces. I had two lost under my command in the charge. In the days fight I lost nine men three killed. The Regt. lost about fifty killed and wounded. The last rays of the setting sun falls in all its granduer on our victorious arms.

The Union attack on the crest of the ridge took place without orders. The soldiers were only to take the Confederate rifle pits near the base of the mountain, but once those were captured, the men surged forward on their own, and the impetuosity of their assault completely routed the Confederates, who were entrenched in strong positions along the crest. Were it not for a heroic stand by a portion of Major General Benjamin Cheatham's corps under the command of General E.C. Walthall, Bragg's army might have been totally destroyed.[29]

THURSDAY NOV. 26:

Lying on Mission[ary] Ridge. There has been some very large fires in the distance. I think the Rebs are burning some bridges. Our forces are following them up.

FRIDAY NOV. 27:

Left Mission[ary] Ridge at ten o'clock last night and returned to camp. There has been some heavy canonadeing in the direction of Reingold [Ringgold]. I guess our fellows are shelling Mr. Bragg's rear at this 5 P.M. We have orders to be ready to march at 4 in the morning with four days rations. Our advance has been fighting again today about Reingold [Ringgold]. They charged then took a lot of artillery and many prisoners. Good evening Johny Reb.

SATURDAY NOV. 28TH:

Regt. and Brigade left camp near Chat[tanooga] at 1 P.M. moveing up the river. Marched four miles and camped in a wood near the Knoxvill[e] Rail Road. Had a big rain this forenoon. Road very muddy. My Co. (A) and Co. D was consolidated and put under my command. It is but a small company yet but they can't be beat.

SUNDAY NOV. 29TH 1863:

Left camp at 6 A.M. Came onto the Cleveland Road about 10 A.M. Marched ten miles and camped at Harrison a small county town. Nothing occurred today worthy of note. Weather very cold freezing all day.

The Sixth Ohio was marching to the support of General Ambrose E. Burnside's army at Knoxville, Tennessee. General James Longstreet, with his corps from the Army of Northern Virginia, had been detached from Bragg's army prior to Grant's attack on Missionary Ridge to threaten the Union Army in that city. It was hoped that this demonstration against Knoxville would induce Grant to weaken his forces at Chattanooga to reinforce Burnside. Longstreet had attacked the Federals at Campbell's Station, just outside of the city. Although Burnside abandoned the field to the Confederates, his army had had much the better of the fight. The Federals retired to the city of Knoxville to defend prepared positions. The issue would be decided before the Sixth Ohio and the rest of the Union relief force could arrive on the scene. In fact, it was already pretty much settled before they undertook their march. On November 28, after numerous delays, Longstreet finally launched an attack on what he considered to be the weak point of the Federal line, an earthwork called Fort Sanders. The attack proved to be a disaster for the Confederates, and they were thrown back in confusion. This setback, combined with news that Bragg had been defeated at Chattanooga and that there were relief columns heading for Burnside's support, caused Longstreet to call off his campaign to capture Knoxville, and he began a withdrawal into southwest Virginia.[30]

MONDAY NOV. 30TH:

Column moved at 5 A.M. passed through a place called George Town where we was cheered by the sight of the national colors as they proudly waved in front of nearly every house. Marched 20 miles and camped one mile from the Tennessee River. Day very cold.

General Sherman had been given overall command of the expedition sent to relieve Burnside's forces at Knoxville, then threatened by Longstreet's corps. Sherman relates the events: "I had already reached the town of Charleston, when General Wilson arrived with a letter from General Grant at Chattanooga informing me that the latest authentic accounts from Knoxville were to the 27th, at which time General Burnside was completely invested, and had provisions only to include the 3rd of December; that General Granger had left Chattanooga for Knoxville by the river road, with a steamboat following him in the river; but he feared that General Granger could not reach Knoxville in time, and ordered me to take command of all troops moving for the relief of Knoxville and hasten to General Burnside. Seven days before we had left our camps on the other side of the Tennessee with two days' rations, without change of clothing — stripped for the fight, with but a single blanket or coat per man, from myself to the private included.

"Of course we had no provisions save what we gathered by the road, and were ill supplied for such a march. But we learned that twelve thousand of our fellow-soldiers were beleaguered in the mountain town of Knoxville, eighty-four miles distant — that they needed relief, and must have it in three days. This was enough, and it had to be done." It was done, through the series of hard marches that Glisan describes. Sherman brought the army to the relief of Knoxville in time.[31]

TUESDAY DEC. 1ST 1863:

Layed quiet this forenoon to draw rations. Moved at one P.M. Marched two miles and came to the Hiawassie River, which we crossed on a steam boat Paint Rock Creek near the mouth. It was dark before the Brigade got over so we only moved one mile farther and went into camp. Weather moderating some.

Period print showing the battle of Knoxville. The Sixth Ohio marched to the relief of Burnside's Union forces there, but the Confederates withdrew before they arrived (U.S. Army War College).

WEDNESDAY DEC. 2D:

Very cold last night. Marched at 5 A.M. passed through Decatur at 12 m[idday]. A small county town. Our march was through a beautiful valley. Roads very bad in places. Made twenty two miles. Plenty of forage in this country.

THURSDAY DEC. 3RD 1863:

Marched at 6 A.M. takeing the London Road. Made twenty miles and camped at Sweet Water a beautiful little town situated on the East Tennessee Rail Road. This has been a very hard day's march. I feel very tired. We have just got into camp at this 10 P.M. I am sitting by a rail fire writing while the Staley Bridge Infant is getting supplies. I have just finished my frugal meal of coffee, crackers, some corn meal flap jack, and mutton chops, and now I must tailor awhile on my pants. They have got a bad breakout.

FRIDAY DEC. 4TH 1863:

On the march at 5 A.M. Took the Morgan Town Road and marched twelve miles. Went into camp at 2 P.M. Regt. on picket tonight. Days pleasant but the nights are very cold.

SATURDAY DEC. 5TH:

Marched at 6 A.M. Crossed the little Tennessee River at Morgan town. made 18 miles. I am almost played tonight and rations are very short. Rained some today.

SUNDAY DEC. 6TH:

On the road at 6 A.M. Passed through Marysvill[e] a county town. Marched 8 miles and went into camp at 12 m[idday]. had a heavy sleet this morning. We are within twelve miles of Knoxvill[e] but they say friend Longstreet has lit out. I quip it was about time. It has cleared off this after- noon and got quite pleasant. I have just finished a big supper and I feel as if I didn't care whether the war goes on or not. I thought for awhile today that I would have to go to bed supperless but the Lord still provides for the soldiers. One of my boys presented me with a chicken, a basket of potatoes, and some molasses that with some meal made a fine supper. Bully for Co. A.

MONDAY DEC. 7TH 1863:

Moved at 8 A.M. Crossed Little River at Rockvill[e]. A small town composed of a cotton factory of about two dozen houses filled with fac- tory girls. Marched twelve miles and camped within two miles of Knoxville in sight of Burnsides' fortifications.

TUESDAY DEC. 8TH:

No move today and if they all felt as I do I suppose they were glad to get a day's rest. We have no tents with us. So we are scattered around loose all through the woods. It is raining some now and I think it will be a wet night.

WEDNESDAY DEC. 9TH 1863:

Still in the woods. No news and but few rations. We haven't had any thing but corn meal and meat for the last four or five days. This has been a beautiful day. Wrote two letters, one to Father and one to Emmie. I wish we would get a mail if it was only a female I wouldn't care either.

THURSDAY DEC. 10TH:

Got a pass this morning and went into the noted City to see where all the martyrs lived. It has been a very nice town before the war but it looks desolate now. The surrounding country is very broken and affords great facilities for defences. I ran around town the most of the day and returned to camp at 4 P.M. with headache enough for a whole family. We have been with out sugar and coffee for the last three days and I suppose we will be without until we get back to Chat[tanooga].

FRIDAY DEC. 11TH:

Got marching orders last night but they were countermanded this morning so the poor little babes have had to spend another day in the woods. No news of any kind from the front for several days.

SATURDAY DEC. 12TH 1863:

Regt. on picket. Got some coffee this morning and a good union Lady brought me in a pumpkin pie so the Babes are all right again. No mail no news. Weather cloudy with appearances of rain.

SUNDAY DEC. 13TH:

Rained all night very hard and the poor little babes got very wet in the woods. Was relieved from picket at 7 A.M. by the Ninety-third Ohio. Came into our bivouacks and breakfasted at 9 A.M. on Beef steak and onions with some sinkers and coffee. Company drill at 3 P.M. Weather still cloudy.

MONDAY DEC. 14TH 1863:

Rained very hard last night and turned quite cold today. Battalion Drill this afternoon. We had splendid grub no coffee or sugar, sinkers, and meat with water for breakfast, and meat sinkers and water for dinner and by the time supper comes the thoughts of the sinkers you have eaten satisfies you for the remainder of the day.

The "sinkers" Glisan refers to were fried corn meal. It was common for the soldiers to cook some salt-pork in a frying pan and then just pour the corn meal into the grease, making a sort of a corn meal mush, which, while filling, was not very appetizing.

TUESDAY DEC. 15TH:

Got a horse and a pass and went out in the country ten miles. Got some chickens and some butter. Found some very fine society. Had a good time. Returned to camp at dark found the Brig. had moved. I started in pursuit and overtook them at 10 P.M. in camp four miles north of Knoxvill[e].

WEDNESDAY 16TH:

Moved at 5 A.M. Road very muddy. Meet the trains of Foster's cavalry returning to Knoxvill[e] with a train of ambulances loaded with wounded. There has been a fight in front the report that the men with the train gave us is that our forces is falling back. There was about two hundred Rebs prisoners with them. Marched 16 miles and camped at Blains Cross Roads.

Foster's cavalry, part of Brigadier General James Shackleford's division, had been at Bean's Station when Longstreet's column passed by there on its march toward south western Virginia. Longstreet attacked these three cavalry brigades, numbering some ten thousand men, in hopes of acquiring much-needed supplies for his men. Confederate cavalry failed to cut off the escape route of the Federals, as had been ordered, and General Bushrod Johnson's twenty-four hundred–man division bore the brunt of the fighting, with little support from the Confederate troopers. Longstreet's only spoils from the engagement were a few wagons of supplies. The Sixth Ohio would be part of the Federal pursuit that was making sure that Longstreet was leaving the area and not just falling back to reform for another try at Knoxville.[32]

THURSDAY DEC. 17TH 1863:

Had a very hard rain last night. Woke up about midnight and found a gentle stream of water flowing around me. Changed our position one mile today and formed in line of Battle. I suppose we will have a fight here before many days. It is said that Longstreet has been reinforced by Ewells corps and he is now advancing on our forces. There has been considerable artillery firing in front today. Our Brig. is in position at one of the passes in Clinch Mountain. There is a Brig. of cavalry just passing to the front. Day cloudy.

FRIDAY DEC. 18TH 1863:

Turned very cold last night. Snowed a little today. Got my shirt washed and went without any while it was being done. I had worn it twenty days without washing and it was getting very lively. All quiet in front. Got orders at 7 P.M. Regt. moved one mile to the front and went on picket and at this 10 P.M. I am on the outpost jerking the picket.

SATURDAY DEC. 19TH:

Still on picket with no prospects of being relieved tonight. The Sun shone out today but the wind is piercing cold. All quiet.

SUNDAY DEC. 20TH 1863:

Very cold last night. I thought I would freeze before morning. The Recall was sounded at 9 A.M. the pickets were drawn in. Regt. formed and moved to the rear one mile and a half and bivouaced at the foot of Clinch Mt. Range. Issued some clothing to my co. then I got romantic and started to explore the top of the mt. and at this 4 P.M. I "with friend Charlie and another comrade" am sitting on the table rock of one of the highest peaks of the Clinch mts. It is about two thousand feet above the level. The scenery is magnificent for miles around. The valleys are dotted with the tents of the Union Army while far away in the distance can be seen the Halston River winding its way to join the waters of the Clinch many miles below. The Sun is just sinking to rest behind the western horizon and as its last Rays are guiding the mountains to my mind [which] is wandering far away to the loved ones at home. It is pleasant to sit and muse upon the grandeur of nature but I must return to camp as darkness closes in around me. 7 P.M. In camp and have just finished my frugal meal.

MONDAY DEC. 21ST 1863:

Remained in camp until after dinner and then started upon the mt. again. The day was clear and I took a glass with me which gave me a splendid view of the surrounding country. I saw Cumberland Gap, Knoxvill[e] and Rutledge the former being distant forty miles. Returned to camp at 6 P.M. The wire in camp is that the rebs have left our front.

The Confederates had indeed left the Union front. Longstreet had marched his corps to a position between Russellville and Greenville, Tennessee, where he made preparations for a winter camp, having given up the idea of any further active operations that season. His army remained there for the winter, moving to Bristol, a border town on the Tennessee-Virginia line, in March of 1864, and from there, it was ordered to rejoin the Army of Northern Virginia, then preparing to meet the Army of the Potomac in the Wilderness.[33]

TUESDAY DEC. 22ND:

In camp all day. Had a big dinner composed of Roasted Turkey, corn cakes, and coffee which cost two dollars and fifty cents. Day pleasant. No news from the front.

WEDNESDAY DEC. 23RD 1863:

In camp. Day cloudy and very cold. I haven't been able to get warm all day. We have a large fire but while I burn on one side I am freezing on the other. We drawed five days ¾ rations this afternoon of hard bread, coffee, shugar, and meat, the largest rations we have drawn since we left Chat[tanooga].

THURSDAY DEC. 24TH:

Still in our bivouac camp. Day clear and cold. There was some artillery fireing on our right but I have heard no news of any kind. We have the order to reinlist vet.[eran] vol.[unteer] but the Boys can't see it.

FRIDAY DEC. 25TH 1863:

I suppose at home this day has been celebrated as Christmas but here it has been nothing more than the 25th of Dec. although I have spent the day quite pleasantly. My friend Penington of Co. K with some of his messmates got up a very nice dinner and invited me to join them which I readily done as I had no very brilliant prospects for a dinner of my own. It was composed of Roasted turkey and chicken with nicely seasoned mashed potatoes, bread, and coffee. It was not sumptuous, but I have reason to believe that we enjoyed it full as well as if it had been the most sumptuous meal at home. This afternoon Dr. Bedell and I took a walk up to the top of the mt. and passed the remainder of the day in pleasant conversation. Thank God it is my last Christmas in the service. No news from the front. The day has been cloudy and at this 5 P.M. it is sleeting and I fear it will be a bad night.

SATURDAY DEC. 26TH:
Considerable artillery fireing in front. Raining most of the day.

SUNDAY DEC. 27TH 1863:
Rode out in front this afternoon to see some friends in the 23rd A.[rmy] C.[orps] but when I got there I found them on the march to the rear so I returned to my bivouac. Day cloudy and raining very hard at this 5 P.M.

MONDAY DEC. 28TH:
Rained all night but stopped this morning and turned very cold. I do hope they will do something with us soon either go ahead and fight or take us where we can be comfortable. No news from the front. All quiet.

The rigors of a winter camp were always hard on the soldiers. It was a trying way to live, even when one had all of the "comforts" that usually accompanied an army in camp. In the case of the Sixth Ohio and the rest of the Union force that had marched to relieve Knoxville, none of these "comforts" were at hand. The Northern troops who huddled around campfires in the mountainous Tennessee countryside did so without the benefit of tents or even of extra clothing.

TUESDAY DEC. 29TH 1863:
The only excitement in camp is in regard to enlisting veteran vol. They seem to hold out for large inducements but the boys can't see it and I hope they won't. Wrote a letter to sister Mary. Day pleasant.

WEDNESDAY DEC. 30TH:
This has been one of the lonliest days I have most ever spent. The forenoon was very pleasant but it has clouded up again and I think we will

Christmas on the Rappahannock

"Christmas on the Rappahannock." Winter campaigning was always a severe hardship on the troops. This was especially true when the soldiers were without basic winter necessities such as greatcoats and tents. The men of the Sixth Ohio suffered greatly from exposure to the elements during their participation in the Knoxville Campaign (U.S. Army War College).

have a wet night. There is no news of any kind from the front. We were promised a mail to day but were disappointed.

THURSDAY DEC. 31ST 1863:

Farewell Old/63 your race is run. Oh! How thankful I ought to be to "God" for his goodness and kindness towards me. While thousands of my fellow man have been called to try the realities of an unknown world my unprofitable life has been spared to see the close of another eventful year. I pray God that he will infuse into our hearts a feeling of thankfulness for our preservation as a people. And may the time speedily come when he will restore to us peace and harmony as a nation. And to him be all the praise now and forever. Raining.

FRIDAY JAN. 1ST 1864:

Last night I think was one of the wildest nights I ever experienced in the army. It rained and stormed until midnight and then turned freezing cold. I arose this morning with my limbs benumbed with cold to see the top of Clinch Mt. covered with snow. It cleared off this afternoon but the wind is piercing cold. in truth, it has been about as miserable day as I ever spent. Many a poor soldier will think of home and a bright fire side to night. Oh my country how I suffer for thee. All quiet.

SATURDAY JAN. 2D 1864:

Nothing occurred to disturb the usual dull monotany of camp life. Day cloudy and very cold. I am out of rations and I think I will have to retire to my virtuous couch to night without supper.

SUNDAY JAN 3:

Got some corn meal this afternoon and come coffee and sugar this afternoon so we will live a few days more. It has moderated some but it is still cloudy and cold.

MONDAY JAN. 4TH 1864:

This has been a wet disagreeable day and a fair prospect for a wet night. Wrote a letter to Miss Annie Harper. All quiet in front.

TUESDAY JAN. 5TH 1864:

Rained the most of last night but cleared off this morning and it has been quite pleasant to day. The 41st Ohio has nearly all went into the veteran service. They with some other Regts. of the Div. Started home on a thirty day furlough. Bully for us. We got mail. The first since we left Chat[tanooga]. I got four letters. A few cannon shots fired in front a few minutes ago.

WEDNESDAY JAN 6TH:

Snowed most of the day. The ground is covered. It has stopped snowing at this 5 P.M. but it is getting very cold. Wrote a letter to Emma. All quiet in front.

THURSDAY JAN 7TH 1864:

Snowing off and on all day at this 6 P.M. It is snowing and looks very stormy. I think it will be a rough night. I have had a very distressing headache to day but it is better this evening.

FRIDAY JAN 8TH:

Regt. left our bivouacks at 6 A.M. for picket. Snow about two inches deep and oh! how cold. It moderated some through the day but at this 10

P.M. it is getting very cold and I think it will snow again before morning. I have a dreadful pain in one of my knees.

SATURDAY JAN. 9TH 1864:
Between the pain in my knee and the cold I got but little sleep last night. Was relieved from picket at 7 A.M. and come to camp. Got a mail this afternoon. I got three letters ... one from Annie Anderson.

SUNDAY JAN. 10TH:
Moved camp one ½ mile. Had no axes to build my Shebang with so I will have to play freeze out to night and I expect to get beat. There was a Div. of Cavalry returned from the front. They say there is no enemy for forty miles. Received nine letters.

MONDAY JAN. 11TH 1864:
I have just finished my Shebang which I have been working at all day. Weather clear and cold.

A shebang was a crude, homemade shelter, which usually incorporated the soldier's shelter tent along with whatever materials were at hand. In the case of the Sixth Ohio, the shelters were probably constructed using branches and what clothing could be spared, as the company had no tents.

TUESDAY JAN. 12TH:
Everything quiet in camp. The boys are all busy fixing up their quarters so as to be as comfortable as possible. I had to stay in my domicile most of the day while I got my clothes washed.

WEDNESDAY JAN 13TH:
Day cloudy with appearances of snow. Have been laying around my Shebang all day. Wrote one letter to W.F. Mitchell. Orders to march in the morning.

THURSDAY JAN. 14TH 1864:
Left our bivouac camp at the foot of Clinch mt. at 6 A.M. Moveing South we crossed the Holston River at Strawberry Plains and took the Dandridge Road. Marched sixteen miles and camped at 5 P.M. Feel very tired and sore. Day pleasant.

FRIDAY JAN. 15TH:
Moved at 7 A.M. Passed through Dandridge at 11 A.M. and went into camp one mile from town. Marched 8 miles. Roads very bad. I am so sore that I am scarcely able to move. Our wagons are not up yet and for want of rations we will have to do without supper.

SATURDAY JAN. 16TH 1864:

Got some corn meal and had breakfast at 12 m[idday] the first I have had to eat since yesterday morning. Our Brave young Col. has just returned from home where he has been since the Battle of Chickamauga. Some Skirmishing between our pickets in front. Day clear and pleasant. On picket at this 7 P.M. Things are getting quite interesting in front.

This reference is to Colonel Nicholas Anderson, who was wounded during the fighting at Chickamauga.[34]

SUNDAY JAN. 17TH:

All quiet on picket last night. Was relieved at 8 A.M. and returned to our bivouac camp. The Rebs attact our advance at 4 P.M. The long Roll was sounded. Battalions and lines of Battle formed. The fighting was severe and lasted until dark when it closed. We stacked arms and are laying under orders to be ready to move at a moment's notice. There is different wires as to the result so I don't know which to believe. Considerable picket fireing at this 9 P.M. I am afraid if they don't stop their foolishness that we will have to go to the front yet and then some one might get hurt. They are a little madder than we are that's what's the matter. Orders to march some time to night.

Late in the day on the 17, the Confederates attacked the outposts of the Sixth Ohio, causing some heavy skirmishing until they were eventually driven off. The command was notified that it was to prepare for a retreat during the night and that anything that could not be carried with them was to be destroyed. The regiment started the march at 3:00 A.M. and continued till 5:00 that afternoon, finally making camp five miles southeast of Strawberry Plains.[35]

MONDAY JAN 18TH 1864:

Got to sleep last night. Marched at 3 A.M. Makeing a retrograde movement towards Strawberry Plains. Rained the most of the day. The Rebs attact our rear guard about 9 A.M. and skirmished with them several miles. Roads terrible. Had to burn three wagons of our train. I have just finished a big supper the first I have eat in twenty four hours. Made twelve miles and camped in line of battle.

TUESDAY JAN. 19TH:

Woke up this morning and found snow about three inches deep on my blanket. Moved at 7 A.M. Our Regt. being the rear guard. the Enemy did not trouble us. Recrossed the 'Holston' at the plains. Took the R.R.

Marched three miles and went into camp at 5 P.M. It seems that the whole army is falling back to Knoxvill[e]. There is a great many refugees—men, women, and children going back with us. I think there is trouble in camp some where. Made nine miles.

WEDNESDAY JAN. 20TH:
     Remained quiet until 2 P.M. when we moved out. Marched out six miles and camped at 5 P.M. within nine miles of Knoxvill[e]. Day pleasant. Roads very muddy. Wrote a letter to Emmie.

THURSDAY JAN. 21ST:
     Moved at 6 A.M. Passed through Knoxvill[e] at 11 A.M., crossed the Holston River and went into camp two miles south of town. Marched 11 miles. Regt. on picket tonight.

For the next five weeks the Sixth Ohio, along with the rest of Woods's division, would be occupied in guarding the roads and approaches to Knoxville. Rumors were rampant, and one that had gained credence with the men was that General Richard Ewell's corps, from the Army of Northern Virginia, had reinforced Longstreet and the Confederates were massed in front of the Union position ready to resume an offensive. This, of course, was false, but many a Sixth Ohio boy worried over the validity of the rumor and the possibility that they would have to face one more pitched battle before their term of enlistment was over.[36]

FRIDAY JAN. 22D:
     Got orders to march this morning but before we got in motion the order was countermanded. Wrote a letter to Carrie this forenoon and this afternoon I went into town and have just returned.

SATURDAY JAN. 23RD 1864:
     Column moved at 12 m[idday]. Recrossed the Holston passed through Knoxville. Took the London Road. Marched ten miles and camped at dark in a woods by the road side. I not heard any news from the front. Day beautiful.

SUNDAY JAN. 24TH:
     Left camp at 7 A.M. Marched five miles to Campbell's Station. When our Regt. was detached and left to guard the R.R. We have been hard at work this afternoon putting up a barricade. I have felt very sad all the day and I can't tell why. Weather beautiful indeed.

The barricade Glisan refers to was a wooden stockade fort that was built at this railroad station, fourteen miles from Knoxville. It took the regiment four days to construct the fort.[37]

MONDAY JAN. 25TH 1864:

My Company was on picket last [night] and to day but I was not with them. The remainder of the Regt. that was not on picket has been working on the barricade. This has been a regular spring day. Wrote a letter to Brother Jim. I have just returned from a solitary walk.

TUESDAY JAN 26TH:

Regt. still working on the barricade. The citizens report a force of Reb cavalry with in ten miles of us. If they want to ride the wagon is greezed. I was over to town this after noon. It is composed of about one dozen houses and they bear marks of the conflict between Burnsides and Longstreets forces. The surrounding country is mostly level and there is some very fine farms and I should think it a very pleasant place to live in times of peace. The weather continues to be fine. Capt. Russell went out forageing and has just returned with some chickens, potatoes, onions, and some crout. How we do live. Bully for Rus[sell] or any other man.

WEDNESDAY JAN. 27TH:

Company D went to Concord two miles from here to guard that point. My old woman is gone so I had to break up house keeping and now I am left alone. She took the Shanty with her. So I had to build myself a she-bang. The old thing will want to come back some of these days but if she don't look out I will get some other damsell.

Glisan is obviously jokingly referring to a messmate, with whom he was sharing quarters.

THURSDAY JAN. 28TH:

Worked some on the barricade with my co. this forenoon. This afternoon I went out in the country about six miles. Saw lots of girls. Got a pressing invitation to stay all night at one house but I could not for which I was very sorry. Got some butter. I have just got in camp at this 8 P.M.

On this date, Congress officially voted General Burnside its thanks for his successful defense of Knoxville. Congress felt that the danger had passed and the Confederate threat had been totally repulsed. Burnside had already left the city, being relieved, at his own request, on December 12.[38]

FRIDAY JAN. 29TH 1864:

Worked some on the barricade with my co. this forenoon. The Remainder of the day I have been loafing. No news. Day pleasant with prospects of rain. 7 P.M. I have just received an invitation to a country dance and I am going if it kills me.

SATURDAY JAN. 30TH:

Had a fine time last night. Did not get into camp until nearly day light. I have an invitation to an other dance next Monday night but I fear I will not get to go. Got orders and marched at 10 A.M. Arrived at Lenoir at 2 P.M. where we joined our Brig. and went into camp. Distance ten miles.

SUNDAY JAN. 31ST 1864:

Rained some last night. I have been engaged to day building myself a Shebang and writing a letter to A.J. Gardner. no news of any kind from the front.

MONDAY FEB. 1ST 1864:

Rained and Stormed very hard last night. The wind blowed the top off my Shebang and I got very wet. It cleared off to day and has been quite pleasant. Wrote a letter to Emma.

TUESDAY FEB. 2D:

Received orders and marched for Knoxvill[e] at day light. Got three miles and were ordered back to our old camp. Wrote a letter to father. Turning very cold.

WEDNESDAY FEB. 3RD 1864:

Had a very hard wind storm accompanied with some rain last night. On picket to day. Weather clear and cold.

THURSDAY FEB. 4TH:

Relieved from picket at 8 A.M. and came into camp. Co. D returned from Concord. My old Gal. is back now and I had to build a larger house so I have been hard at work all afternoon. No news from the front.

FRIDAY FEB. 5TH:

Nothing transpired worthy of note to day. Weather cloudy with appearances of rain.

SATURDAY FEB. 6TH:

Rained some to day. My friend Gardner called on me this morning. He is mail agt. for the Dept. of the Ohio. I got a pass and came up on the train with him to this place Knoxvill[e]. At this 6 P.M. I am with him at his Boarding House, Mr. Scotts. There is two very fine looking young ladies here. They appear very sociable and I think I will have a pleasant time.

SUNDAY FEB. 7TH:

Have spent a pleasant day this forenoon. Gardner and I went out to his Regt. to see an old friend. This afternoon we went with the young ladies to church. Very nice. I wish it could last.

MONDAY FEB. 8TH 1864:

Bid adieu to Gardner and the young ladies at 8 A.M. Come to the depot got on the train and arrived at Lenoir at 11 A.M. and at this 8 P.M. I am on the discontented field with my Regt. Weather clear and cold.

TUESDAY FEB. 9TH:

On picket. Day made up of clouds and sunshine. The air is very cold while far away can be seen the peaks of the Smokey mountains covered with snow. Rec'd a mail. Got two letters one from Jennie and one from brother with his Phot[o]. I should never have known him.

WEDNESDAY FEB. 10TH 1864:

Very cold last night. Was relieved from picket and come into camp at 8 A.M. We had battalion drill this afternoon. I spent the remainder of the day building a house. It is built of logs and chinked and doubed with mud. It is almost finished. It has a fine chimney and at this 7 P.M. I am sitting by a nice fire feeling quite cozy.

THURSDAY FEB. 11TH:

Officer of Fatigue party working on the breast works. Rec'd our baggage from Chat[tanooga] and tomorrow I will have a change of cloths. Day pleasant.

On February 11, the regiment finally received a portion of the baggage it had left in Chattanooga when it began the march toward Knoxville before the end of the year. After almost two months, the troops were finally afforded a small amount of comfort.[39]

FRIDAY FEB. 12TH 1864:

Very busy makeing out my monthly returns. No news from the front. Day pleasant with prospects of rain.

SATURDAY FEB. 13TH:

Engaged most of the day makeing out master rolls. The Paymaster was in camp and i think we will get some green backs in a day or two. Wrote a letter to Emma.

SUNDAY FEB. 14TH:

Working all day on my co. pay rolls. Raining everything looks dreary.

MONDAY FEB. 15TH:
Finished my Pay Rolls and sent them in. Still raining. Orders to march in the morning.

TUESDAY FEB. 16TH 1864:
Revillie at 3 and marched at 5 A.M. takeing the Knoxvill[e] Road. Marched twenty one miles and went into camp at 4 P.M. three miles from town. Feel tired to night. Day clear and cold.

WEDNESDAY FEB. 17TH:
Very cold last night. Drempt I had cold feet and no wonder. Changed our position one mile to the rear and are waiting further orders.

THURSDAY FEB. 18TH:
Snowing most of the day and very cold. No news of any importance from the front. Wrote a letter to Jennie.

FRIDAY FEB. 19TH 1864:
Got a pass and went to town to see my friend Gardner he being absent I called on the misses Scotts and spent a few hours very pleasantly. Returned to camp at 5 P.M. Day very cold.

SATURDAY FEB. 20TH:
Brigade inspected and reviewed by Lt. Col. Comstock at 10 A.M. This afternoon the Regt. was payed for two months. I received $205.00. Got a mail. I got an Illustrated Paper from the 'Unknown.'

SUNDAY FEB. 21ST:
Had a large snow storm in the forenoon but it cleared off this afternoon and got quite pleasant. Made out my ordnance report for the 4th Quarter of 63 and forwarded it to the war Dept. at this 6 P.M. I have Headache enough to supply a whole family.

MONDAY FEB. 22D:
Sent our baggage to Knoxvill[e] to be stored. Got orders and marched at 6 P.M. Crossed the Holston at Knoxvill[e]. Went into camp at 10 P.M. two miles from town. Made five miles.

TUESDAY FEB. 23D:
Marched at 1 A.M. Halted at daylight. Twelve miles from Knoxvill[e] for breakfast. While we were at breakfast we were informed that there was no enemy in front so we rested until 12 m[idday] and started back. Arrived in camp at 6 P.M. haveing marched a distance of twenty seven miles in less than 12 hours. Feel very tired.

The orders the regiment had received on February 22 were for a rapid march to attack a Confederate force at Shuck's Gap, some twelve miles southeast of Knoxville. The regiment got under way just after dark. They marched the ten miles to Shuck's Gap only to find that the enemy had already gone. It was decided to return to camp immediately, and the men were given little time to rest before retracing their steps in the cold and snow-covered landscape.[40]

WEDNESDAY FEB. 24TH:

Wrote a letter to Emma. Moved at 8 A.M. passing through Knoxvill[e]. We took the Strawberry Plains Road. Marched seventeen miles and camped for the night three miles from the plains. Day fine.

The Confederates had left the area, and Longstreet had made plans to put his men in winter quarters and cease offensive operations for the winter. The main reason why the Sixth Ohio and the rest of the Union forces that were with it remained in the area around Knoxville was not to guard against an impending threat from the enemy. General Grant wanted a strong presence in the region because he envisioned it to be of great importance when active campaigning resumed in the spring. Grant thought that the next major undertaking of the war would be an advance by his army through east Tennessee and into Virginia from the southwest. By doing so, he would be able to catch Robert E. Lee's Army of Northern Virginia between his own army and the Army of the Potomac. Grant could not know that in a few short months he would be the overall commander of the Union armies or that he would be personally leading the Army of the Potomac against the enemy.[41]

THURSDAY FEB. 25TH:

Remained in camp. All quiet. The steamer ran up this far and brought us a mail. Weather very windy and disagreeable.

FRIDAY FEB. 26TH:

No news of importance from the front. It is rumored that the Rebs have lit out also that we start in pursuit tomorrow. Capt. Russell has been sent back to Knoxvill[e] to bring up cloths for the officers so I suppose there is something in the report. My book is full and I have no other so I fear I will have to stop takeing notes of our adventures. Day very pleasant.

The regiment continued to serve in east Tennessee until it was sent back to Ohio to muster out on June 23, 1864. Although the regiment did not have the required number of men reenlist to allow it to remain in the service, many members enlisted on gunboats and with General Winfield S. Hancock's corps. Several of the noncommissioned officers also stayed in the army, receiving commissions in other regiments. William Glisan was not among the number who reenlisted. From the Campaign in West Virginia, to Shiloh, to Stones River, to Chickamauga, he had seen enough of war in his three-year term of service.[42]

During its tour of duty, the Sixth Ohio Infantry lost 144 men killed in battle, died of wounds, or died of disease. A large number to be sure, but relatively low considering the numerous and bloody battles in which the regiment was engaged. The regiment was mustered out of the service on June 23, 1864, at Camp Dennison, Ohio.[43]

After the war, Glisan resided in Allegheny County, Maryland, and Pittsburgh, Pennsylvania, where he earned a living as a laborer. In later years, he applied for an invalid pension, citing a sunstroke he received while on a forced march to Philippi, West Virginia, on July 4, 1861, as being the cause of his disabilities, which included heart problems and vertigo. William Glisan died in Pittsburgh on June 3, 1909, at seventy-two years of age.[44]

Capsule History of the Sixth Ohio Infantry

The Sixth Ohio Infantry was organized at Camp Dennison, Ohio, on June 18, 1861. From there, it was moved to Fetterman, West Virginia, between June 29 and July 1, 1861, and attached to the First Brigade, Army of Occupation, West Virginia. It took part in the march to Philippi on July 4 and was at Laurel Hill on July 8 and Carrick's Ford on July 13.

From August 6, till November 19, 1861, it was camped at Elkwater, West Virginia, during which time it took part in the Cheat Mountain Campaign in September. From November 19–30, 1861, it was moved to Louisville, Kentucky, where it did duty at Camp Buell until December 9.

During the month of February 1862, the regiment marched in support of General Ulysses S. Grant's army at Fort Donelson and then took part in the operations against Nashville, Tennessee. On February 25, it was the first Union regiment to enter the city of Nashville. It performed duty in Nashville and Savannah, Tennessee, until April 6, when it took part in the great battle of Shiloh on April 6–7, 1862. Following that battle, the regiment did duty at Pittsburgh Landing until May. It then participated in the seige of Corinth, Mississippi, May 24–30 and the pursuit of the Confederate Army to Booneville till July 12. The regiment was ordered to

Athens, Alabama, on July 12 and served there until July 17, when it was sent to Murfreesboro, Tennessee. From Murfreesboro, the regiment took part in the Kentucky Campaign, which culminated in the battle of Perryville on October 8, 1862.

The Sixth Ohio marched to Nashville on October 22, 1862, and performed duty there until December 26. It then participated in the battle of Stones River, December 30, 1862–January 1, 1863. After the battle, the regiment did duty in the area of Murfreesboro until June of 1863. It then took part in the Tullahoma Campaign, which culminated in the battle of Chickamauga, September 19–20. The Sixth Ohio was part of Major General William S. Roscrans's beseiged army at Chattanooga from September 24 to November 23. On October 27, it took part in the engagement at Brown's Ferry that opened a supply line to the city, and on November 25 it took part in the storming of Missionary Ridge, which broke the seige of Chattanooga. The regiment then marched to the relief of Major General Ambrose E. Burnsides, whose army was beseiged in Knoxville, from November 28 to December 8. From December of 1863 to April of 1864, the Sixth Ohio took part in operations in east Tennessee before being sent to perform garrison duty at Cleveland, Tennessee, from April 12 to May 17, 1864. They were then ordered to Resaca, Georgia, where they guarded the railroad bridge over the Oostanaula River until June 6, 1864. On that date, the regiment was ordered to the rear to be mustered out of the service. It traveled to Camp Dennison, Ohio, where the men were discharged on June 23, 1864, upon the expiration of their enlistments.

During the war, the Sixth Ohio lost 86 men killed and mortally wounded and 58 men who died from disease.[45]

Muster Roll of Company D, Sixth Ohio Infantry

This company roster, obtained from the regimental history, was compiled by the regimental historian many years after the war.

Captain Ezekial H. Tatem (accidentally killed in a railroad accident July 15, 1862)

Captain Charles B. Russell

1st Lieutenant Oliver Parker (resigned February 15, 1862)

1st Lieutenant George W. Morris

2nd Lieutenant Thomas H. Boylan (resigned February 14, 1862)

2nd Lieutenant Harry Gee (resigned September 11, 1862)

2nd Lieutenant Joseph L. Antram (transferred to Company H April 17, 1863)

2nd Lieutenant William R. Glisan

1st Sergeant William F. Balming

1st Sergeant James H. Cochnower (discharged for promotion in another command December 13, 1861)

Sergeants

William Bowers

Thomas Daniels (dropped from rolls May 7, 1862)

George T. Marshall (discharged November 29, 1862)

James W. Morgan (discharged August 26, 1862(

James F. McGregor (killed or died of wounds September 20, 1863)

Ewell West

Amos Willoughby

Dennis O'Brien

Corporals

Willaim A. Clockenburg

William Hawkins (discharged February 24, 1863)

Wallace Hume (discharged January 19, 1863)

James Johnson (discharged February 5, 1862)

Giles Richards (discharged March 23, 1863)

William A. Yates

William H. Drips

John Turner

Augustus W. Young (killed or died of wounds November 25, 1863)

Musicians

William A. Cormany

Oliver D. Blakeslee

Privates

Fred H. Alms (transferred to Signal Corps January 16, 1864)

Joseph Anter

Frederick H. Bastian

Charles H. Bausley

Joseph Bender (discharged May 1, 1863)

John Birnbaum (discharged December 29, 1862)

August Bristol

Herman Brockman

George W. Brown

John Butcher

Luther Carpenter

Edward Chattin (dropped from rolls April 1, 1862)

C. Columbus Cones (discharged August 1862 for promotion in another command)

William Darby

Charles DeLeon (discharged March 26, 1863)

Frank Dellar

Joseph Desar

William F. Dill

William F. Doepke (transferred to Signal Corps January 16, 1864)

Albert C. Drips (discharged March 9, 1863)

Hugo Elder

William F. Failor (absent at Chattanooga)

John Ferrill (absent at Chattanooga)

Alex K. Green

Jacob Gross (discharged February 13, 1863)

Conrad Herring

Thomas Herring

Reinhold Hoffman

Adam Hugel (killed or died of wounds February 5, 1863)

Antoine Imer

Joseph Imm (killed or died of wounds November 25, 1863)

Liberty H. Jenkes (transferred to Veteran Reserve Corps August 31, 1863)

Samuel Keller (discharged August 28, 1861)

George K. Kopp (killed or died of wounds September 20, 1863)

Frank Korte

Fred Lancaster (discharged March 19, 1863)

Henry H. Lanius (discharged November 13, 1862)

George W. Lawrence (transferred to Veteran Reserve Corps August 31, 1863)

Joseph Lively (dropped from rolls June 30, 1861)

John J. Lodge
Thomas H.B. McNeil
James H. Mahon (dropped)
Frank A. Manns
Albert H. Marthens
John Mechley
Charles Mitchell (discharged May 16, 1863)
Thomas J. Morgan
George F. Mosher
Levi L. Pritzell (transferred to Company H June 18, 1861)
John E. Rees (discharged September 29, 1861)
William C. Rees
Andrew Remlinger
Michael Renner
George Richater
Thomas J. Rice
Adam Roberts (dropped from rolls April 1, 1862)
George G. Sabin
William Saxon
Thomas Scannel
Edwin D. Smith (transferred to Battery M, Fourth U.S. Artillery October 23, 1862)

Frederick Soghan
Frederick Speck
Samuel W. Stepehnson (killed or died of wounds October 10, 1863)
Kellian Strassler (transferred to Company H June 18, 1861)
Nicholas Stumpf (transferred to Company H June 18, 1861)
Edward Ulm (transferred to Company H June 18, 1861)
William Vout
John Wakeman
George W. Weiss (discharged)
Simeon Weeks (killed or died of wounds November 30, 1863)
Stephen H. Weeks
William H. Weeks
John Wiederecht (absent)
Martin Wiederecht (absent in hospital–Missionary Ridge wounds)
John Williams
William W. Williams (discharged April 14, 1863)
Thomas Wolcott (discharged October 9, 1862)
John F. Wolflick (discharged July 31, 1862)[46]

TWO

Sergeant Will Duncan,
Second Pennsylvania
Militia Battalion

Will Duncan enlisted in the Union Army as a result of the Militia Act of 1863. On June 9, 1863, the War Department, in response to the impending threat of the invasion of the North by Robert E. Lee's army, created two new military districts in Pennsylvania: The Monongahela and the Susquehanna. Both President Lincoln and Pennsylvania Governor Andrew Curtin made impassioned appeals for men to volunteer in the militia. Lincoln called for one hundred thousand men to meet the emergency, half of them to be from Pennsylvania. Volunteers were slow to enlist initially, as most thought that the Confederate invasion of Pennsylvania was little more than a nervous rumor from the War Department. On June 12, 1863, Governor Curtin issued a proclamation stating "Information has been obtained by the War Department, that a large rebel force, composed of cavalry, artillery, and mounted infantry, has been prepared for the purpose of making a raid into Pennsylvania." Even this proclamation failed to cause large numbers of men to swell the ranks of the militia. It was not until Lee's army crossed the Pennsylvania border that the men of the state answered the call to arms in droves.

Lincoln's call for militia stated that the men were to be enlisted for a period not to exceed six months and further stated that those who volunteered could be mustered out of the army sooner than that, once the emergency passed and the militia was no longer necessary. Although there are several instances where these six-month units actually saw combat, most of them guarded regional points of strategic value and served out their terms as home guards. For the vast majority, their terms of enlistment were spent performing the function of garrison troops, not front line combat soldiers. This is not to devalue their service or cast aspersions on their patriotic fervor in any way. Those who volunteered did so during a period of extreme emergency and uncertainty. They volunteered, ready and will-ing to do their part to repel the invaders of their native soil, and had not Meade and his army overtaken Lee's Confederates at Gettysburg, many of these volunteer militia would probably have seen combat against seasoned Southern troops.[1] As a short-term militia unit that saw no real combat, the Second Pennsylvania Militia Battalion had no regimental histories written about it and, in fact, there is very little in the official records to even commemorate its existence. The monumental set of Pennsylvania reg-imental histories written by Samuel Bates, which lists the unit histories and muster rolls for every unit that served from the state, merely lists that the unit existed, with no information about its service and the scantest of information in its muster roll.

Will Duncan was not an average volunteer. He was a sixty-eight-year-old resident of Buffington Township, Indiana County, Pennsylvania, when he enlisted on July 1, 1863, during the height of the panic caused by Lee's invasion of Pennsylvania. The battle of Gettysburg had already been fought and the Confederate Army removed from the state by the time the battal-ion was formally mustered into Federal service on July 14 in Pittsburgh. Born in Dauphin County in 1795, Duncan had moved with his family to Indiana County when he was fourteen years of age.[2]

Company F, Second Pennsylvania Militia, in which Duncan eventu-ally found himself, was one of sixteen companies raised in Indiana County in response to Governor Curtin's call for volunteers. More than eleven hundred men from the county answered the call. It was commanded by Samuel Campbell, who had just recently been discharged from the 135th Pennsylvania, a nine-month regiment that had just fought at Chan-cellorsville. Forty percent of the males of Indiana County between the ages of fifteen and forty enlisted in the army during the course of the war.[3]

JULY 24 1863:

Company D moved today 2 miles east to guard a bridge on the Bal-timore and Ohio railroad.

These Union forces were actually retaking the area in and around Cum-berland, Maryland. The city had been evacuated for a short time by North-ern troops on June 16, following the defeat of Union forces under the command of Brigadier General Robert Milroy at Winchester, during Lee's march north. Cumberland was surrendered to Confederate cavalry under the command of Brigadier General John Imboden on June 17. The Rebels only stayed in town long enough to destroy the telegraph lines and such railroad stock as had not already been removed before following after the rest of the Confederate Army into Pennsylvania. During Imboden's short stay, local merchants were reported to have done a thriving business selling the Confederates a large quantity of hats, clothes, and boots and receiving their payment in Confederate currency. The Confederates had fired a couple of artillery rounds into the town before presenting a demand for its surrender, but no one in Cumberland had been hurt by the shells. The only casualty of the Confederate occupation came when Imboden's troopers had already left the city and were heading north again. A farmer just outside of town availed himself of the opportunity to fire at the Rebel cavalry and was shot dead.[4]

JULY 25:

Was redding up our new camp ground, the cars were on a trip on the road today, as far as our camp. Although in camp, today is hailed with pleasure. A party of persons went out today on a scout and returned with two horses and 3 chickens.

JULY 27:

Was out today on picket, formed an acquaintance with Hannah Smith, a full blooded Virginian. She plays cards and swears, but treated us kindly. Some of the boys kill two sheep today.

The area south of Cumberland and around Old Town was in close proximity to the Potomac River and the West Virginia and Virginia borders. This proximity, combined with the fact that Maryland was itself a Southern state, meant that there was a segment of the local populace with strong Southern sentiments.

JULY 28:

Volunteered for scout today, traveled 5 miles and returned with 3 chickens.

All Union forces in the area were on the alert to guard against the Confederate cavalry of General John Hunt Morgan. Morgan had undertaken another of his celebrated raids on July 2, traveling through Kentucky, Indiana, and Ohio and reaching the Ohio River and the Ohio–West Virginia border on July 18. Although Morgan's force was attacked and badly mauled in the battle of Buffington Island, the remainder had crossed into West Virginia and made their way through the Little Kanawha Valley. Morgan's force was followed and dogged by Union pursuers until it eventually

crossed into Virginia from Sulphur Springs, West Virginia. Morgan had begun his raid with more than twenty-two hundred men under his command. By the time he was captured at Salineville, Ohio, on July 26, there were only about three hundred men with him. Stragglers from the raid continued to be captured in West Virginia for a few weeks after the surrender of Morgan's main body, and their presence in the area was a constant cause for alarm.[5]

JULY 29:

Nothing Important today. Gathered a lot of blackberries and had a nice supper consisting of blackberries and hard tack.

JULY 30:

A very warm day. Lying in the shade this forenoon. A tremendous heavy rain in the evening running through all the tents.

JULY 31:

Started this morning after boards for our tents. I got them in the old school house, made a raft and came down the river. Got a good dinner near the river, found two fishing lines on the bank.

AUG. 1:

Today was a day of rejoicing to us for Sam Hill came to camp with a squad of recruits, he also had a new shirt for me, and one letter from home. Also got a letter from some of the female friends.

AUG 2:

Wrote a letter today. Had preaching today by a methodist preacher. Went up on a pinnacle of rock, saw the Col. riding up the tow path. He saw us and waved his hat. G. Snyder and I crossed the river this evening and got a canteen full of milk.

The tow path that Duncan refers to is for the Cheasapeake and Ohio Canal, a major line of supply for western Maryland and southwestern Pennsylvania. In an effort to disrupt the shipment of coal on the canal, the Confederates made numerous raids against it. Even with the placement of Union troops such as the Second Pennsylvania Militia, the raiders were

Opposite: Map of Cumberland, Maryland. This city, nestled in the mountains of western Maryland, was an important staging area for operations launched into West Virginia and the Shenandoah Valley. All though it changed hands a couple times during the war, it was generally the home of a large force of Federal garrison troops. The map is from 1873, but little had changed in the city from the end of the war to that date (Allegheny County, Maryland, Historical Society).

usually successful in damaging the canal and temporarily disrupting com-
merce from being shipped. A.C. Greene, director of the canal, believed that
the raids would continue despite the presence of Union troops and that the
only way they could be avoided was if there were sufficient rain to make
the Potomac River unfordable for the Confederates.[6]

AUG. 3:

Was on picket today guarding the bridge.

AUG. 4:

Was very unwell today, excused from drill.

AUG. 5:

Am better today, Allison received a can of butter today from his home.
Keller and I got some milk and cheese and had a good supper.

AUG. 6:

Sam Hood and I went to Old Town [Maryland] today, was in the hospital.

Familiar scene of traffic on the Cheasepeake and Ohio Canal, south of Cumberland, Maryland. The canal was a major artery of commerce for the region, and
its strategic importance to the war effort necessitated that it be guarded against
Confederate raids, The Second Pennsylvania Militia battalion served as a part
of that garrison force (Allegheny County, Maryland, Historical Society).

AUG. 7:

Wrote a letter today. Gunfire started out on the picket this evening.

AUG. 8:

Another foggy morning and sorrowful news to the regiment for another soldier is gone. He died at the hospital this morning at 4 o'clock, his name is Rattigan.

AUG. 9:

Today will long be remembered by Co. J, the news came that Co. J was to be disolved to fill up other Co.'s we were to be divided into 4 squads. Sorrowful was the news. I was at church today at 10 o'clock and went to Mr. McAlters and got some milk and had a good supper.

AUG. 10:

The news that alarmed us proved false. Mr. Fitzjhons took very sick today, so much so that we were obliged to take him to the hospital in a flat boat.

AUG. 11:

Caught a mess of fish today and had a good supper.

AUG. 12:

Company J and G undertook to drain a large pond to get fish, worked hard all day, went out on picket this evening.

AUG. 13:

Nothing important today.

AUG. 14:

Allison got a nice pone today for 10 cents. Last night a squad of six men went out on a scout and returned with a rebel by the name of Tailor as prisoner.

AUG. 15:

Stan Drum went to town today and got drunk and came part of the way home and then lay down and was unable to go further.

AUG. 16:

Drum came to camp this morning. This is Sunday evening and I am sitting on a high point of rocks 60 ft. from the level of the river.

AUG. 17:

Yesterday evening at 6 o'clock Sgt. Taylor, a member of G company died in the hospital. his disease was consumption. He was from or near shelocata. Sam Hood and I were out fishing today and waded the river to get some bait.

The Cresap House Inn at Oldtown, Maryland. The Inn was a central point in the little town that Duncan visited many times (Allegheny County, Maryland, Historical Society).

Cumberland and nearby Clarysville had been established by the Union Army as major regional hospital facilities. The establishment in Clarysville consisted of seventeen buildings, the main hospital being built in the shape of a wagon wheel, with ward rooms extending out from the central hub. Although it had bed space for a few thousand patients, the facility at Clarysville was insufficient for the needs of the army, and there were an additional fifteen hospital buildings scattered throughout the city of Cumberland.[7]

The military hospital at Clarysville, Maryland. Cumberland and the surrounding area was home to a number of military hospitals. This one, located at Clarysville, was the largest and the best. Picture is from a period drawing done in 1863 (Allegheny County, Maryland, Historical Society).

Aug. 18:

Charles Allison was very unwell today. N. Hood and I went down the railroad today and bought a chicken for Allison for 18 cents and promised to return tomorrow and pay for it.

Aug. 19:

N. Hood and I returned today and payed for our chicken with some sugar that we had saved, we also brought some corn meal with us (that we begged) to be made into bread, and while the pone is cooking I am writing.

Aug. 20:

Lingenfelter, Jamison, Douglas and myself are on picket today, we had a nice mess of corn for dinner.

Aug. 21:

The camp was surprised last night on account of us pickets firing, and we fired because the pickets at camp Lininger fired. The camp were all out in line of battle. After coming off picket I jumped on the cars and rode down to Capon to see Capt. Moos's company. Found them all well. Took dinner with D. Simpson and returned in the evening. Allison is still unwell.

False alarms were not uncommon for troops on guard duty along the B&O Railroad and C&O Canal. Rebel partisan rangers were known to operate in the area, and there was the occasional raid by regular Confederate cavalry. Soldiers often adopted the philosophy of "shoot first, ask questions later" as they fired at moonbeams in the dark.

AUG. 22:

This morning I took some washing up to Mr. Frenches. When I returned Allison consented to go to the hospital. We took him across the river in a flat and got him in a canal boat, in this way got him to the hospital, appeared better when we left.

The Baltimore and Ohio Railroad, leading out of the city of Cumberland. The B&O was not only a major supply source for the Union Army, it was also an important means by which to move troops from one place to another. Raids against the B&O were frequent, especially in the sparsely populated areas in which the Second Pennsylvania Milita were garrisoned (Allegheny County, Maryland, Historical Society).

The Civil War witnessed the first major use of the railroads as a means of conveying troops over long distances. Will Duncan records seeing many military trains, just like this one, passing by his camp, carrying reinforcements to General William S. Rosecrans' army in Chattanooga, Tennessee (U.S. Army War College).

AUG. 23:

Was out on a scout today, some 2 miles. Wrote 2 letters today, one to jo and one to mary. Am quite unwell this evening. Made a whiskey stew and went to bed. Allison is no better.

AUG. 24:

Was very sick last night, feel some better this morning. D. Lewis and D. Simpson came to camp today. I feel better this evening. Allison sent word to come to the hospital if I was not better.

AUG. 25:

Our visitors yesterday stayed all night. It rained today and I felt very sick, felt as though I was taking the chills.

AUG. 26:

Last night the sad news came to us that Allison was dying, 4 men went up to the hospital, S. Hood, J. Anderson, M. Kerr, S. Drum. I was unable to go. They returned this morning with the news of his death which took place about 12 o'clock. This day must have been decreed to be a day of sorrow and gloom to our company, for we were not only to bear the sorrows of a deceased friend but company J was dissolved in compliance with an order from Gen. Brooks. I am too ill to write more today.

Aug. 27:

Allison was buried yesterday evening at 6 o'clock in the honors of war, but before he was buried our company was divided. Capt. Marshall and 14 men went to Ritcheys Co. Lt. McHenry and 19 men into Capt. Finkbernz. Lt. Bell and 10 men into Altimes. This was all done yesterday. Our squad went to company F in the evening and I was taken up on a hand car with more of the unwell. Co. F received marching orders this morning, we were to go down to the south branch where we had just come from, which was good news for the 19 Co. G boys but sorrowful news for the rest of the company. They dreaded going tomorrow as they thought it so sickly, for most of us from there are sick. I felt better this morning but when we started in the sun I nearly gave out and when we got near the camp grounds, I lay down in the shade while my mess mates were building a tent. The vacancy in my mess made so by the death of Allison, has been filled by M. Munshower.

Located as it was near the banks of the Potomac and the line of the C&O Canal, the camp of the Second Pennsylvania Militia was an unhealthy place during the hot months of the summer. Medical science had not yet identified the causes of the various fevers that were claiming so many lives in the regiment, primarily the mosquitoes that were so plentiful at the water's edge. The fevers shakes, and chills that Duncan states he was afflicted with sound like the symptoms of malaria.

Aug. 28:

The fever has left me and I feel some better. Both Co,'s have moved their position 10 rods to higher ground. I am spending the day lying under a shade tree.

Aug. 29:

Camped with Hoods boys last night, our tent not being finished. Still felt unwell. Sam Hill and I both took a notion to go to the hospital. Went up to the hospital on a boat and had a chill after dinner and a very high fever after.

Aug. 30:

Felt quite well today and had a good dinner. Rev. Latshaw came to the hospital, we had bible class in the afternoon, had worship at night.

Aug. 31:

This is the day I should have had a shake, but had none, therefor feel as though the fever has broken. M.C. Bell came from Cumberland today.

A camp at Fort Hill, Cumberland, Maryland. This permanent camp was but one of many in and around the city to accomodate garrison soldiers. Troops stationed here were less exposed to the elements and to the malarial sicknesses that plagued Will Duncan and his comrades. Picture was taken in 1863, during the time the Second Pennsylvania Militia was serving in the area (Allegheny County, Maryland, Historical Society).

SEPT. 1:

Today two months is up. Sam Hill and I gathered a bucket of berries for the hospital.

SEPT. 2:

The hospital Steward informed us this morning that 10 men were to return to their Co.'s, among that number were Hill and myself accordingly after dinner we left for camp and found the boys pretty well in camp and glad to see us return.

SEPT. 3:

Felt tolerable well today, wrote a letter to Sallie.

SEPT. 4:

Got a letter from Mary and two newspapers from father.

SEPT. 5:

Munshower caught some fish today. Wrote a letter to cousin B. Griffith. Sam Smay called today to see me from Co. X [?]. Had a good supper consisting of pot pie and sweet milk. Paid 10 cents for a canteen full of milk.

SEPT. 6:

Was a beautiful sabbath. Had preaching today by Lt. Latshaw. McHenry put on his new uniform today.

SEPT. 7:

Got a pass today, went to Mr. Longs, had a talk with the daughter. Got a hassock full of apples and canteen full of milk and some potatoes, had a fine supper this evening.

SEPT. 8:

Went out on picket this morning for the first time in two weeks. Went into camp for dinner. Harbison had a nice lot of potatoes fried.

SEPT. 9:

Wm Munshower got a fine lot of peaches and potatoes today, had peaches and milk for supper, received a letter from father today with 2 dollars in it.

SEPT. 10:

Went to Old Town today and bought a coffee pot for 40 cents, got some milk coming home for nothing. Had a peach pot pie for supper. Wrote a letter to father and mary.

The Second Pennsylvania Militia was fortunate to be stationed in an area that had not been subjected to the ravages of war. They could readily supplement their scanty army rations with fresh fruits and vegetables purchased from farmers in the surrounding countryside. Many soldiers, on both sides, were not so lucky.

SEPT. 11:

Received a letter today from M.G.C., got my pants and shirt washed for 5 cents each.

SEPT. 12:

Got a fine lot of apples today. A. Woodward received a box from home in which was a vest and 3 cans of fruit for myself from home.

SEPT. 13:

I was detailed for guard last night at 9 o'clock in place of Wm. Meyers, he being sick. Our camp is reported to be in danger. A new picket post was made today, we have 27 men on guard all the time.

SEPT. 28:

Slept part of the time last night lying very comfortably on the dusty road. Soldiers passing all night in the trains, some going today.

Following the defeat of Major General William S. Rosecrans's Union Army at the battle of Chickamauga, some twenty-two thousand Federal troops were transferred to Rosecrans's command. These reinforcements were all sent on the Baltimore & Ohio Railroad, and under the supervision of railroad president John Garrett, the transfer of all twenty-two thousand troops took only eleven days.[8]

SEPT. 29:

Made a door for our tent this morning, Munshower and I went over into Maryland in the afternoon, tried to trade soap for some milk but failed. Went to a place where no one was at home, took a tin and some apples. Coming home we saw some rifle pits that it is said were made under Gen. Washington. Succeeded in trading my soap for two loaves of bread. Soldiers continuing to go westward.

SEPT. 30:

Felt unwell last evening, better this morning. Went on picket on the Romney road. The sun was very warm and I was not on duty long before I took a chill, then a burning fever, after which I went to camp and went to bed.

Romney, in Hardy County, West Virginia, was known to be a hotbed of Southern sympathy. A large number of Confederate soldiers had volunteered from the town, and many of the citizens were supportive of the Southern irregular cavalry units that frequented the area. Although the records show that of the 19,189 votes cast in a special election to decide if West Virginia should dissolve its affiliation with the rest of Virginia and form its own state, 18,408 were in the affirmative, this is not an accurate estimate of the sentiments of the area. True, the measure won by an overwhelming margin, but dissenting votes were not cast, either because the voters were already in the Confederate Army, or because those at home were afraid to make their feelings known and risk retaliation by Union-supporting neighbors or by the Federal forces that occupied the counties.[9]

OCT. 1:

Felt pretty well this morning, ate breakfast, at noon another chill and fever. Ate no dinner. A member of Co. C died last night in the hospital, by the name of_____. Got a letter today.

OCT. 2:

Could not sleep last night, took some quinine. Ate some breakfast after which I took a chill and a very hard fever, was deranged part of the time. It commenced raining this morning and rained hard all day. Some of the tents were nearly swimming. Doc. Tom called today to see me and gave me some medicine.

OCT. 3:

Felt better today, still confined to my tent. I opened a can of apple sauce today but don't feel like eating. G. Clark came to see me twice today and brought me the Advocate.

OCT. 4:

Slept tolerable, took medicine today which made me very sick. The day was pleasant. Drawed all our rations today and took to own cooking.

OCT. 5:

M.C. Bell came from Cumberland today on business. I feel better today. Sent to Old Town and got ½ pound of cheese for 10 cents, also bought ½ pie for 5 cents.

OCT. 6:

Better today. A horse race in Old Town. Some of the 54th Penn. Reg. are in camp from Romney.

The Fifty-fourth Pennsylvania Infantry was a veteran unit to the area in which Duncan and his comrades were operating. Having enlisted in the fall of 1861, the Fifty-fourth had spent the majority of its time in the service in the general area of Capon Bridge, Romney, and New Creek (present-day Keyser) West Virginia. 10

OCT. 7:

Nothing important today. Wrote a letter, Jas. Anderson and J. Anthony started for home today. Saw a drove of wild ducks.

OCT. 8:

Munshower and Harbison are on picket today and I am cook. I had beans for dinner and beef for supper. We were paid off today, I received $26.00. Isaac Myers got a box from home today. Capt. Altimis and C. Low had a race this evening.

Duncan's pay was for two months of service. The standard rate of pay for a private in the army was a mere $13.00 per month.

OCT. 9:

Went to Old Town and traded some rice for some syrup at the rate of 5 cents per pound. Sold two pounds of sugar for 15 cents per pound, some coffee 25 cents per pound. Sent my money home today by G. Young. Wrote a letter home to father. Sam Douglas came down from Cumberland to see us. W. Munshower and J. Ricket went to Cumberland today. I sold one of my cans for 10 cents today.

OCT. 10:

Harbison and I are on camp guard today. We made a grist mill today out of a piece of old tin by punching holes in it with a nail. Munshower ground cornmeal last night, enough for a meal of mush for breakfast. David Richard was to see us today from Capon. Countersign last night was Garibaldi.

OCT. 11:

Munshower is on picket today. I got on a coal train this morning and went to the south branch. Took dinner with Lingenfelter and Kierr and then went to Mr. Longs and got some apples, then came to camp on a canal boat near sundown.

OCT. 12:

Harbison and I are on guard today. I was in Old Town on patrol duty guarding a prisoner. Ten of us slept in the guard house with a good fire. Old Mr. Eastman brought on a lot of pies, apples, cakes, cigars and cheese.

OCT. 13:

Came off guard this morning. Sam Hood and I got aboard the cars and went down to Capon. Took dinner with D. Richard, went across the river and got on a canal boat and started for Camp Lininger. A nigger wench gave us a pie, bread, cup of tea and meat for 5 cents all with good will. We left her wishing she might never go hungry.

OCT. 14:

Repaired our fireplace today, got a lot of corn ears and grated it, made some mush and fried it for supper. Got some beer at the post office. Report of rebels east of us on the railroad. Held an election yesterday and resulted in a large majority for Christian.

> *The election would have been for company officers. It was a common practice in both armies for the men in the ranks to elect their company-level officers. In some cases, this could have the effect of placing inept officers in positions of responsibility, as soldiers sometimes voted based on popularity, instead of ability.*

OCT. 15:

On picket today, Harbison and I. I am on the post they call the bluff, Harbison is on the Romney road. I traded 4 pounds of meat today for apple butter, the meat at 7 cents a pound, the butter at 10 cent a pint. We have a picket post or picket house built this evening of poles and clay. This evening is cloudy with a good prospect of a wet night.

OCT. 16:

Last night was slightly wet. Sam Hood and I slept from 9 to 1 then stood guard till morning. Countersign was Alleghany River. Borrowed a mess pan last night but found a hole in it and had to throw it away. Got a can full of milk. Had corn cakes for supper. Received a letter from mary.

OCT. 17:

A wet morning but a pleasant afternoon, sold 4 pounds of sugar today for 60 cents and some coffee. Two men from indiana county, Sam Lydick and a man by the name of McElly got a letter today. Paid 15 cents for mending my shoes. The boys tore down old Mr. Eastman's shaving saloon last night. Got a letter today.

OCT. 18:

On guard today at the canal bridge. It's a pleasant autumn day. Got some paw paw's from a boat, save some seeds. The river rose so much yesterday that the pontoons were likely to break, swinging it to one side. Came across this morning on a skiff. Munshower was cook today and had beans for dinner which was very excellent.

OCT. 20:

Mr. Eastman is in camp today with his suttlers shop selling pies, cakes, lager beer. The river rose considerable last night. So much so that it has become dangerous to cross in a skiff. Harbison and I made some more cornmeal last night and fried it for breakfast this morning. Got a pint of apple butter today for 10 cents.

OCT. 21:

In Old Town today on guard. Harbison received a box from home today with bread, apples, pies, and clothing. Saw a load of apples in Old Town for sale at $1.00 per bushel. Six deserters came to camp from the rebel army wanting to go to Ohio. A beautiful indian summer day. August Latimer and Ros. McCoy were put on a bull ring for going to Cumberland without a pass. Four boys coming off picket this morning in crossing the river in a skiff, upset, they fell in, losing their guns and nearly drowning.

Corporal punishment was much enforced in both armies during the war for offenses great and small. Men who committed offenses could be exposed to punishments like riding the wooden horse, which consisted of the soldier being forced to straddle a pole or board that was suspended high in the air with his ankles tied together. They could also be bucked and gagged or forced to wear a ball and chain. Being tied by his thumbs so that the soldier had to stand on his tip-toes to prevent them from being pulled out of their sockets or having a log placed across his shoulders with outstretched arms tied to the log, were other popular forms of punishment. Any infraction of the rules could bring about this severe sort of treatment, and a major violation such as desertion or cowardice could result in capital punishment before a firing squad.[11]

Oct. 22:

Wrote a letter today to F.M. Sunter. Saw a drove of wild ducks. The boys recovered the guns that were lost yesterday.

Oct. 23:

Company F had a game of ball today. I sent a ring to Capon to get plated for Sallie. Cold raw day.

Baseball had not yet become America's pastime, but it had attained a level of popularity with the soldiers in camp. Many men got their first introduction to the sport while serving in the army.

Oct. 24:

Harbison and I are on picket today. Munshower relieved me this afternoon as I felt unwell, and he wanted me to draw rations. Saw a very large drove of ducks and one of geese wending their way southward.

Oct. 25:

Last night was a very frosty night. We kept a brisk fire up all night on picket. W. Hood and I got a knapsack full of persimmons this morning. Got a letter from father this morning with the sad news of Sarah's illness and of my uncle and aunt being there from Ohio. I went this afternoon to Mr. Dorseys and got a pint of apple butter. This evening 17 rebel prisoners, well guarded, were brought to Old Town. They looked pretty rough in their suits of muddy grey.

Oct. 26:

This morning our orderly called to Harbison and me to be ready for a scout at 7 o'clock, so we got up and had breakfast before daylight. About 8 o'clock 18 of us started but it proved to be nothing more than to guard four wagons that were sent for hay into Virginia seven miles up the south branch. We ate our dinner while the wagons were loading, which was dry bread and butter. Daniel Lydick was buried today, he died from the effects of a bruise he received at the south branch.

Oct. 27:

This morning the news reached us that Lowman, another member of Co. G died in the Old Town hospital from typhoid fever, and this evening

I was one of the bearers that bore him to his last resting place on the hill above Old Town, where, when the last glimmering of the setting sun rested on the western sky, we laid him in his grave to sleep his last long sleep. G. Clark spent the evening with us. Had beans for supper.

OCT. 28:

On camp guard, Harbison and Munshower and I, washed a shirt and one pair of socks. Wm. Lingenfelter and Dr. Tom called to see us this evening. G. Clark got a box from home today with a lot of good things. He gave me a share of his preserves. Got my blouse mended this morning for 5 cents.

OCT. 29:

Came off guard this morning, got on the wagon train and went to Capon. Took dinner with D.H. Lewis. Came home in the wagon train. Invitation to dinner with G.H. Clark which consisted of sweet cakes and caned pears. A letter from Sallie today.

OCT. 30:

Munshower was on picket today, Harbison and I were detailed to guard the hay wagons, to haul hay. In my travels I bought a pie for 10 cents. Came home this evening tired and hungry. Got a letter from father this morning with $2.00 in it with some more things coming in Snyders box tomorrow.

OCT. 31:

Munshower and J. Meyers killed a pig yesterday on picket. W. Hood and I went out last night and brought it in. We salted ours in a crock. Snyders box came today with my boots, socks, pr. overpants and some apples therein. I plated a ring today for myself. Went to Old Town in the evening, traded some rice for molasses and bought a haversack full of cornmeal for 20 cents.

The reason Duncan and a comrade went to retrieve the killed pig after it had been shot by the pickets was that the soldiers were not permitted to forage in the surrounding countryside. Western Maryland was considered to be Union territory, and the residents of the area were supposed to be under the protection of the army. Duncan and his four comrades would have faced stern punishment for killing the pig if they had been caught by an officer.

NOV. 1:

Harbison and myself were detailed for picket this morning, but Munshower took my place and I am to take his tomorrow as he wants to plate some rings. This is a very pleasant day. I cooked beans and beef for dinner, wrote half a letter to Sallie Munshower and Wm. wrote the rest.

Nov. 2:

Wrote a letter this morning before daylight to father. Went on guard to Old Town. Two deserters from the rebel army came in today. Lt. McHenry took them with one we had to Cumberland in the evening.

Nov. 3:

Last night a lot of the 54th got on a drunk about eleven o'clock went to a tavern, tried to get in, kicked in the door. The landlord got up and drew his revolver and fired at one outside, the ball missed him and came near hitting one of the guards, it striking the ground between them and throwing mud on their heads. We went in to arrest them but they skedaddled. Our Sgt. Cohoe got slightly drunk. Was introduced this morning to Mr. Young of the 54th by his brother in law G. Clark. Col. Linger came home this morning with his wife and 3 children. Mr. Smith died today in the hospital.

Nov. 4:

Today is election day in Maryland, a guard was sent to Old Town of 24 men under Lt. McHenry to quell any disturbance that may arise. I washed a shirt and pr of drawers, warming water in the mess pan and using an old crock for a wash sink. A very fine day.

Union authorities in Maryland were ever fearful of Southern interference or Democratic victory in the fall elections. As such, Major General Robert Schenck, commander of the Middle Department, issued General Order 53, which gave all provost marshals and Union commanders in Maryland the authority to arrest any person thought to be disloyal to the Union. This included all Southern sympathizers, who would have voted Democratic in the election. Governor Bradford of Maryland protested the order strongly, but Schenck was upheld in his actions by President Lincoln.[12]

Nov. 5:

On guard in Old Town today, put a doctor from Romney in the guard house for getting drunk, his wife was with him and cried. Sam Hill went to the hospital yesterday, was crazy all last night. Sent a telegraph to his brother N. Hill of his illness. Capt. Dickson got leave in the afternoon to send him home. N. Hood was to go with him but Sam thought he would stay until his brother would come. Got my hair cut today by Wm. Meyers.

Nov. 6:

I went to the hospital last night to see Hill. He told me he was no better or no worse. He asked me what post I was on. He then asked me if there was any light upstairs. I told him yes. He then said he wanted to wash his feet and change his socks, and then he became flighty wanting to get up. We left him and the news this morning is that Sam Hill is no more. The Col. received a dispatch from Romney that General Imboden was going to make another raid on the railroad. The Col. went to South Branch and Patterson Creek to arrange matters for his reception. The boys in camp were replenished with ammunition. Col. McHenry went to Cumberland today for a coffin for Hill and intends returning tomorrow.

Nov. 7:

McHenry returned today at 8 o'clock with a coffin for Hill costing $40.00. the company raised $57.00 to send him home. Sam Hood, Harbison and myself got a team and brought the coffin from the hospital to the cars this evening, got it aboard and McHenry started for home with it by way of Somerset [Pennsylvania].

Sick and wounded men spent long, tedious hours in ward rooms such as this. Although doctors, nurses, and civilian volunteers did what they could to alleviate the suffering of the patients, medical science and the resources of the medical department could not keep up with the demands placed on them by the war (U.S. Army War College).

Four hundred fourteen men from Indiana County died of all causes during the war. Of this total, 168 died of disease, accounting for over 40 percent of those who perished. In his diary, Duncan refers to a large number of men in his outfit who all died of various diseases.[13]

NOV. 8:

Munshower is unwell, Harbison and I are on duty. He is on picket, I in Old Town guarding. A very cold windy day. The Col.'s wife was out at dress parade this evening.

NOV. 9:

Slept in the guard house last night. Commenced snowing today for the first day, made a ring today for a young man and got 25 cents for it.

NOV. 14:

Was paid today, 2 months wages, paid Anderson 25 cents for cooking. A nice warm day.

NOV. 15:

Very wet morning and forenoon, wrote a letter to M. G. C., read an account of Robinson's [Rosecrans'] campaign.

NOV. 16:

A great many boys got drunk, two from company E were out in the guard house for fighting. One had a case knife. Got a letter from some of the girls.

NOV. 17:

Plated a ring today, which sold for 50 cents. Got a letter today.

NOV. 18:

A cold rainy day.

NOV. 19:

M. E. Bell was with us last night. Our meat had to last through this morning. The coldest day we have had yet. Lt. McHenry and I left this evening for Methodist Church some two and one half miles from here in rebeldom.

Although Duncan reports seeing no action in his diary entries, the area in which the Second Pennsylvania Battalion was operating was commonly raided by both regular and irregular Confederate cavalry. McNeil's Rangers made frequent raids into the region, and although Duncan and his comrades were never engaged with them, many a Union soldier performing guard duty on the B&O Railroad and C&O Canal was captured by this active band of partisan rangers whose base of operations was in Moorefield, West Virginia.

Nov. 20:

Quite a cold night, last night, cold enough for a frost. The lieutenants with their men are in camp this morning having returned last night. They heard a good sermon. Ten men out of each company went today including our two lieutenants and preacher Latshaw. I was along, heard a good sermon, saw some fine ladies. Stood picket, had a good dinner and returned to camp. But a serious accident occurred, man by the name of Gamble accidently discharged his revolver, the ball passing through his fingers.

Nov. 21:

Was very busy repairing our tent, preparing for winter, last night being very cold with a heavy frost this morning.

Nov. 22:

Working on the tent. Got some apples at Mr. Longs, bought a pound of butter for 10 cents. Got a letter from Sallie and answered it.

Nov. 23:

Still working at the tent. Munshower received a box from home with a chicken, pears, pie, apples, prunes, peaches, pound cake, shirts and paper.

Nov. 24:

Another sad day to our company. We had our tent just finished when the news came for us to leave for Camp Lininger. Many curses were heaped on the Col.'s head for this trouble.

Nov. 25:

A very busy day hauling our tent boards to Camp Lininger and putting up our tents. Received two cannon today in camp, 12 men were detailed for guard.

Captain Hans McNeil. His band of partisan rangers were an active and constant threat to the supply and communication lines in western Maryland and West Virginia (U.S. Army War College).

Nov. 26:

Another busy day hauling bricks and building a chimney in which we put some fire and it drew beautiful. Went to Old Town, got some grapes. A large wagon train in our camp with excellent mules. Cavalry company left this morning for Romney, one of the men, being in liquor fell from his horse and was much injured. Received two pieces of cannon yesterday.

Nov. 27:

Was detailed for picket with D. Stevens, W. Hood. Last night was so cold that it froze ice. A corps of soldiers from the Potomac army passed yesterday and last night to reinforce Rosecranz. I write this evening with my face toward the setting sun, blue mountains in view westward. Camp Lininger half mile distant in the west, the Potomac fllows at the floor of the hill to my right. Beyond and in view lies Old Town. While this is all in view a regiment of soldiers is passing on the railroad between me and the river on their way to Rosecranz.

Thus ends Will Duncan's diary. It details but the first half of his nine-month enlistment. After completing his term of enlistment with the Second Pennsylvania Militia Battalion, one would think that Duncan had certainly done his duty to his country, but obviously Duncan himself did not think so. He enlisted in the 206th Pennsylvania Infantry on August 31, 1864, for a one-year term and was mustered out on June 26, 1865. The death of Duncan's wife in 1864 may have had a great deal to do with his motivation to reenlist for another tour of duty. During this time, Duncan served as a first sergeant with the regiment. The regiment was attached to the Army of the James in October of 1864. Although it saw duty in the trenches before Petersburg, it took part in no pitched battles. The 206th was a part of the force that occupied Richmond after its evacuation by the Confederate army, and then the regiment did provost guard duty at Richmond and Lynchburg.[14] After the war, Duncan returned to his farm in Indiana County, where he died on June 11, 1873, at the age of seventy-eight. He was survived by six children. William Duncan is buried in the East Union Cemetery in Buffington Township, Indiana County, Pennsylvania.[15]

Capsule History of Second Battalion, Pennsylvania Militia

The Second Battalion, Pennsylvania Militia was officially mustered into the Federal Service on July 23, 1863, having been recruited during the months of June and July. The battalion was raised largely in Indiana County, Pennsylvania, and was recruited to serve for a period of six months. It was mustered under the Militia Act of 1863, which called for one hundred thousand short-term volunteers to defend against Robert E. Lee's invasion of Pennsylvania during the Gettysburg Campaign. The battalion performed its entire tour of service doing garrison and guard duty in the Cumberland and Old Town areas of western Maryland, along the lines of the C&O Canal and the B&O Railroad. During its enlistment, the battalion fought in no major battles and had precious few brushes with the enemy. According to Samuel P. Bates's book History of Pennsylvania Volunteers, 1861–1865, the battalion was mustered out of the service on January 29, 1864. Dyer's Compendium lists the date as January 21, 1864. Neither source provides any personal information on the soldiers in the unit or battalion returns regarding losses.[16]

Muster Roll for Company I, Second Battalion Pennsylvania Militia

The records for militia units were often incomplete. In this case, Samuel Bates, the compiler of the unit histories for the state of Pennsylvania, did not even designate this unit as the Second Battalion, merely as "Independant Battalion." His listing of Duncan's company lettering is also incorrect, as Duncan was in Company J originally and then was consolidated into Company F. Bates lists it as Company I. Personal information is noted for members of the majority of the regiments in Bates's collective works, but there are no such listings for any of the militia units. The personal notation for Samuel Hill is from Duncan's diary. Note the scant number of men listed in this roster when compared with those of the other regiments in this book.

First Lieutenant William B. Marshall
Sergeant William Duncan

Privates

James Anderson
Amos T. Anthony
Andrew S. Buchannon
Moses C. Bell
Joseph Barnett
Edward Boring
Samuel Douglass

Daniel S. Drum
Anthony Ewing
George N. Foukes
Samuel M. Hood
Matthew Harbison
Samuel Hill (Died of Disease)
George W. Hood
John T. Jamison
Martin Kier
David S. Kerr
Augustus Lattemer

William Lingenfelter
Noah Livingston
James Myers
William Munshower
Isaac N. Myers
Robert D. McClure
John D. McClarren
Robert M. McClarren
William W. McCrackin
Oliver M'Henry
Anthony Riffel
William W. Rankin

John M. Ray
Richard W. Rowe
John H. Rodkey
George H. Snyder
William Shields
Daniel Snyder
Theodore Shank
Adam Smith
Frederick Smith
William Snyder
Michael C. Woodward
Robert A. Young

THREE

Private John M. Kelly
Thirty-ninth Illinois
Volunteer Infantry

The Thirty-ninth Illinois Volunteer Infantry, commonly known as Yates Phalanx in honor of the governor of the state, was mustered into Federal service on October 11, 1861. It was sent east and saw initial duty guarding the B&O Railroad at Williamsport and Hancock, Maryland. It participated in the battles at Kernstown and Winchester before being sent to join McClellan's main force at Harrison's Landing, Virginia. After a brief stint as garrison troops at Fortress Monroe, the regiment was sent to Suffolk, Virginia. From there it was sent to New Bern, North Carolina, and then to Port Royal, South Carolina. The Thirty-ninth ended up at St. Helens Island, South Carolina, at the beginning of 1863, where it became a part of the Union Army engaged in operations against the forts and fortifications of Charleston, South Carolina. For the remainder of 1863, the regiment would take part in expeditions against Forts Wagner, Gregg, and Sumter as well as Morris Island. Wagner and Gregg were captured on September 7 of that year. The regiment had sufficient members reenlist to allow it the distinction of being a veteran regiment, and the members were given furlough for thirty days on January 1, 1864. When the men returned from furlough, they were sent to Yorktown, Virginia, and attached to General Ben Butler's Army of the James. They took part in the operations against Bermuda Hundred, Petersburg, and Richmond, which is where Private Kelly's diary ends.[1]

John Kelly was a seventeen-year-old farmer from Huntingdon County, Pennsylvania, when he signed up with the regiment. He was tall for the time, standing at five feet, ten inches and had black hair, hazel eyes, and a fair complexion.[2]

DEC. 20, 1862:
My Birthday. No one knows it yet. A cold day.

SUNDAY, DEC. 21, 1862:
Still Remains cold.

DEC. 22, 1862:
On picket today.

DEC. 23, 1862:
Releived of picket today.

DEC. 24, 1862:
We prepared 3 days Rations for a march today. We expect to move soon.

DEC. 25, 1862:
Christmas [Day]. I received a box from home this evening.

DEC. 26, 1862:
Still Rumor of [a march].

DEC. 27, 1862:
Rained some today.

SUNDAY, DEC. 28, 1862:
Spinola's Brigade left today.

DEC. 29, 1862:
Part of Corcoran's Brigade came to this place today.

DEC. 30, 1862:
2 Regts. more of Corcoran's Brigade came in today and the 67th Ohio of Ferry's Brigade left on train for Norfolk.

DEC. 31, 1862:
The 62nd Ohio left on the cars for Norfolk, also the 174th [?] P.[ennsylvania] V.[olunteers].

The 174th Pennsylvania Infantry was a nine-month unit that had just been mustered into the service in November of 1862. Like the Thirty-ninth Illinois, it was to be attached to the Tenth Army Corps and see service in the Hilton Head and Charleston areas of South Carolina, being mustered out of the service in August of 1863.

THURSDAY, JAN 1, 1863
The day came in windy and cold. Dress parade.

JAN. 2, 1863:
A warm day. Battalion drill at 10 A.M.

JAN 3, 1863:
Dress parade today.

SUNDAY, JAN. 18, 1863:
The Illinois State Flag (sent by Governor Yates) was presented to the Regt. by Col. [acting Brig. Gen.] Osborn on Dress parade this evening. Regimental inspection at 10 o'clock this morning.

JAN 19, 1863:
Company inspection today at 9 A.M. Dress parade at 6 P.M.

JAN. 20, 1863:
A Review was ordered to come off at 10 A.M. [we formed] at the time, but it commenced to rain and we were ordered back to Camp again. It stopped raining and we had Batt[alion] drill at 3 P.M. It commenced raining about 4 P.M. again & continued to rain up to 8 P.M.

JAN. 21, 1863:
It rained by degrees all day today. Batt. Drill at 3 P.M. and Dress parade at 6.

JAN. 22, 1863:
Rained some again today.

JAN. 23, 1863:
The 62nd and 67th Regts, Ohio Vols, left here today. Destination unknown. Batt. Drill & Dress parade. Orderly Kingsbury of Co. E was promoted to 2nd Lieutenant & [?] 4th Sergt. appointed in Kingsbury's place. The Company is [happy] with the appointment.

These two Ohio regiments were also being transferred to the Tenth Army Corps in South Carolina. They were merely two of the first regiments in Kelly's camp area to be forwarded to that destination. Kelly and the rest of the Thirty-ninth Illinois would soon join them.[3]

JAN. 24, 1863:
I went to town this morning & Returned at 1 P.M. Battalion Drill and Dress parade today.

SUNDAY, JAN. 25, 1863:
We received orders last night at 9 P.M. to March this morning & about 7 A.M. all preparations being made, we started to the Depot at Newbern &

got on the cars & about 10 A.M. we started for Beaufort & arrived there about 1 P.M. & immediately boarded the boat and moved out into the Harbor & anchored.

JAN. 26, 1863:
We laid On the Boat Gen. [Meigs] about 9 P.M. Co E & C moved to the Boat "Skirmisher," a schooner of about 180 tons Burthen.

JAN. 27, 1863:
We are much pleased with our change of Boats. It is Raining some and the wind is Blowing some.

JAN. 28, 1863:
The wind is raising very high and the waves can be seen out on the Sea raising like mountains. It is still raining and it's very disagreeable on deck.

JAN. 29, 1863:
It is clear today but the wind blows very cold.... About 2 P.M. we [weighed anchor] and went out to sea.

JAN. 30, 1863:
We sailed on today. The wind is still blowing very high.

JAN. 31, 1863:
The wind is fair today & we sail southwest bound for Port Royal, North [South] Carolina.

> *The capture of Port Royal had been among the first of the North's important victories in the first year of the war. It provided the Union Navy with a much-needed port and coaling facility, without which establishing or maintaining the blockade against the Confederate coastline would have been an almost impossible task.*

SUNDAY, FEB. 1, 1863:
The wind has turned today. We have to tack again.

FEB. 2, 1863:
We sailed on today. The wind is the same. Had inspection today.

FEB. 3, 1863:
Very windy today. We arrived in Port Royal Harbor about 5 P.M.

FEB. 9TH:
We landed today and went into Camp where the balance of the Regiment were already in Camp. The day is warm & Pleasant.

10TH:

On Guard at General Ferry's Head Qrs. Went on at 12½ o'c P.M. His Head Qrs. is in a small white house on the River Bank. The day is very warm, making it pleasant in the shade.

11TH:

Relieved of [guard] at 12½ P.M. Still warm.

12TH:

Fog Rolled in this Morning. We were signed by [Paymaster] & about 5 P.M. were paid off 4 months pay. I received $40.00.

13TH:

The boys are making a Christmas of today as apples, candy & c. are plenty in the camp. Early this morning we received the sad news of the death of John A. Laughlin. He died at Port Royal in the Hospital. His disease is supposed to have been consumption. It is cloudy & windy & somewhat cooler today. This day one [year ago] I left Orbisonia on my way to the 39th which was then at Patterson's Creek, Va. [The] party consisted of J.L. Ripple, Wm. B. Ripple, A. Laughlin, D.S. Rutter in charge of the coach & myself. We had a pleasant Ride.

All of the companions Kelly mentions traveling to Patterson Creek with were Huntingdon County boys who joined the Thirty-ninth Illinois. The reason they opted to join this Illinois regiment in preference to a local Pennsylvania unit was probably for the bounty that was being offered. The bounty system was put in place to offset the Conscription Act that the Federal Government had enacted. A draft was only instituted in a Congressional District if volunteer enlistments from that district fell below the quota of men assigned to it. When enlistments fell below that level, then the draft was instituted to make up the difference. The draft was so unpopular that many states and cities began offering bounties to men who would enlist in an effort to raise the quota of men without drafting. This bounty system proved very successful, as thousands of men were induced to join by the large amounts of money being offered. The bounty system also alleviated a great deal of civil strife in the North. Many Northerners who were willing to volunteer to serve their country could not understand how free men, in a free nation, could be compelled to do so. Resistance to the draft reached the point of armed insurrection in many places, and army officers who were placed in charge of draft offices were often in fear for their lives.

14TH:

We left Bloody Run [Everrett], Pa. this morning one year ago on our way to Cumberland, Md. We got to Cumberland about sunset in the

Evening of that day & put up at a hotel. Windy this Morning & about 3 P.M. it commenced Raining. Dress parade at 4½ P.M.

15TH:
    Sunday. Clear & warm today. Regimental inspection at 10 A.M. We had preaching at [?] o'c P.M. Dress parade at 4½ P.M. This makes [1 year] since I came to the [Regt.] which was then at Patterson's Creek, Va. along the Potomac.

16TH:
    Windy & cool today. Battalion Drill at 10 A.M. Company drill at 3 P.M. Dress parade at 4½ P.M. Inspection, Co., at 9 A.M.

17TH:
    On Camp Guard today. Cloudy & cool. Inspection & Battalion Drill in the forenoon. Orders came for us to prepare to move at 2 hours notice. Dress parade at 4½ P.M.

The officers of the Thirty-ninth were strict disciplinarians when it came to drilling the men. Even though the regiment had been in the service for over a year, the men were required to perform drill twice daily — two hours of company drill in the morning, and two hours of battalion drill in the afternoon. The constant drilling made the Thirty-ninth one of the most proficient regiments in the Department. When reviewed by a United States General Inspector, they were pronounced to be "the best drilled and disciplined regiment in the Department of the South."[4]

18TH:
    Raining this morning & very windy. Relieved of guard at 8 A.M. Dress parade at 4½ P.M. when [orders] for leaving was countermanded. Brigade [review] ordered for tomorrow. Clear & warm today.

19TH:
    Clear & warm today. Order for review today put off for the present. Battalion drill at 10 A.M. Company drill at 2 P.M. Dress parade at 4 P.M.

20TH:
    Clear & cool today. Drills & c. the same.

21ST:
    Clear, windy & cool. Drills & c. The same as before. Dress parade at 4½ P.M. An order for Brigade inspection tomorrow at 2 P.M. was read. George Lyons of Co. A Died at the Hospital here about 9 P.M. this evening. Disease Typhoid fever. He is brother of Sidney Lyons, Co. B.

The hospital, one of two, was located on Hilton Head Island, as was General Hunter's headquarters, the quartermaster's and commissary's depots, and a quantity of sutlers and photographers. One of the hospitals was under the matronship of Mrs. General Frederick Lander, who was a well-known actress and more commonly known to the public as Julia Davenport.[5]

22ND:

Sunday [In honor] of Washington's [birthday] Schooners in the [river] are covered with [pennants] of various kinds. Company inspection, Brigade inspection, Dress parade at 4½ P.M. George Lyons, Co. A, was buried at about 6 P.M. with the usual ceremonies & c. It rained a little this morning but cleared up this Evening.

23RD:

Orders to build up beds in the tents from the ground. No Drill till 2 P.M., then Battalion drill. I was not out. Dress parade at 4 P.M. The day is clear and middling warm.

24TH:

[Drum] beat for Review [and we] were soon [out and] stacked arms. Soon [we were called] out and Marched out about 5 miles N.E. and formed for Review and waited about ½ hours for Gen. Hunter and as soon as he came, he reviewed Neglee's and Terry's Divisions. The day cloudy & cool and some signs of Rain. Dress parade at 4½ P.M.

25TH:

Clear & warm. I sent $25.10 home this morning by express. Battalion Drill at 10 A.M. Company Drill at 3 P.M. Dress parade at 5.

FEB. 26TH:

St. Helens Island. On fatigue.... Relieved at 11 A.M. The 116th Pa. [Volunteers of] this Brigade left on a Boat for Beaufort ... Battalion Drill at 11 A.M. Dress parade at 5 P.M.

27TH:

Clear and warm. Drill as usual today.

28TH:

Inspection & Muster for pay this morning & Company drill & Dress parade this evening. Rained some about 8 o'clock P.M.

MARCH 1ST:

Sunday. Cloudy & warm. On Guard today, 2nd Relief, don't have to stand at night. Mail came in today. Busy writing & reading letters this evening.

2ND:

Warm. Relieved of guard at 8 A.M.

3RD:

Regimental inspection [?] A.M. Battalion Drill at [?] P.M. Dress parade at 5 P.M. Col. [acting Brig. Gen.] Osburn made a speech to the 39th after Dress parade, subject—condition of the Country at the present time. He spoke of the Divided North and of enemies at our homes & tryd to encourage us from getting down Hearted. The days is warm & pleasant. We drawed clothing today, also rubber blankets which we should have had more than one year ago.

The rubber blankets Kelly refers to were almost a necessity for the soldiers. They were an essential part of a soldier's bedding, used as a ground cloth to keep moisture from coming up from the ground or placed over the soldier to fend off dew and condensation while he slept.

MARCH 4TH:

St. Helens Island. Windy & quite cold this morning. Battalion Drill at [?] also at 3 P.M. Dress parade at 5 P.M.

5TH:

This day is still cold and windy. On Company guard today. Battalion drill at 10 A.M. Companies inspected by Capt. Linton & Capt. Philips & Adjt. Warner this afternoon & c. Mail came in today, a letter for me. Dress parade at 5 P.M. On orders to prepare for inspection tomorrow morning.

6TH:

Regt. Inspected by a Capt. of Regular U. States Artillery. Drilled by him also. The day is warm. Dress parade at 5 P.M.

8TH:

On Camp guard. Regimental inspection at [?] A.M. after which Lt. [?] read part of the "Articles of War" to the Regiment. Dress parade.

9TH:

Came of[f] guard this morning. Drills the same as before. A fine day.

10TH:

A warm day. Drills as usual & c.

11TH:

Raining this morning. Brigade drill this Evening by Col. T.O. Osburn.

12TH:

Windy & cool. Battalion Drill at 9 A.M. Co. [drill] at 3 P.M. & Dress parade at 5 P.M.

13TH:

Windy & cool this day. On Camp guard today. Battalion drill at 9 A.M. The widow of the late Gen. Lander, Dec'd, paid us a visit this afternoon. The 62nd O.[hio] V.[olunteers] coming by first & gave 3 cheers for her & the 39th then came out & gave her 3 cheers. Dress parade at 5 P.M.

Brigadier General Frederick W. Lander had died on March 2 of the previous year. He had led an attack on Bloomery Gap, West Virginia, in February of that year and had applied to be relieved following that engagement. The general was ill, and he reported "my health too much broken to do any severe work." His replacement was not immediately forthcoming, however, and within two weeks he died of what was termed a "congestive chill."[6]

14TH:

Some warmer today. Relieved of guard at 8 A.M. About 11 A.M., an order came for us to prepare to fall in line in 15 minutes with everything

we had. We marched to the Landing, boarded the Boat & went up the River about 10 miles & landed in small boats & drilled in firing & c. for about 2 hours, then boarded the Boat & Returned to Camp, arriving about 5 P.M. Somewhat tired and Hungry. I fired [?] Rounds while out.

15TH:

Sunday. Warm today. Regimental inspection at 10 o'c this morning and Dress parade at 5 P.M.

16TH:

Very warm. Battalion Drill & Brigade Drill & Dress parade today.

Colonel Thomas Osburn, commander of the Thirty-ninth Illinois Infantry (U.S. Army War College).

17TH:

Pleasant morning. On fatigue, putting up a target to shoot at today. Drills as usual. Some fireing by Cos. H & I.

18TH:

A Pleasant day. Co. E had a turn at target fireing this Evening. Best shot fired by Wm. Anderson.

Contrary to popular opinion, not all Americans of this period were "crack shots." In fact, overall marksmanship in the Civil War was poor. Some historians have estimated that in some battles, for every man hit, his own weight had been fired in bullets. Volley firing, by company or by regiment, was one way that officers compensated for this lack of accuracy. Kelly describes a volley fire by the Sixty-second Ohio the following day.

MARCH 19, 1863:

St. Helens Island. Cloudy today.... The 62nd Ohio Vol. fired one Round today. Battalion & Company Drill and Dress parade. Cool evening.

20TH:

Cool morning. Drills as usual. Rained some through the day. News came of the fight at Yazoo City on the Yazoo River & 8 Transports captured & 7000 or 8000 men captured by our forces.

These were reports of General Grant's opening operations against Vicksburg, Mississippi. They were highly exaggerated.

21ST:

Cool today & Raining most of the day. Batt. Drill at 10 A.M. but Rain prevented Company Drill. Mail came in today.

22ND:

St. Helens Island. Pleasant day. Cool morning, warm day. Regimental inspection at 10 A.M. I went on fatigue Building fence around cattle to keep them together. Turn of Extra duty. Dress parade at 5 P.M.

23RD:

Warm day. On Camp guard today assigned to the "Post of Honor" at Col. Mann's Headquarters. Battalion drill at 10 A.M. Company drill at 3 P.M. Dress parade at 5 P.M.

24TH:

Rained very hard last night & still raining today. Relieved of Guard at 8 A.M. Mail came in about 2 P.M. Company drill about 3 P.M. Warm & pleasant Evening.

MARCH 25, 1863:

St. Helens Island. Warm & [pleasant] today. Regimental inspection at 10 A.M. by Col. Osburn & Staff. Dress parade at 5 P.M. mail came in today. 1 Letter for me.

26TH:

A pleasant day. An order for Review for 10 A.M. and we were out at the appointed [time] And properly in line near the River and were Reviewed by Gen. Hunter. Every thing passed off [fine], and also Done "Right up the the Handle." We returned to Camp for dinner. Dress Parade at 5 P.M.... Col. Howell, 85 P.V. as Senior Colonel takes Col. Osburn's place as Commander of the Brigade. Captain L.S. Linton Received his commission for Major & other Lieuts. also got commissions as Captains, & c. The Companies are changed on line again, owing to the Late [?] & Co. K, which was on the left took the Right. Cos. E & H also put on the Right & Cos. I, G, & D, which had been on the Right were placed on the left of the Regt.

27TH:

Warm & pleasant today. Battalion drill at 10 A.M. No Company drill by E on account of fixing up Shade & onrnamental [?] & c. Dress parade at 5 P.M.

28TH:

Cloudy & pleasant day. On fatigue at Col. Howell's Head Quarters. No Drills. Dress parade as usual.

29TH:

Sunday. It rained all day. Co. Drill & [inspection of] Brigade this day.

30TH:

Rained some today. Windy & cool. Drill as Usual. Dress parade.

31ST:

Rainy windy & cool. Battalion Drill 10 A.M. by Maj. Linton. Company Drill at 3 P.M. by Lt. Warner. Dress parade at 5 P.M., major Linton in Charge.

APR. 1ST:

Orders came about 11 o'clock last night to prepare to move. Had Battalion Drill at 10 A.M., packed up in the afternoon, struck tents just at dark, [loaded] them on wagons & set [out] to the wharf to be loaded on transports. An order came to Bivouac for the night. The day clear.

2ND:

 Called up at 4 A.M. I was detailed for guard on the boats at daylight & went to the wharf. Got on board the Steamer "New England," sidewheel, & posted on board the Deck. The Regt. came [aboard] about 7½ A.M. The first [?] about 8 A.M., started to sea but Returned again for a Scow with Surf Boats. Went out again and anchored off Port Royal till about 7 P.M., then went to Sea. The wind blowing pretty hard, waves high.

3RD:

 We Run all night but anchored a short time just after daylight, then started again, then went into mouth of North Edisto River where 6 Gun Boat monitors were anchored & laid the Remainder of the day. The wind is still high.

4TH:

 We started up again ... went [up the] Inlet & anchored ... landed in the small [boats] about noon on the Cole's Island where the 100th New York Volunteers have been for a week or so. Got to Camp & got our tents put up soon afterwards and then I was detailed for fatigue to unload provisions off the Boat about 4 P.M. Not Relieved till about 8 P.M. The tide came up & we had to wade through water to get to Camp. This day is clear & warm.

 This was part of General Hunter's expedition against Folly Island. In addition to the Thirty-ninth Illinois, Hunter's expeditionary force included the 100th New York, the Sixty-second Ohio, the Sixty-seventh Ohio, and the Eighty-fifth Pennsylvania. Once the force was all ashore, they made their camp near the beach and in close proximity to Folly Island, which was in Confederate hands.[7]

APR. 5TH:

 Coles Island. Busy fixing things today. I was detailed for guard at Sunset. They expect an attack tonight & moved the Camp which is much [exposed] to the Beach about 8 o'clock P.M. I was relieved of guard at 10 o'clock & Returned to Regt.

 Hunter and his officers were greatly concerned that the Confederates would mount an attack on this night to try to force the Federals off the island. The men were busily engaged in throwing up earthworks and in mounting cannon. At dusk came the order to extinguish all lights so as not to betray their position to the Rebels if the attack should come. At 10 P.M., the order was given to strike the tents and prepare for a movement against Folly Island.[8]

APR. 6TH:

We left Camp at 1 o'clock this morning, went to the Landing, went aboard a Boat & went to Folly island & Landed about 3 o'c, got laid down about 4 o'c & laid till morn[ing], then Marched 7 miles North along the Beach & Bivouaced in an open space but the tide came up and Routed us out. We got on higher ground and laid till Dawn again. The Day was fine.

The Union force swept the entire seven-mile length of the island with a strong skirmish line preceding the line of battle and with two twelve-pounder cannon drawn by hand by a detachment of Marines. No Confederates were to be found, however, as they had already abandoned the island.[9]

APR. 7TH:

Folly Island, S.C. We were aroused at [?] this morning & went up the Beach about 2 miles & laid till daylight, then Marched back ½ miles and Camped, leaving Co's G&H on picket. Some cannonading heard about 10 A.M. & at half past 2 P.M. the Rebel guns on Fort Sumpter & surrounding Batteries opened on the Federal Monitors which had entered the Harbor & the gunboats soon responded to their fire. Was kept up till 5 P.M. when the Boats retired & the firing ceased. We were situated on a piece of ground about 6 miles from Fort Sumpter & could see it but [they] could not see us.... Rations very scarce....

At 2:00 P.M., Admiral Henry Du Pont's naval squadron entered the shipping channel at Charleston. The attacking vessels consisted of the Weehawken, Ironsides, Passaic, Montauk, Patapsco, Catskill, Nantucket, Nahant, *and* Keokuk. *At 2:30 P.M., the guns of Fort Sumter opened on the fleet, and for the next hour, the Union ships endured one of the most terrific bombardments seen in the war as the Confederate batteries on Morris and Sullivan's Islands added their fire to the bombardment. Because the shipping channel had been mined with torpedoes, the attacking ships could approach no closer than eight hundred feet from the fort. Five of the ironclads were reported as being wholly or partially disabled by the fire from the fort. The Keokuk, a ship having only thin armor plating, took some ninety hits from the Rebel guns and was completely disabled. Her commander and crew were able, through the use of pumps, to sail her away from the fort, but she eventually sank near the entrance to the harbor, and the Confederates were able to salvage her guns for use in their fortifications. Although the situation in the harbor was such that an attack by the Union naval forces was a forlorn hope, dissatisfaction with the failure, both from the public and the Administration, led to Du Pont's removal from command.*[10]

Fort Moultrie, one of the many fortifications that ringed the seaside approaches to Charleston and had to be taken one at a time by the besieging Union forces (U.S. Army War College).

8TH:

Clear & pleasant day. Received Rations this morning. We also got mail. We Marched down the Beach 3 Miles & left our knapsacks & then drawed a Battery of 6 guns [12 pounders] 3 miles up the Beach where we had started from & laid till after dark, then Drawed it back to get out from the tide, then went back to the Old Camp & laid down to Rest.

APR. 9TH:

We were roused up at [?] this Morning & went and got our knapsacks and Marched back from the Beach 2 miles & Camped & laid till 3 o'c P.M. when I with 6 others from Co. E was Detailed for fatigue, but [was] soon Relieved and about 5 P.M. Co. E was sent out North of Camp for a Reserve for the picket guards. The Regt. changed it's front this morning, putting Right where the left had been before.

10TH:

Clear and pleasant Day. Firing heard toward Charleston, also toward Hilton Head. It commenced at 10 A.M. but Did not continue long. As it was the choice of the Boys of Co. E, we did not move our position today as it is a good place to stay.

APRIL 11TH, 1863:

Follys Island, S.C. All quiet.... The 39th was ordered to fall [out] and Deploy as skirmishers & skirmish the Island over in pursuit of Rebels that are supposed to be on the Island but we did not find any and Returned to Camp about 5 P.M. quite tired & Hungry.

> *On the night of April 11, approximately three hundred Confederates approached Folly Island in small boats, with the purpose of capturing the Union outposts. They were discovered and driven away, but not before they had killed one member of the 100th New York, and captured two others.*[11]

12TH:

We fell in line about 9 A.M. & Marched up the Island about 2½ Miles & Camped. I was Detailed to pack shot & shell from one place on the Beach down about ½ Mile in the Timber. After that was done, the Regt. fell in to drag the cannon down the Beach 1 Mile to where the ammunition had been deposited.

> *The Union artillery was being moved here and there for two reasons. First, the gunners were trying to find positions from which their fire could be the most effective. Second, they were attempting to change positions so as not to allow the Confederate gunners the opportunity of zeroing in on their positions.*

13TH:

[The 100th] N.Y.V. left their [camp this] Morning early for [the beach] & the 39th Camped [in the place] which had been occupied by them. I was detailed for Camp guard about 5 P.M. Stood before Col. Osborn's Head Quarters.

APR. 14:

Relieved of Camp guard at noon today. Captain Rogers, Co. I, 62 Ohio, was shot Dead last night by one of Co. D, 62 Ohio Vol. while on picket. It is supposed he took the guard for a Rebel & turned to Run when the guard shot him through the Body & he soon bled to Death. Co. E was out on picket up the Beach. It commenced Raining before we started & Poured down in torrents.

15TH:

Relieved of picket. Returned to Camp at Daylingt this morning. Clear & pleasant but the wind blows higher out at sea. All quiet today.

16TH:

I was detailed for [guard] & we got to our Posts before noon today N.W. of Camp.

17TH:

Came off picket at 12 M[idday] today. A Rebel Battery was preparing to rake the Island from the point of Morris Island about 11 A.M. today but our gunboats soon stopped their fun by throwing a few shot & shell among them. They fired a few shots but [did no damage].

APR. 19TH:

Sunday. We laid back in the timber to prevent the Rebels from seeing us. I stood on post today.

Union officers had forbidden the sounding of reveille or any other calls out of concern that the Confederates on Morris Island would be able to determine the location of the troops and shell them. The officers need not have been so concerned, however, for the opposing soldiers had established a sort of truce between themselves. A great deal of trading took place between the Confederates on Morris Island and the Federals on Folly Island. Coffee for tobacco was the prime exchange in the bartering, but the soldiers would also trade newspapers and other articles. The items would be sent across the channel in little hand-made dugouts and floats complete with sails. This trading was done in secret from the officers because the men knew that they would put a stop to it. In fact, when a duty officer approached the picket line, the pickets would then, and only then, engage in a lively fire toward the enemy, shooting high so as not to injure the enemy who had not been given a warning previous to the beginning of the firing.[12]

20TH:

We [signed] the [payroll] today & were paid off 4 months pay. I stood post tonight again.

21ST:

All quiet today. Stood on guard again today.

23RD:

The Enemy tried to [shell] a Battery on the Island [but] the gunboats

Routed them. Co. J was Relieved of picket this evening. Returned to Camp about 7 o'clock P.M.

24:

The Regt. having moved Camp while we were out, we had a [hard time] Reading off [the] Company ground [but] got it done.... The weather was fine while we were out on picket but the gnats were very Bad when the wind was still. I Bathed twice in the Ocean today which is 4 times since we came to this Island.

25:

We laid in Camp today without being Disturbed except by the fire which some [one] started on the Island.

26:

Sunday. All quiet today. We Received Mail today. Weather fine but [very] windy.

APRIL 27TH:

Folly Island. I was Detailed in the Morning [for picket] about 1 A.M....

28:

Cloudy & [cool]. Relieved of picket & Returned to Camp.

29TH:

With Leo H. [corporal] Received [orders] to the point of the Island. Got my picture taken & Returned to Camp at sunset...

Photography had not become generally available to the masses until the latter half of the 1850s. As such, it was still a relatively novel experience. Prior to that, only the very wealthy could afford to leave images of themselves for posterity through hiring an artist to paint their portraits. The advent of photography made it possible for almost everyone to leave a visual legacy to future generations. Most images of people from the era show a solemn, almost stern visage in their demeanor. This was due both to the feeling that having one's picture taken was an event too important for levity and to the slow exposure time of cameras of the time. For most young men, the photographs they had taken while in the army would be the first time they had ever been before a camera.

30:

We were mustered for pay at 10 A.M. by the Major of the 85 Pa. Vols. I was Detailed for Camp guard...

Three members of the Union Tenth Corps that participated in the operations against Charleston. The backmarks on these CDVs states that they were taken by the official photographer of the Tenth Corps on Hilton Head Island. Kelly probably had his picture taken by this same photographer.

2ND:

Came off picket [in the] morning. All quiet today.

3RD:

Sunday. Cool & pleasant today.

4:

Raining this Morning. Went on picket at 9 A.M. Cleared up about noon.

5:

Relieved of picket at 9½ A.M. Dress parade at 10 A.M. Rained hard in the afternoon & night.

6:

Clear & warm today. We got our tents from the Point today & put them up & had Dress parade at 8 A.M.

7:

Drill at 6 A.M. Dress parade at 8 A.M. I went to the Point with J.L. R.[iddle] & had a picture taken.

MAY 8:

Folly island. On fatigue detail on foot today. Not [feeling] well in the afternoon. Drill & Dress parade the same.

9:

Nothing of importance transpired today.

10:

All quiet today also.

11:

On fatigue today cutting timber in front of the Lookout that is being erected in front of Camp. Relieved at 11 A.M.

12:

News came today that Gen. Hooker is in Richmond but not credited generally.

These were rumors and reports of General Joe Hooker's Chancellorsville Campaign. Although the battle of Chancellorsville had taken place on May 3, news of the action was just reaching South Carolina, and the rumors the soldiers were receiving were grossly inaccurate.

13:

On fatigue working on the fortifications today. Very warm day.

14:

The Regt. went out this morning to work on the fortification. Very warm again.

MAY 15:

Cloudy & Rained some today & the wind is high.

16:

Raining today. Cool, clear & pleasant, the sea is very calm today.

17:

Inspection & dress parade at 8 o'clock this morning.

18:

Went on picket at 9 A.M. today to the Landing on Folly Creek. Cloudy, looks for Rain.

19:

Relieved from picket & Returned to Camp today. The Mail came in today with news of Hooker's retreat back to Falmouth & rumor of his advancement toward Richmond again.

20:

Cloudy & warm. Another Boat ran the Blockade last night. One boat also was captured. Report that the Mail Boat is captured.

MAY 21ST, 1863:

Folly Island, S.C. On fatigue. Cleaning off the Regimental [grounds] today. Very warm.

22:

Orders for Co. E to go to the point of the Island [Northern] to do picket duty and we got to post at Sunset.

23:

Warm day. Some firing from the Boats last night. Capt Whipple with 7 men went out towards James Island 2 miles through mud & water to a bunch of timber to see what could be seen, but saw nothing. Soon returned.

24:

Sunday. Warm & pleasant. A salute of 13 guns was fired from Fort Sumpter today. Supposed to be a salute for some General.

MAY 25:

I stood on Post last night, all quiet through the night. Warm today.

26:

A warm day. A few shots were fired by the Blockade fleet last night. We learn today that a Boat was captured & c.

The captured vessel was the blockade runner Ruby. It had successfully slipped through the blockading fleet only to become stranded on a sand bar at the mouth of the inlet. The vessel was midway between Morris Island and Folly Island. The Confederates made several visits to the ship to try to take off as much of the cargo as they could. A party of soldiers from the Thirty-ninth Illinois acquired a boat and cautiously rowed out to the stranded vessel so as not to attract the attention or fire of the enemy. The party helped themselves to as much of the cargo as they could carry, including pineapples, cigars, and Scotch whiskey.[13]

27:

We were Relieved of picket & Returned to Camp about 5 P.M. Very windy & Rained some during the Day. I stood on Post last night.

28:

Raining & storming out at Sea.

29:

Still raining & windy.

30:

A man of Co. I was drowned today while Bathing in the Water.

31:

Clear & pleasant. Inspection this morning. Baker Died, Co. I, was Buried today here.

JUNE 1, 1863:

Folly island, S.C. Clear & pleasant. On picket today. Landing on Folly Island.

JUNE 2ND:

I came off picket at noon today. Thunder storms this Evening accompanied with wind.

3RD:

Cleared up this morning & is very pleasant. Co. E went out on picket up the Beach. Looks for rain as we go out to Post.

4TH:

I stood on Post last night at a piece of Artillery planted on a Sand bank near the sea shore. We returned to Camp at day break — still cloudy.

5TH:

Cloudy but pleasant, looks for rain this Evening at 5 o'clock. We have set shade trees around the tent and [fixed] it up so that [there is shade]. Better than it had been for a few weeks Back. It has now quite a rural appearance.

6TH:

A pleasant day. We Received Mail today. We also Drew clothing which we very much needed, especially Socks & Shoes.

7:

Sunday. A pleasant day. Dress parade at 8 A.M. Preaching by Rev. Mr. Wright, a Missionary from Philadelphia, at the Head Quarters of the 67 Ohio at 3 P.M. His text was the 12 Chapters, 23, 24 & 25 Verses of Hebrews.

The area of operations of the Tenth Army Corps was a favorite destination for missionaries from Philadelphia, New York, and Boston, who came to bring religion to the many ex-slaves in the region who were now within Union lines.

8:

Cool & pleasant day. Nothing of importance transpired today.

9:

7 Companies on fatigue today. Quite warm.

JUNE 10, 1863:

Folly Island, S.C. Warm this day. I am on Camp guard today & c.

11:

Heavy firing about 1 o'clock this Morning by the Blockade and at Daylight a boat can be seen on the bar near the N.W. point of the Island. It was on fire when we first saw it but the fire went out by some means about 9 A.M. this Morning. I was Relieved of Camp guard at 10 A.M. Our Artillery throwed several shots to get the range of the Boat. Co. E was detailed to drag a small boat across the [bar] to The Beach of the Island. It commenced raining just as we started & was very dark after we got the boat to the point. We returned to Camp.

JUNE 12:

A party of our men went aboard the Boat about 11 o'clock last night & a 2nd party in the after part of the night. They found the boat to be loaded with lemons, oranges, limes, apples, whiskey, & c. A negro belonging to Co. K 39th was killed with a shell that the Rebels threw from Morris Island last night. About 2 P.M. today, the Rebel Battery's on [Morris] Island opened fire on our pickets at the N.W. point of the Island & some began to shell our Camp & the Lookout here. They threw one shell into the Camp of the 62 Ohio but did no Damage. Afterwards, they threw one into our Camp, cutting off a pine tree 15 feet from the ground. The tree fell on some of the tents of Co. K, wounding one man of Co. K slightly. The tree is 20 in. in Diameter.

JUNE 13:

No Boat went out to the Steamer last night. The Rebs threw a shell at our Camp at daylight this Morning, did no harm. The Blockade Boats are firing out to Sea at some Boat that we cannot see from here. The Sky keeps cloudy & threatens Rain but still keeps very warm. The Rebels opened fire on this Island this afternoon. Our men returned the Compliment soon after. No harm done to our side.

Blockade runners were built to be small, fast ships, having a low profile and burning anthracite coal so as not to leave a visible plume of smoke from their stacks. Most attempts to make Confederate ports were at night to gain further advantage over the ships of the Federal blockading fleet whose mission it was to keep the Rebel ships from making port. The odds were definitely in favor of the blockade runner, but by the last two years of the war, those odds were getting slimmer. Most runners made only one or two successful trips before being captured or sunk. Even so, the soaring prices for consumer items in the South caused by the blockade made it possible for an owner to still turn a handsome profit, even if he did lose his ship after only one or two runs. Federal blockaders adopted the use of calcium flares or rockets in an effort to illuminate the night-time sky to search for runners. By the end of the war, some Union ships had been equipped with powerful searchlights taken from railroad locomotives.[14]

JUNE 14, 1863:
    Folly Island, S.C. The Enemy fired at us from [Morris Island] commencing at 6 P.M. They confined the fire to the pickets and did not fire at our Camp.

    On June 14, Generals Quincy Gilmore and Truman Seymour arrived at Charleston Harbor. Gilmore had been sent to replace General Hunter in command of the land forces. He had already been successful in directing operations against coastal fortifications, having been in command of the assault that had captured Fort Pulaski in Savannah, Georgia.[15]

15:
    The men were all moved from Camp along the Beach last night as it was thought the Enemy intended shelling our Camp with heavy mortars during the night but they did not undertake it. We returned to our tents about Midnight. The Rebs threw shell[s] at the pickets at intervals of about 30 minutes during the night. All quiet this morning. They exchanged shell[s] this Evening. I went out on picket Reserve at Sunset.

16:
    I stood on Post last night 3 hours. The Rebs threw Shell[s] at [us] from a Mortar at intervals through the night. We Returned to Camp at daybreak. The Rebels commenced shelling again at 3 P.M. & threw some shell[s] near our Camp but did no harm. The Regt. was moved out of Camp down the Beach to avoid the shells after 4 P.M. & returned about 5½ P.M.

17:

Co's E, I & J are on fatigue today, Co. E on the Magazine at the Beach. Heavy cannonading on James Island...

18:

On picket at [the magazine] near the Beach today but relieved about 2 P.M. & the Co. struck tents & started for the point. Reached there at Sunset & stopped for a Boat to take us to Cole's Island.

19:

We laid over night without blankets or overcoat[s]. The Boat came about 3 P.M. & we crossed to Cole's Island. It rained a hard shower this Morning & we became very wet. Still cloudy & looks for rain.

20:

I am on fatigue carrying baggage & c. for the Adjt. Relieved at [?] A.M. & fixed up my tent & c. this Evening.

21:

Sunday. Inspection this Morning. On fatigue this Morning again carrying plank for a wharf, relieved at 11 A.M. as usual. Co's I & C went on a Scout to James Island this morning.

22:

Co's E & A went out to relieve Co's I & C this Morning with 3 days Rations. Detailed to stand on Post tonight. Rained some this Afternoon.

JUNE 23:

Folly island. We fell [in at] 10 P.M. tonight [on picket] till morning [then] turned to post near Lower Bridge across Marsh, fell back again at night. Still raining.

24:

Returned to post this Morning again and Remained on post tonight. Remains cloudy.

25:

We were Relieved by Co. K & returned to Camp about 11 A.M. and Received two months pay. Still Cloudy — thundering & appearance of rain. We Drew Hats & Musketo Bars this Evening & c.

26:

Cloudy & cool Day. Dress parade at 8 A.M.

28:

Sunday. Cloudy & Warm. Dress parade & Inspection in the Morning. Still Raining.

29:

The Company went on Picket this Morning for one Day. On Post at the Lower Bridge N.W. of Camp.

30:

Relieved of Picket by Co. I. All except 2 Co's left Cole's Island yesterday & went to Folly Island. Co's I & E are left here. Mustered for pay at 4 P.M....

The constant fatigue and picket duty had greatly worn down the members of the Thirty-ninth Illinois and they were ordered to Cole's Island for a well-deserved rest period. Company E was briefly left behind with Company I when the regiment returned to Folly Island.[16]

JULY 1, 1863:

Coles Island. Some rain today. Nothing of importance transpired today. The Monitor Gunboat "Nantucket" came into the Inlet this Evening & anchored. 3 other Monitors were seen going toward Charleston Harbor.

2ND:

Heavy Showers today. I helped Sail a boat to the point of Folly I[sland], also up to the pickets opposite the White House to carry water to them.

Although they were surrounded by water, fresh drinking water was a constant supply problem for the troops.

3RD:

On fatigue today moving Major T.S. Linton's tent, got it moved & set up again by 10 A.M.

4TH:

Independence Day — Boat in the harbor covered with flags [of] all colors & sizes. Salutes were fired by the Gunboats, also by land Batteries on Folly Island. Nothing worthy of Note transpired on this Island. The day is fine & clear & pretty warm. I took a boat ride to the Landing on Folly Island at about 10 o'clock A.M.

Kelly was not yet aware of it, but the Union soldiers in South Carolina had good reason to celebrate this Independence Day. General Robert E. Lee's Invasion of Pennsylvania had been turned back in the three-day battle at Gettysburg, and the Confederate citadel of Vicksburg, Mississippi, had fallen to the Federal Army under General U.S. Grant.

5TH:

Sunday — Inspection at 9 A.M. Very warm & clear sky.

6:

I went on 5 days Picket with Co B & got to post a little after dark. The post is advanced. Pickets a mile farther than before.

7:

The Rebels fired a few shots across the River at us but no one was hurt. We fired one shot in return.

8 & 9:

Still on Picket. No one disturbing us but an occasional shot from the Enemy about dark on the 9th. Some of our Gunboats came up the channel near us & threw some shells among the Rebel Pickets & by mistake threw a few shots at us but fortunately did no harm.

10:

We were awakened [last] night by Musket fire across the River from us. It proved to be our men Landing near the Rebel pickets who fired at them. Our Batterys on the point of Folly Island opened fire on Morris Island. The Rebels soon fired too but our guns soon silenced theirs & our men Landed on the Island & made a charge on them & move[d] them back, capturing 300 Prisoners & several pieces of Artillery. We were relieved in the afternoon & went to Camp, from there we proceeded to the Regt on Folly Island, leaving our knapsacks. Marched to the point of the Isle where the fight had been in the Morning.

The musket fire Kelly had heard was an assault on Morris Island. The Thirty-ninth was part of a three thousand man force that had been sent to James Island under the command of Brigadier General Alfred Terry to divert the attention of the Confederates away from what was to be the main assault. The attacking force, under the command of Brigadier General George Strong, was composed of the Forty-eighth New York, Sixty-seventh Pennsylvania, Sixth and Seventh Connecticut, Third New Hampshire, and Ninth Maine. The assaulting force was conveyed across the inlet on small boats and was supported by four Union monitors. Once ashore, the Federals quickly captured the first two lines of Confederate rifle pits and advanced to within rifle shot of Fort Wagner. The Confederates had been completely surprised and were reeling in confusion. A more determined effort might have been able to carry the fort, but the Union forces were halted while Strong planned an assault on the fortification to take place the following day. Union losses were reported as 53 killed and wounded, while those of the Confederates were 294, with 127 of that number captured.[17]

11:

3 o'clock this morning relieving the 67th Ohio of their post. Cannonading was kept up through the day by Gunboats. A charge was made on Fort Wagner by our men before day[light] this morning but [we] were repulsed with some loss. The 76 Pa. V.[olunteers] suffered the most, being foremost in the charge, several Prisoners taken by both sides.

The assault of Battery Wagner was made by the Seventy-Sixth Pennsylvania, Ninth Maine, and Seventh Connecticut. The Seventh Connecticut advanced as far as the parapet of the works but was at last repulsed. Casualties were 340 killed and wounded on the Union side. Following this repulse, it was decided that there would be no further attempts against the fortifications until the works could be sufficiently damaged by a concentrated land and sea bombardment.

A Confederate account of the battle appeared in the Charleston newspaper on July 18: "At peep of day my attention was called to a dark mass approaching my front. When about twenty-five yards off I ordered to the videttes to 'fire by file,' which they did; then the whole battalion rose, formed lines, and gave an almost simultaneous 'yell.' This meant for me 'all right' for Battery Wagner, 'They are coming.' My first line had come to a 'ready'; we could see the beard on the faces of the Federals. 'Aim- fire!' Then a sheet of flame bursts into the advancing line; this doubles up their front, but on comes the body at a 'double-quick.' We fall back, loading as we retire, and form on the left of the second line, coming to a 'ready, aim- fire!' and we poured another volley into their faces. Their front staggers, but on come the survivors at a stately 'double-quick.' We fall back to the third line, the whole battalion coming to a 'ready'; they are now within ten steps of us. 'Aim-fire!' for the last time. The effect is terrific — it appears as when the wind strikes the stalks of a wheatfield. I actually felt sorry for them. It was 'war' hence 'fair,' but it did seem to me that we were taking unfair advantage of them; they could not stop to fire upon us, for time was all-important to them; their success depended on reaching the battery without delay, and hence they had to receive these dreadful volleys without responding. The enemy dashed on, but barely gave us time to reach the inside of the works before they were repulsed."[18]

JULY 12, 13, 14, 15, 16, 17 & 18:

[Much time] spent in preparing for another attack on the Rebels by moving cannon ammunition, mortars & Provisions from Folly to Morris

Island. Meanwhile, our gunboats were not idle but kept a firing & continued annoyance to the Rebels, sinking one of their Boats & burning it under the guns of the Rebel Forts. On the 16th, the Rebels attacked Gen. Ferry on James Isle early in the Morning but the Negro Regt. [54th Massachusetts] drove them and had some of their men taken prisoners. The [men] in [the] 7 days mentioned were continually on Fatigue Loading Artillery Shot & Shell on the Boats & sending them to Morris Island. On the 18th, the Monitor Gunboats entered the Harbor, 11 in number with the New Ironsides to back them & a warm fire was kept up in the afternoon. The weather has been very unfavorable for Soldering the Last 2 weeks as it has rained nearly every day & having no tents, we were exposed to all kinds of weather.

JULY 19:

Sunday. Morris Island, S.C. A charge was [made] on Fort Wagner last night again but was driven back with heavy loss on our side. The 39th were ordered out about Midnight last night & Crossed to Morris Island but were too late to be of any service in the charge. We laid on the Beach till night, then went on Picket up near Fort Wagner.

This second assault against Battery Wagner was made by the same units that had participated in the first attack, with the addition of the Fifty-fourth Massachusetts Infantry, which was selected to spearhead the assault. Approximately nine thousand shells had been fired at the fort before the order was given for the infantry to go in, at 7:00 P.M. Fifty-fourth Massachusetts made

Effects of the Union breeching battery against the masonry walls of Fort Sumter (U.S. Army War College).

a gallant assault, gaining the parapets, where a fierce hand-to-hand combat was fought. Their colonel, Robert Gould Shaw, fought at the head of his men, where he was shot dead. They were eventually driven back, however, with frightful losses. Although this attempt at capturing Battery Wagner was a failure, the bravery of the Fifty-fourth Massachusetts in making it greatly aided in convincing many skeptics that Black troops would fight. By the end of the war, over 180,000 Black men would enlist in the army. The Thirty-ninth Illinois did not participate in the assault.[19]

20:

A few shots were fired at us after we got to our position last night. We laid in Rifle pits today. The gunboats & Land Batteries opened on Fort Wagner about 2 P.M. today & were ordered to fire on the Rebel gunners but we soon found the distance too great for us & ceased firing. We returned to Camp after dark.

21ST:

We had a good nights sleep last night and were quite Merry this Morning. We moved Camp a little further from the Beach. I went on fatigue to the North end of our Entrenchment. The Shelling was kept up today By both sides. We signed the Payrolls today. Relieved of fatigue at sunset.

22:

We Received 2 months pay today. Went out on picket to the beach after Sunset.

23:

No firing done today on either side except sharp shooters. We were relieved after sunset & Returned to Camp.

24:

We were in line at 3 o'clock & marched toward Fort Wagner on the Beach. Returned to Camp after Sunrise. The Monitors & Land Batteries opened a heavy fire on the Rebel Forts at Sunrise. The Rebels sent a Flag of Truce to the Admiral about 11 A.M. & all firing ceased for the time. The meaning of the Flag is not known in the Lower echelon but our men fired [no] more through the day.

A few days after the failed assault on Battery Wagner, a number of the regiments were ordered away to Hilton Head and to Florida. The Thirty-ninth Illinois remained at Charleston, along with the rest of General Alfred Terry's division.[20]

JULY 25:

A large detail was made in the Regt for fatigue at dark last night & we went to throwing up Entrenchments in Parallel lines advancing on Fort Wagner. The Rebs kept shelling us through the night but did no hurt. We Came to Camp about 3 P.M. The firing was kept up all day today. The 39th on Picket again tonight.

26:

The Enemy Shelled us all night & today but none of the 39th was hurt. Relieved at [?] P.M. at night.

27:

We fell in line on the Beach at 3 A.M. & it rained till daylight. Returned to Camp. All quiet through the day.

28:

Brisk firing on Both sides today by Gunboats & Land Batteries. The 39th on Picket tonight.

29:

We laid in front under a Bomb proof today. The firing kept up through the day. One man [of] Pioneer Regt killed last night & several wounded by grape & cannister & 5 wounded by shell. we came to Camp about 10 P.M.

JULY 30, 1863:

Morris Island, S.C. We fell in at 3 A.M. on the Beach, laid till Sunrise, firing as usual. We had Dress parade at [?]

31:

Firing as usual today. The 39th went on picket this evening.

AUG. 1ST:

The day passed of[f] as usual. We came to camp after Sunset this evening.

2ND:

Sunday — Heavy firing in the afternoon & night. Company Inspection at 10 A.M. Dress parade at 6 P.M.

3RD:

Corp. J.W. Whiteman who left us at Suffolk, Va. returned to Company today. Very little firing done to day.

4:

We got some [?] — today & made beds of them which makes it more comfortable in the tent.

5:

Very sultry. Thunder. Appearance of rain. A few scattering shots only are fired from Fort Johnson today. On Camp guard today. Regimental Inspection at 8 o'c A.M.

6:

Relieved of Camp guard at 8 A.M. and detailed for fatigue at 4 P.M. & went to the front at 6 P.M.

7:

Relieved of fatigue at 3 this Morning & returned to camp. Inspection and review at 5 o'clock of Howell's Brigade by Brig. Gen. [?]

AUG. 8, 1863:

Morris Island S.C. Howell's Brigade went to the front. Picket this Evening. 39th in front of the fortifications.

9:

Sunday — The Rebs shelled us all night from Sumter & Johnson. All quiet till Evening today when the shelling commenced again. 4 or 5 men were wounded during last night & today. We returned to Camp at 8 P.M. tonight.

10:

Dress parade at 5 P.M. An order was read prohibiting writing of the Strength and position of Gillmore's Army at present.

11:

The Rebels attacked [our] men at work on [earth] works in front. About 2 A.M. last night, [the] men fell back a short distance & opened on them with grape, soon driving them back. Our Brigade ordered out at 3 A.M. & came in at sunrise. I am on Camp guard. Today very warm. The Regt went out on fatigue at night.

12:

Relieved of Guard at 2 P.M.

13:

Everything quiet in Camp. Some firing in front.

14:

Howell's Brigade on picket tonight.

15:

Co. E 39th on guard on the Beach to the rear of Batteries. M. was shot in the Head by [sharp] shooters this Morning. The [wound] is slight as it was a spent ball that struck him. One man in Co H was wounded in foot by a piece of shell. we returned to camp about 8 o'clock P.M.

16TH:
Sunday. Heavy firing last night in front. inspection at 6 P.M. by Col. Mann. A large detail went on picket about 9 P.M.

17TH:
We were relieved of picket & came to Camp at daybreak. Opened on the Rebel forts with the large cannon this Morning. The Gunboats also opened fire. Several holes made in Sumter's walls by Shell shot. The firing ceased at 8 P.M. entirely — shower this Evening.

18TH:
Bombardment kept up today by the Navy and Land Batteries. Detailed for fatigue at 4 P.M. Very windy. The waves roll high at dark.

On this day, General Gillmore sent, under a flag of truce, a message to General Beauregard in Charleston. Gillmore stated that, unless the Confederates surrendered Fort Sumter and Batteries Wagner and Gregg to the Federal Army, he was prepared to initiate the bombardment of the city of Charleston itself. Beauregard refused to capitulate, and the bombardment of the city began the following day.[21]

19TH:
We were relieved of fatigue about 10 P.M. last night & returned to Camp. The Bombarding kept up as usual.

20:
Fell in line at 3 this Morning & went up the Beach about ¾ mile & laid till sunrise and returned to Camp. Went to the front on picket tonight.

On August 20, Colonel Osborn of the Thirty-ninth Illinois assumed command of the brigade as the result of a freak accident to Colonel Howell, the regular commander. Howell was severely wounded when the bombproof he was staying at caved in. Once he had received medical attention and was well enough to travel, Howell was given a furlough to return home to Philadelphia.[22]

21:
Rebels Shell & grape came thick & fast around us today. None hurt in 39th. About 30 men were wounded in 85 Pa. V.[olunteers] by shell falling on Bomb Proof and going through it. We were relieved and got to Camp about 8 P.M.

Fort Sumter, South Carolina, showing the effects of Union bombardment. The fort was a major target of the North for the entire war and many attempts were made to capture it. It remained in Confederate hands until it was finally evacuated at the end of the war because of the threat of General William T. Sherman's army, marching up the coast from Savannah, Georgia (U.S. Army War College).

22:

Detailed to help erect a bake oven for the Regt. Worked all the day. It rained some this afternoon.

23:

Company Inspection at 7 A.M. Regimental Inspection and Muster at 8 A.M. Dress parade at 8½ P.M. This day [being Sunday] off quietly in Camp but the Bombardment of Sumter & Wagner kept up as usual. Nothing more important Transpired.

Fort Sumter was the recipient of an almost continual bombardment from the Federal fleet and the Union land batteries on the beach. By the 24th of August, it had been so materially damaged as to lead General Gillmore to report to his superiors that the fort was nothing more than a mass of ruins, but the Confederate defenders continued to resist from behind the piles of rubble. In fact, their position was even stronger, and they were harder to dislodge from it after the masonry walls had been battered down.[23]

24TH:

I was detailed this Morning with a Corporal and 3 others to go with Lieutenant Booker, Co C to Folly Island for some men that were there belonging to the Regt. It was a long walk and coming back, we got a wagon to ride back to the upper end of Folley. We got to Camp about 9 o'clock P.M.

25TH:

It rained hard and steady last night after 11 o'clock. Cleared up this morning. The firing ceased till about 3 P.M., then opened again. The 39th to go on picket again tonight to the front.

AUG. 26:

Morris Island. We got to post tonight about 8 P.M. and the shell[s] from James Island came flying thick and fast. The shelling was stopped about 10 P.M. Co E moved back this morning to get shelter from the shell[s]. All quiet through the day but at night the 24th Mass. Vol. went up and charged on the Rifle pits and took about 100 Prisoners & gained their Rifle pits. Our Batteries were all opened on Wagner and James Island. Batteries opened on Fort Gregg also—a few shots. After our guns ceased, the Rebels threw grape from Wagner. The 39th were relieved about 8 P.M. & returned to Camp with the loss of one killed & one wounded, Co K, two wounded, Co G, one wounded Co. D.

27:

Corporal [?], Co K was buried this morning. Myself & 3 others of Co E were Pall Bearers. We had Dress parade and Inspection this Evening at 8 P.M.

28:

The 39th to go on picket tonight again. We started out at 6 P.M. raining hard. We [were] on guard on the Beach.

AUG. 29TH:

Morris Island. The Rebels fired an occasional shot from Sullivan's Island today which was the first from that Island since we came to this

Union troops in Fort Johnson, Charleston, South Carolina (U.S. Army War College).

Island. The[y] did no harm. Co E were not troubled by shell and grape. We were relieved at 7 P.M. & returned to Camp. It ceased raining early last night and we had a pleasant day.

30:

Sunday. rained some in the Day. Regt. Detailed for picket again tonight. Heavy firing today on both sides. The Lieut. Col. of 85 Pa. V.[olunrteers] killed this Morning by shell.

31st:

We were further front today than heretofore. The Rebels threw some grape & shell but we all came out unhurt tonight except Major S. Linton, [Wounded] slightly on head.

> *Kelly's first diary ends with this last entry, just prior to the capture of the prize for which they had so long struggled: Battery Wagner. Following the second assault on the fortification, the Union Army set to work digging parallel trenches to the fort so that the soldiers could get close without being subjected to the fire of the defenders. Several mortars and artillery pieces were moved forward in these trenches until it became almost certain death for the Confederates to show themselves above or outside of their works. A tremen-*

*dous bombardment was opened by the Union land batteries on September 5,
and the following night a deserter from the fort came into the Federal lines
to announce that the works had been abandoned by the Rebels. A call was
made for five volunteers to go into the fort and verify the validity of the
deserter's statement, and Private Cornelius Cox of the Thirty-ninth Illinois
was one of the volunteers. The following is his account of the mission: "Some
time after midnight September 7th, a man came in from Battery Wagner,
having swam out in the water to elude detection, and reported to the commanding officer of the trenches that Wagner was being evacuated. Soon after,
Major Linton, came around and called for volunteers from each company to
enter the fort and ascertain whether the report was true or false. I volunteered
for Company G. There were five of us. We separated, and passed around on
top of the parapet until opposite each other, and then came through the fort
in the center. While we were doing this, the rebels fired two shots from their
small mortars, which was the last of them. After looking around and finding
some of the guns spiked, one of the five was sent back to report the fort evacuated, after which the regiment marched in and took possession. This was
just at daybreak. I did not see any lighted fuse [the fort was reported to be
prepared to be blown up] but was informed afterwards that one of the five
before mentioned did find a lighted fuse, supposed to lead to the magazine,
and cut it. I do not think any particular officer, man, or company is entitled
to credit for first occupying the fort after the fact had been established that it
had been evacuated. I do not write this because I wish to figure as a hero, for
I am aware that it would be unjust to mention names, unless all that did
their duty could be mentioned; but I do think five men from the regiment,
regardless of any particular company, are entitled to the credit of first entering Fort Wagner under very perilous conditions. I may add that we each
received a complimentary 'furlough' of thirty days indorsed by General Quincy
A. Gillmore and Lieutenant Colonel Orrin L. Mann."[24]*

The capture of Battery Wagner placed the whole of Morris Island under
the control of the Federals, giving their army a position that was now closer
to Fort Sumter and the city of Charleston. The Thirty-ninth Illinois moved
to Morris Island, spending a considerable period of time garrisoning Battery Wagner, while siege operations against the city continued. In December of 1863, the regiment was ordered back to Hilton Head for a break
from front-line duty. It is during this rest period that Kelly once more took
up the task of keeping a journal of his experiences.[25]

FRIDAY, JANUARY 1, 1864:

Hilton Head, S.C. The New Year came in Windy and Cold. The
Officers of the 39th prepared a dinner for the Regt. which was eaten about

The City of Charleston during the time that Private Kelly and the Thirty-ninth Illinois were engaged in operations against the city and its defenses (U.S. Army War College).

2 P.M. after which Col. Osborn and others made short speeches to the Boys. Subject Relative to Veterans.

SATURDAY 2:

All quiet today. Veteran excitement pretty much past. Two men more from Co. E enlisted today, making in all 29 men from Co. E and about 280 from the Regiment. The 39th are determined to see the end of the War.

SUNDAY 3:

On Camp Guard today, 2nd Relief No. 4 at Hospital. Cloudy with some rain. The enlistment of Veterans still continues. There are about 320 this evening, if they keep coming in, we will all go home together yet. Hope we may.

MONDAY, JANUARY 4, 1864:

Hilton Head, S.C.—Rainy and disagreeable for Guards last night. Relieved at 9½ A.M. The Regt. fell into line and Col. Osborn made another speech to us, urging all to reenlist who had not enlisted. Near 400 have now gone in.

TUESDAY 5:

A rainy day. The old Guard that came of[f] yesterday on police today. The time of enlisting on the Veterans and receiving the $402 bounty ends this day. Near 400 of the 39th have reenlisted. All but 3 of 60 [Co] E that are present have gone in again.

It was considered to be a great honor in the army to receive the designation of being a "veteran" unit. In order for this to happen, enough men of the regiment had to reenlist so that the regiment could continue to be an effective fighting force. In the case of the Sixth Ohio, as mentioned in the first chapter, not enough men signed up for another tour of duty to keep that regiment in existence. The Thirty-ninth Illinois did muster the required numbers to see the war through as a unit and to earn the special designation of being "veterans."

WEDNESDAY 6:

Still wet and uncomfortable outdoors today so we sat in our tents reading newspapers, writing letters & c. I spent part of [the] evening helping Sgt. Ripple, as Ord. Sgt. to make out the Quarterly Ordnance Returns.

THURSDAY, JANUARY 7, 1864:

Raining slow but steady all day. The weather somewhat cooler than it has been the last few days. I laid and sat in different tents all day, talking over old times and discussing the Hopes of the future.

FRIDAY 8:

No Rain today but still cloudy. We had no Drills except Dress parade at 5 o'clock P.M. We received mail from the North tonight but no news of importance, but nothing to discourage the Union Soldier.

SATURDAY 9:

Clear and quite cool today. On Camp Guard today—3rd Relief No 4 near Hospital. Nothing of importance transpired during the day. Countersign Hanover.

SUNDAY, JANUARY 10, 1864:

Hilton Head, S.C.—relieved of Camp Guard at 9½ A.M. Came to Quarters. Received a Corporal Warrant dating Jan. 1st, 1864. Regimental

Union troops gathered around a store at Hilton Head. Note the black teamster and the black soldiers on the porch of the store.

inspection at 1 P.M. Examined today by Surg. Woodard and passed for a Veteran. Dress parade at 5 P.M.

Kelly was put in for promotion to corporal this day. It would be the rank he would hold for the rest of his time in the army.

MONDAY 11:

On fatigue this afternoon. Brigade Drill from 2 to 4 o'clock P.M., the first in this month. We received the order for continuing the reenlistment of Soldiers as Veterans till the 1st [of] March 1864, today.

TUESDAY 12:

Rained some last night. Company Drill at 9½ A.M. Brigade Drill as usual. It commenced raining about 4 P.M. and rained till dark, preventing Dress parade this evening. Still raining at tapps.

WEDNESDAY, JANUARY 13, 1864:

A rainy and disagreeable day. We laid in our Quarters all day. Nothing working. Nothing transpired. The time passed away very slowly and seemed rather lonesome.

THURSDAY 14:

Pleasant today. Battalion Drill at 10 A.M. The Regt. was divided into three Companies, practiced in Skirmish Drill. First two Companies deployed, commands by bugle. Dress parade at usual hour.

FRIDAY 15:

Company Drill at 10 A.M. Brigade Drill from 2 to 4 P.M. It commenced raining about 4½ P.M. and prevented us from having Dress parade. We received mail this day but nothing for me.

SATURDAY, JANUARY 16, 1864:

Pleasant day. The forenoon was spent preparing for inspection and we were inspected at 1 P.M. by Capt. Dawson 85th Pa. Vol., Brigade Inspector. The Regiment was in good condition. I spent the evening helping make out Mustering Out Rolls.

SUNDAY 17:

Clear and pleasant this day. Company inspection at 9½ o'clock A.M. After inspection, a few sections of the Regulations was read to Col. by Lt. N.C. Warner. Dress parade at 5 P.M. The remainder of the day spent reading papers & c. and writing letters.

MONDAY 18:

It rained all day except a short spell this evening. It stopped raining and we had Dress parade at the usual hour. I spent the afternoon helping write Duplicates of the Veteran Enlistment papers. Finished them about 8 o'clock P.M.

TUESDAY, JANUARY 19, 1864:

Windy and rather cool today. Company Drill at 9½ A.M. The remainder of the day passed by as is usual with the Soldiers. Dress parade at 5 P.M. The Transport Fulton arrived here this evening from N.Y.

WEDNESDAY 20:

A pleasant day. We practiced in Target shooting this Morning. Brigade Drill at the usual hour & c. We had a school of the non-commissioned Officers at Head Qrs. this evening.

THURSDAY 21:

Rather warm today for the season of the year. On Camp Guard today, in charge of 1st Relief. The first time on Guard since I was promoted to Corporal. Got along finely, much better that I expected.

Kelly was lucky. He had at least been given some rudimentary schooling on what would be expected of him as a noncommissioned officer. Many

Civil War officers and noncoms were not so fortunate. For most, it was on-the-job training, and they learned their responsibilities as they went.

FRIDAY, JANUARY 22, 1864:

Relieved of Company Guard at the usual hour. Came to Qrs. cleaned my gun & c. About 11 A.M. an order came for inspection immediately and we were soon in line and inspected by Lt. McKee of Gen. Seymours Staff. Brigade Drill and parade this P.M.

SATURDAY 23:

A pleasant day. On fatigue, policing parade ground in front of Regt. this forenoon. Company Drill at 10 A.M. No Brigade Drills on Saturday. Dress parade as usual. All quiet here.

SUNDAY 24:

Company inspection at 9½ A.M. We had preaching at 3 P.M. by [?] Dress parade at 5 P.M. We put in the day in all sorts of ways, reading, writing, jumping, wrestling & c, & c.

MONDAY, JANUARY 25, 1864:

The Veterans of the Regt. were mustered in at 10 A.M. today. I was not mustered and will not be till after Feb. 12 next, at which time I will be in service 2 years and can draw the the $100 bounty due me.

Since Kelly joined the regiment after it was already in the field, his dates of mustering in and out of the army were different than for many of his comrades. He had also signed up for two years, not three, but his enlistment had taken place long enough after the original muster of the regiment that he would receive his discharge shortly after the rest of the regiment and therefore be eligible for the rest of his signing bounty, having received the first half when he signed up.

TUESDAY 26:

No Drill in the 39th today. All are anxiously awaiting the time for us to start home. I spent the Evening making out the Company Monthly Returns and got them signed by the men. Very warm today.

WEDNESDAY 27:

I signed the Pay Rolls this morning. Nothing to do all day and was somewhat lonesome. I helped to make out some Receipts & Returns of Ordnance and Equipage. The Co. signed the Pay Rolls this evening.

THURSDAY, JANUARY 28, 1864:

Hilton Head, S.C.— The Company paid off early this morning. We struck tents immediately after and prepared to leave. I got my pay [$54.30] just after dinner, fell in line at 3, had a speech by Col. Howell. Cheers for him in old Bri.[gade]. marched to dock escorted by Bri[gade]. Cheers for old Bri[gade], South, Gillmore, Seymour, Howell and got aboard the Mary E. Bordon before dark.

FRIDAY 29:

We left the Harbor about 12 last night, steaming all night and today. On Guard today, 2nd Relief, 3 men. The sea is calm and we have a very pleasant time today and hope it will remain so.

SATURDAY 30:

We ran aground at Frying Pan Shoals this morning but got off without harm. Passed Hatteras Cape this afternoon. Still pleasant. Relieved of Guard at 9 A.M.

SUNDAY, JANUARY 31, 1864.

As we get North, it begins to get cold. The wind has commenced to blow and the waves are raising so that our faithful craft begins to roll from side to side. Some Sea Sickness.

MONDAY, FEBRUARY 1:

The waves increase in size today. Some water casks broke loose and rolled over and wounded five men of Co I, 39th Ill. Vet. Vols. We are nearing New York Harbor. Wish we were in.

Note that Kelly no longer refers to the regiment as the Thirty-ninth Illinois. One can sense his pride in calling it the Thirty-ninth Illinois Veteran Volunteers instead.

TUESDAY 2:

We crossed the Bar at 12 last night and anchored till this Morning. Arrived at N.Y. and landed about 11 P.M. Marched to barracks and left our baggage and took a stroll over the city. At Barnums Museum tonight.

WEDNESDAY, FEBRUARY 3, 1864:

New York City — The Regt. left for Illinois at 8 A.M. I got a furlough for 30 days from here and left for Phila. at 2 P.M. by the Camden and Amboy R.R. Arrived at Phila. and took lodging at Wm. Penn Hotel about 7 P.M. Got our supper and went to theatre on Walnut Street.

THURSDAY 4:

Philadelphia — We lay over here today. We took the opportunity to visit the City. We went to independence Hall — splendid place. We also visited Fairmont Water Works, this is a grand sight. I looked over other parts of the City and then went to theatre on Chesnut Street.

FRIDAY 5:

We took the train at 8 A.M. this morning for Mount Union and arrived at 5½ P.M. and put up at Ault's Hotel. After supper we took a stroll around the town — to bed at 7 P.M.

SATURDAY, FEBRUARY 6, 1864:

Mt. Union, Pa.— Snowed a little here last night. We got conveyance to Orbisonia by Mr. Aults. The roads are very bad, we traveled slowly. Arrived about 12 M. Saw some old friends here, arrived at home at dark. All glad to see me.

SUNDAY 7:

At home — After an abscence of two years, I am again under my Fathers roof. Miss Adaline Morgan paid us a visit and my sisters and I went home with her and stayed till bedtime. I was rather lonesome all day.

MONDAY 8:

It is quite cool today. Susan and I went to school this afternoon. I did not like the teacher very well and soon left again and came home. Supper ready for us when we got in.

TUESDAY, FEBRUARY 9, 1864:

Blacklog, Pa.— The wind is blowing some and quite cold. I stayed at home all day. I went to Spelling School tonight to the School House. We had a good time. I beat the school spelling.

WEDNESDAY 10:

I went to Orbisonia this morning, bought an overcoat. Started home and met some of the Blackloggers going to meeting and went back to town with them. No meeting so I went to the Serenading of [?]. Arrived at home at 11.

THURSDAY 11:

I came home from [?] early this morning. Pleasant day. I laid at home all day reading newspapers & books & c.

FRIDAY, FEBRUARY 12, 1864:

I took a stroll over to Joshua Morgans this afternoon. I stayed till 7 P.M. then Henry, Theodore, Martha and Adaline came home with me and we had a pleasant time.

SATURDAY 13:

I laid at home all day but went to Orbisonia on my way to Monroe. I stayed at Uncle Caleb Kelly's tonight.

SUNDAY 14:

I and Susan left Orbisonia at 10 A.M. Went to Benjamin Rinkers, stayed till night, then went to Monroe to Meeting, heard preaching by Graham. I went to R.D. H.'s after Meeting and stayed over night.

MONDAY, FEBRUARY 15:

Monroe — I paid a visit to L. Hecks this morning, then went to E.A. McKims and spent the day. The day is pleasant but a little cool.

TUESDAY 16:

I went to Monroe School this morning and saw some of my old school mates. Stopped at Mr. Books for my supper, then went to debate at Monroe. The weather very cold today.

WEDNESDAY 17:

This is the coldest day I have experienced for 2 years. I sit by the stove at D.B.'s till after dinner, then went to school again. I stayed at M.A. Books tonight.

THURSDAY, FEBRUARY 18, 1864:

The weather is more mild today. I went to Grandfather A. Miller in Hill Valley today. Returned to Monroe this evening and went to Sugar Grove to preaching by Rev. Falhelm.

FRIDAY 19:

I stayed at Whartons last night and started home this morning. Stopped at Orbisonia till night, then went to B. Hecks (He being sick) with R.A. Kelly and N.J. Kelly. Stayed till midnight & went to D. Hecks.

SATURDAY 20:

I stayed in Orbisonia till after dinner, then started home (R.A.K. with me), arrived at home about 5 P.M. Went to the School House to Singing tonight and got home again about 10 P.M.

SUNDAY, FEBRUARY 21, 1864:

Blacklog — I lay indoors this forenoon. The day is pleasant. I went to J. Morgans this evening in company with R.A.K., M.K. and S.K., had a good time and got home again about 10 P.M.

MONDAY 22:

A warm day. I wrote a letter this evening to J. Kelly, 140 Pa. Vol., Carlisle Barracks, Penna. Washington, Henry, Martha and Adelaide Morgan and Sarah Kelly came and spent the evening with us till 10 o'c P.M.

TUESDAY 23:

I went to school this morning and stayed till evening. Went to Spelling School this evening, a poor turnout and a very poor Spelling.

WEDNESDAY, FEBRUARY 24, 1864:

I went to Monroe this evening for Spelling but found it turned to be a Prayer Meeting. I staid at E.A. McKims for the night. I rec'd a letter from G.M.M. and wrote one to him.

THURSDAY 25:

Monroe, Pa.—I went to school here this morning, left for home at noon. Stopped in Orbisonia a short time, arrived at home about 6 o'c P.M. M.J. and H.J Bolinger spent the evening here.

FRIDAY 26:

Blacklog—Snowing and windy this morning. Cloudy all day. A party of us went to the school to Singing tonight and arrived [home] about 11 P.M.

SATURDAY, FEBRUARY 27, 1864:

Blacklog & Orbisonia—I went to Orbisonia this morning, took dinner with J.L. Ripple. I got three pictures taken, two of them in lockets. I went to singing in Blacklog tonight & c.

SUNDAY 28:

I got ready this morning and left for Orbisonia at 11 A.M. Arrived at Mt. Union at 6 P.M. Christian Ripple took us down in Dearborns. We put up at Aults Hotel.

MONDAY 29:

We took the train at 7 A.M. and arrived at Pittsburg at 1 P.M. and stopped at Exchange House. Spent the day roaming over the City and went to the theatre tonight.

TUESDAY, MARCH 1, 1864:

We started for Chicago, Ills. at 1 A.M. on the Pittsburg, Ft. Wayne and Chicago R. Road. Took supper at Ft. Wayne and arrived at Chicago at 10:50 P.M. and stopped at Union House. No bed.

WEDNESDAY 2:

Chicago, Ill—We took stroll over the city and went to Camp Fry and got leave of absence till the 5th inst. and took the cars & went to Wilmington on the Chicago and St. Louis R.R. at 4 P.M.

The significance of making a trip to Wilmington, Illinois, was that a very large number of the men in Kelly's company hailed from there. Kelly

*and the rest of the Huntington County boys were most certainly made wel-
come among the friends and families of their comrades in arms.*

THURSDAY 3:

I spent the day roaming over the City. I find it to be a nice place. I
took supper at the H.E. Sartells and then went to the Ball in the City. Had
a right good time but did not dance any.

FRIDAY, MARCH 4, 1864:

Wilmington, Ill.—I took a trip out in the country this evening.
Snowed all the afternoon. went to Wm. Baxters, took supper and then went
to Mrs. Hudsons to party in wagon. We had a merry time. Got some little acquaintance with the Ladies of the place.

SATURDAY 5:

We got to Wilmington from the party about 3 this morning. We took
the train at 10:50 A.M. for Chicago and arrived here about 3 P.M. Went to
the Theatre at 215 & 217 Dearborn Street. The performance was dancing.

SUNDAY 6:

I put in the day running over the City. Went to Camp Douglas but
could not get in. I wrote a letter this evening. I went to Baptist Church
tonight, saw the rite of Baptism administered to 5 Soldiers.

*Camp Douglas was a Northern prisoner of war camp. It was a fairly
common practice to allow the prisoners to be "viewed" by those who were
curious to get a look at real, live Rebels. At Elmira, New York, a stairway
and platform had been constructed on the outside of the prison for spec-
tators who came to gawk at those so unfortunate to be confined there.*

MONDAY, MARCH 7, 1864:

Chicago, Ill.—I put in the day roaming over the City and went to the
Circus tonight and saw some splendid horsemanship and other feats of
great daring.

TUESDAY 8:

Camp Fry, Chicago, Ill.—We left the Hotel early this morning and
went to Camp. Stayed a few hours and went to the City for a sword for
J.L. Ripple and stayed in Camp tonight.

WEDNESDAY 9:

I went to the City this morning and stayed till 4 P.M. and returned to
Camp. It rained all day and is very unpleasant in camp as the ground is
low and gets very muddy.

THURSDAY, MARCH 10, 1864:

Camp Fry, Chicago, Ill.—I stayed in Camp this forenoon. Inspection of Arms at 2 P.M. The Regt. marched to Bryan Hall at dusk, escorted Gov. Yates to the hall and had a speech from him followed by remarks from Gen. Benton of Indiana and Adj. Gen. Fuller of Ills. Then we returned to Camp.

FRIDAY 11:

I took Corporal Burtons place on Guard this morning and was posted at a grocery north of Camp. Relieved at 12 M[idday] & came to Camp. Went to the City this evening & returned at 7 P.M. Still raining and very uncomfortable today.

SATURDAY 12:

We had Squad Drill this forenoon. I had 5 men only to drill. It rained this afternoon again. I put in part [of] the time making Commutation papers for the Company. Went to Theatre in the City tonight.

SUNDAY, MARCH 13, 1864:

I stayed last night at Hotel in City & returned to Camp this morning and was engaged this afternoon making out Muster Rolls etc. for Recruits and wrote a letter tonight.

MONDAY 14:

I went to the City this morning and returned about 3 P.M. Got some book portfolios etc. I cannot content myself anywhere since I left home. I only hope we may soon go South again.

TUESDAY 15:

It snowed some last night but it is pleasant today. We packed up and left Camp at 3 P.M. and took the cars on the P.[ittsburgh], Ft. W.[ayne] & C.[hicago] R.R. at 6 P.M. and started for Washington, D.C. We had good cars and we are all merry as we can be.

WEDNESDAY, MARCH 16, 1864:

We stopped for dinner today at Ft. Wayne, Indiana and made two trains of the one, and we got along some faster than we did before. It is rather cool and we stayed inside most [of the] time.

THURSDAY 17:

We got to Pittsburg at 10 A.M. and partook of a good breakfast that the Ladies prepared for us and we laid over till 4 P.M. for cars to convey us to Harrisburg and the[n] we got cattle cars.

FRIDAY 18:

We got to Mt. Union at daybreak this morning. I left cars a short time here. We were welcomed all along the Road, especially at Duncannon and Little York. We did not exchange cars at Harrisburg but went on to B.[altimore]

SATURDAY, MARCH 19, 1864:

We got to Baltimore at Daybreak this morning and got breakfast and laid over till 11 A.M. and then got conveyance to Washington on B&O R.R. Arrived at 3 P.M. Got supper at Soldiers Rest. Had an exhortation this evening in barracks.

SUNDAY 20:

Washington City, D.C.— We had an exhortation by a Mr. Feature, a Chaplain, here this morning and he distributed some books & c. among us and I got a Hymn Book. We left this evening, marched across the Potomac and encamped in tents.

MONDAY 21:

I took a visit around to the different fortifications this morning and [was] put on Camp Guard at 9½ A.M. Had charge of 2nd Relief, numbering 5 men. It is quite cold today and a good fire is very comfortable.

TUESDAY, MARCH 22, 1864:

Near Alexandria, Va.— I was relieved of Guard at 9 A.M. It is growing colder and appearance of a storm. I went to a saloon and got my dinner. It commenced snowing about 5 P.M.

WEDNESDAY 23:

About 6 inches snow fell last night. The sun comes out quite warm today and the snow is thawing fast. We laid quiet in Camp all day. It goes rather hard with us just after returning from home to the field.

THURSDAY 24:

I went to a saloon and got my breakfast. We had Dress parade at 4½ P.M. I went to hear a Lecture on Temperance by Mr. [?] of Ohio at Col. Osborns Head Qrs. Had a short speech from Osborn and others.

FRIDAY, MARCH 25, 1864:

I was out on Drill today as left Guide of the Recruits that were drilling. It commenced raining about 2 P.M. and continued till night. It is very uncomfortable for us. Crowded six of us in 1 tent.

SATURDAY 26:

It is cloudy today and rains by spells. Out on Drill again this morning. Dress parade at 5 P.M. A committee of 3 men appointed to examine persons recommended for promotion in Regt.

SUNDAY 27:

A very pleasant day. On Camp Guard this day. Charge of 3rd Relief, 14 men. We had a pleasant day of it and everything passed off smoothly.

MONDAY, MARCH 28, 1864:

Quite warm today. Relieved of Guard at 9 A.M. and went on Regimental Inspection at 10½ A.M. Moved our tents in afternoon. Dress parade at 5 P.M. We are beginning to get used to Camp life again.

TUESDAY 29:

Cloudy and rather cool today again and some rain this afternoon and commenced to rain in earnest about 6 P.M. Nothing of importance transpired except drilling the new Recruits. Had a visit from Perry Miles, 62 Ohio [Infantry].

WEDNESDAY 30:

It rained all last night and turned to snowing this morning. Very disagreeable all day. We lay in our Quarters most of the day. We passed away the time in amusements of various kinds.

THURSDAY, MARCH 31, 1864:

The recruits of Co. F drew new arms. We had orders to prepare for General Inspection at 11 A.M. and the Regt. was out in line at the appointed time but the Inspector did not come and we were dismissed. The Inspector came about 1 P.M. and we were inspected — allright.

FRIDAY, APRIL 1:

Camp Grant, Va. — April comes in clear and pleasant and appearances of Spring. We drilled the Recruits with arms for the first time this morning. It clouded up and commenced raining about 3 P.M. and continued all night.

SATURDAY 2:

It rained all night and this morning it turned to snowing and continued to snow and rain all day. I took a squad to the Barracks this morning, got my dinner and returned to Camp.

SUNDAY, APRIL 3, 1864:

Camp Grant, Va. — It rained this forenoon but was more pleasant this afternoon and six of us got a pass and went to Convalescent Camp, paid a visit to the Soldiers Library. Returned to Camp about 4 P.M.

MONDAY 4:

Quite pleasant this morning. Co. Drill at 10 A.M. E. Karr and myself procured a pass and went to the Soldiers Library this afternoon, got a book to read, "Little Friends in Council." Com[menced] raining about 2 P.M. and rained till tattoo tonight.

TUESDAY 5:

It continued raining all night and all day and it is too cold to be out of Quarters more than a few minutes at a time. I laid in the tent reading a Book from Soldiers Library entitled "Nina or Lifes Caprices."

WEDNESDAY, APRIL 6, 1864:

It rained nearly all night but cleared up and is pleasant today. I was detailed for Camp Guard this morning and got the 1st Relief, 7 men. 1st Lt. Knapp, Co. I, in command of Guard, Capt. Heritage, Co. B, Officer of the Day.

THURSDAY 7:

Warm and pleasant today. Indication of Spring weather. Relieved of Guard at 9 A.M. Busied the remainder of the day in helping making out my Mustering Papers. Dress parade at 5 P.M.

FRIDAY 8:

I was excused from drills today to make out Mustering and Descriptive Rolls for men that have not yet been mustered into Veteran Service. We got through about 3 P.M. and had parade at 5 P.M. and went to Church to Convalescent Camp.

SATURDAY, APRIL 9, 1864:

Camp Grant, Va.— I went to Washington to be mustered etc. but my papers proved to be wrong and I could not be mustered. I paid a visit to the White House, shook hands with the President. I went to the Capitol, stopped in the House where the Congressmen were assembled & heard them debating etc. Got to Camp again at 5 P.M. Rained all day.

It was a symbol of the innocence of the era that a soldier could just stop by at the White House and shake hands with the President. Lincoln had a special attachment with and to the men in the Northern Army. They viewed him as their commander-in-chief more than any other American President before or since.

SUNDAY 10:

Pleasant today but cloudy this evening. We had Company Inspection this afternoon. I was busied this evening helping make out my Mustering Papers and got them made out again. Dress parade at usual hour.

MONDAY 11:

J.L. Ripple and I went to Washington today again. Visited the Smithsonian Institute early this morning, got to Mustering Office at 10 A.M. I went to the Capitol before dinner. Was in the House and Senate Chamber while there. Then returned to office at 2 P.M. & went back to Capitol this evening. Went to Theatre tonight Varieties and put up at Lutz Hotel.

TUESDAY, APRIL 12, 1864:

We visited the Patent office this morning and went to Mustering Office at 10 A.M. Was mustered up at 11 A.M. and went to Maj. Taylor and rec'd $120.55 in cash & went to Maj. Goula and rec'd check for $73.00 and got it cashed at Treasury. Got to Camp at 5 P.M.

WEDNESDAY 13:

Pleasant day. Drill this morning. I got a pass & went to Convalescent Camp & returned. Had Drill at 2 P.M. It rained some this evening which prevented us from having Dress parade.

THURSDAY 14:

On Camp Guard today, 2nd Relief, 15 men. We had a pleasant day of it, had to stay at Guard House all day except for meals, etc. Dress parade at 5 P.M. A Squad of Co. E went to Washington today for [commissary] money.

FRIDAY, APRIL 15, 1864:

Camp Grant, Va.— Cloudy and pleasant this morning. Relieved of Guard at 9 A.M. On Skirmish Drill this afternoon. Dress parade at 5 P.M. Order for General Inspection on the 18th inst. at 12 M[idday]. rained a little before tattoo.

SATURDAY 16:

Three Recruits came to Co. today. It rained all night slowly and continued to rain all day. No drilling of any kind. Day spent as I usually spend my rainy day, reading, writing letter, reading books & c.

SUNDAY 17:

It rained some this [day], but the sun occassionally peeps out from behind the clouds and is fast drying up the mud this evening. Company Inspection at 2 P.M. by Lt. Warner assisted by Lt. Kingsbury. Dress parade at 5 P.M. Still cloudy & c.

MONDAY, APRIL 18, 1864:

Pleasant day. Squad Inspection of Arms at 8 o'clock. Comp[any] Inspection at 11 A.M. and General Inspection at 2 P.M. by Capt. Suce, A.D.C. [Aide-de-Camp] to Gen. Casey. All passed off quietly. Dress parade at 3 P.M. Order for Review tomorrow.

TUESDAY 19:

The day pleasant but rather warm. We fell in and marched over the hills to a field near the long Bridge and were Reviewed by Gen. Casey and then returned to Camp at 4 P.M.

WEDNESDAY 20:

We laid in Camp all day except drill time. I had a squad of 4 men to drill who had not been drilled before. I had an unpleasant time as I never like to drill men. Cloudy this evening.

THURSDAY, APRIL 21, 1864:

Camp Grant, Va.— Cloudy today. We had a small shower of rain just after dinner. I had my squad of men to drill today. The Regt. had Battalion Drill this evening but I was not out and am not anxious to go on Bat. Drill.

FRIDAY 22:

I went on Camp Guard at 9 A.M. today. Got on 1st Relief. The 25th Ohio Vet. Regt. left for Florida at 2 P.M. Governors Brough of Ohio, Sprague of Rhode Island and Secretary Chase paid the Regt. a short visit this P.M. Remarks by Brough of Ohio.

SATURDAY 23:

It rained a little just at dark last night, then cleared up and was pleasant all night. Relieved of Guard at 9 A.M. today. Dress parade at 5 P.M. No drill this afternoon. The evening spent dancing & c. The day pleasant & warm.

SUNDAY, APRIL 24, 1864:

Warm and pleasant today. Company Inspection at 9½ A.M. Preaching in camp at 11 A.M. I was not present as I was writing a letter. Dress parade at 5 P.M. Orders to leave came this evening and preparations are being made to leave tomorrow at 8 A.M.

MONDAY 25:

Rained all night & some this morning. We struck tents at 7 A.M., left Camp at 8½, arrived at Alexandria at 11 A.M. We got dinner at the Soldiers rest. Got on board the Steamer montauk at 3 P.M. and left the Dock about 4 P.M. We had a pleasant day so far but rather warm for marching.

TUESDAY 26:

We ran all last night and arrived at Fortress Monroe at 10 A.M. and left again about 11 A.M. Arrived at Gloucester Point opposite Yorktown about 3 P.M. Disembarked and got to Camp ½ miles from the River where the Detachment of [the] 39th were encamped. Found the Boys all well and glad to see us.

WEDNESDAY, APRIL 27, 1864:

Gloucester point, Va.— On fatigue at Col. [Act. Brig. gen.] Ponf, 62 Ohio, had charge of 4 men. Went to mill dam & took a bath after we got through with our work. We are 1st Bri.[gade], 1st Div.[ision].

The Thirty-ninth was now part of the Tenth Army Corps, General Quincy Gillmore commanding. This was Gillmore's old command from the Department of the South that had been participating in active operations around Charleston. Ten thousand reinforcements for the Army of the James were added when this corps was transferred north. The Thirty-ninth had served under Gillmore in Charleston, and their commander as well as many of the regiments in the corps would be well known to them.[26]

THURSDAY 28:

Company Inspection at 9 A.M. We were busied all day cleaning up in Camp and getting our tents properly arranged etc. Dress parade at 5 P.M. Cloudy & rather cool.

FRIDAY 29:

General Inspection this morning. Dress parade at 5 P.M. We drew clothes this evening according to order, each man having 2 prs shoes, 3 prs socks, 2 prs drawers, 2 shirts, 1 pr pants, one Blouse, the [?] to be turned over to be stored in.

SATURDAY, APRIL 30, 1864:

We were mustered for pay at 9 A.M. this morning and had Grand Review this afternoon. We were reviewed first by Brig. Gen. Foster & afterwards by Maj. Gen. B.F. Butler. Appearance of rain this P.M.

SUNDAY, MAY 1:

It rained all day today. We lay Quiet in Camp. We got the news of the capture of Brig. Gen. Wessells and Command at Plymouth, N.C. on the 21st ult. Also the victory of Gen. Banks in Louisiana —

The report of the victory of General Nathaniel Banks in Louisiana was erroneous. This is a reference to the failed Red River Campaign in which the Union forces were defeated and forced to retreat by Confederate forces under the commands of Generals Richard Taylor and Kirby Smith.[27]

MONDAY 2:

Pleasant today again. Company Drill at 9 A.M. Preparations are being made for the coming Campaign and we expect to be moving soon.

TUESDAY, MAY 3, 1864:

Gloucester Point, Va.— I went out and got some poles to make a Bunk, got back at 8 A.M. and went on Camp Guard at 9 A.M. Got the 2nd Relief, 24 men. We got orders to march this evening, all are getting ready.

WEDNESDAY 4:

All up at 1 this morning and packed up for a march. I was relieved of guard at daylight and fell in with the Regt. Marched to the Dock, got aboard the Steamer Jolas and anchored in the River. Boys all in good spirits. I have bad cold.

The Thirty-ninth Illinois was preparing to take its part in General Grant's overall campaign strategy for the spring of 1864. For the first time in the war, all of the Union armies were going to act in concert, exerting pressure on the Confederacy that the South had not before seen. In the past, an army in the east might be idle while a western army was fighting a pitched battle. An army in the deep South might be maneuvering for position while one in the middle states was falling back to regroup and reorganize. Under Grant's strategy, all of the armies of the North would act as one, engaging whatever Confederate forces were in their area of operations, holding on to them, and not giving them a chance to use interior lines of travel to reinforce one another. Grant planned to use the superior numbers of manpower that the North could field to its utmost advantage and to wear the South down in a war it could not hope to win. On May 4, 1864, Grant and the Army of the Potomac crossed the Rapidan River to make contact with Robert E. Lee and the Army of Northern Virginia. The Thirty-ninth Illinois was enroute to undertake its role in the overall campaign on the Virginia Peninsula in the vicinity of Bermuda Hundred. That army, under General Ben Butler, would be in a position to threaten Richmond as well as the rear of General Lee's Confederate Army while Grant's force engaged Lee from the front.[28]

THURSDAY 5:

We started down the River about 11 last night, got fast on the Bar and laid some time. Got to and passed Ft. Monroe about 7 A.M. Moving up the James River at the slow rate of about 4 knots per hour.

FRIDAY, MAY 6, 1864:

We ran aground again last night and laid 2 or 3 hours. Arrived and landed at City Point at 6 A.M. and marched about 3 miles up the River. Our Company was deployed as Skirmishers this evening. Very warm. Relieved as Skir[mishers] at dark and fell back.

Grant's orders to Ben Butler were: "When you are notifed to move, take City Point with as much force as possible. Fortify, or rather intrench, at once and concentrate all your troops for the field there as rapidly as you can. From City Point directions cannot be given at this time for your further movements. The fact that has been already stated — that is, Richmond is to be your objective point, and that there is to be cooperation between your force and the Army of the Potomac — must be your guide. This indicates the necessity of your holding close to the south bank of the James River as you advance. Then should the enemy be forced into his entrenchments in Richmond the Army of the Potomac would follow, and by means of transports the two armies would become a unit."[29]

SATURDAY 7:

We laid back last night, were up in line at 3 A.M. & laid till daylight. Moved forward about 9 A.M. along Rifle pits. Brisk skirmish in front by the 100 N.Y [Infantry]. On our side R.R. ½ mile destroyed, loss on either side not known yet. Great many sunstruck. The 100 N.Y. relieved at dark. We lay in old positions. Rations scarce.

SUNDAY 8:

We were in line at 3 as usual. We went out on picket about 9 A.M., laid till night on post, then Relieved and fell back 1 mile. The weather is very warm and being in the heavy timber, we get little air. Boys all very lively and want to go front.

MONDAY, MAY 9, 1864:

In the Field near Ft. Darling, Va.— We were up at 3 A.M. and ordered to prepare to march with 2 days Rations without knapsacks. We started at daylight and advanced 2 miles. Stopped at Church till 10 A.M., then 6 Cos. From left, Co. E included. We were on right on the River — laid till night, then Relieved by Co. F & fell back to Church. Some Skirmishing by Negro Cav., one or two of them wounded.

TUESDAY 10:

We laid near the Church till night supporting a Battery. Heavy fighting in front between 9 & 1 o'clock. The 13th Ind., 67 Ohio, 169 N.Y and some Cav. And Artillery were engaged. Our side victorious in the end. We fell back at 8 P.M. 2 miles. Relieved by other forces. Good news from the Army of the Potomac this evening. Reinforcements coming.

WEDNESDAY 11:

We laid quiet till 11 A.M., then moved back and encamped in line of Battle and put up our tents and laid quietly till night except a fatigue post was called for from the Regt. I was not on it.

The operations Kelly describes were the Federal attacks against Fort Darling and Ware Bottom Church. Although the Thirty-ninth Illinois took little part in these actions, they would have their opportunity in a little more than a week. A number of men from the regiment would become casualties at Ware Bottom Church on May 20.

Fort Darling at Drewry's Bluff, Virginia. The assault of the Thirty-ninth Illinois against this Confederate stronghold was one of the regiment's bloodiest encounters of the war (U.S. Army War College).

THURSDAY, MAY 12, 1864:

It was reported that the Rebs were advancing last night and we lay in readiness to fall out at a moments warning. We went out to support a Battery at daylight. Relieved at 9 A.M. On fatigue from 11 to 4½ P.M. Some fighting today, no particulars.

FRIDAY 13:

It has been raining the last 2 days, cleared up today. We lay quiet all night and today. Rained some again this evening. Reported that fighting was done this evening in front about 5 miles. 8 P.M. Report confirmed, no particulars.

SATURDAY 14:

We were up at 3 this morning and returned to the front. Guarded Baggage trains—got out to support a Battery at sunset, laid in field. E. Karr and S. Benson killed by Rebel shell fire. [?] wounded, arm amputated. [?] wounded in face, all Co. E. Some others were wounded in Regt.

SUNDAY, MAY 15, 1864:

Line of Battle 11 miles from Richmond. We lay all day in the open field. I moved up [to] Entrenchments in front of us this evening. Some 5 or 6 in the Regt. wounded through the day by Rebel Shell & Musketry. Some rain through the day.

With Grant's Army of the Potomac occupying Lee's Army of Northern Virginia at the Wilderness, it was hoped that Ben Butler's Army of the James, to which the Thirty-ninth Illinois now belonged, would have an almost unobstructed road to Richmond. He would be opposed by Confederate forces under the command of General P.G.T. Beauregard. Butler had attacked the Confederate position at Drewry's Bluff, some 15 miles from Richmond, on May 15. The assault went well initially, with Butler's men capturing the outer line of defenses, and the attack was to be continued the following day. If Beauregard could be brushed away, the road to Richmond and possibly the end of the war would be open.[30]

MONDAY 16:

The Rebs advanced in force in line of battle. The 55 Pa. V.[olunteers] gave way on our right. We fell back a short distance, rallied again, held our right till flanked. Major Linton wounded, Capt. Wightman & Adj, Walner mortally wounded. Lt Kingsbury wounded in arm.

On May 16, the Confederates assumed the offensive. Butler's army was attacked by three divisions under the command of Generals Robert Hoke, W.H.C. Whiting, and Robert Ransom. Ransom's attack flanked the Union right and forced it to fall back. The Confederates could possibly have routed Butler's army, but General Whiting chose not to make his scheduled assault on the Federal left. After advancing but a short distance, Whiting turned back and retired to Petersburg, stating that he had just been placed in command of that city's defenses and that he was concerned over its safety. Butler's army was permitted an escape route to Bermuda Hundred, where it dug in and assumed the defensive. Grant's hopes that the Army of the James might capture Petersburg and Richmond were foiled, and Butler's army was effectively bottled up in their defenses.[31]

Although the Thirty-ninth Illinois had been under fire on many previous occasions, Drewry's Bluff was the first real infantry battle that it had participated in. At one point in the battle, the regiment was practically surrounded, but it fought its way out with a number of bayonet charges and hand-to-hand combat. The battle lasted thirteen hours and cost Butler's army three thousand casualties. The Thirty-ninth Illinois lost 119 men killed, wounded, and missing.[32]

TUESDAY 17:

We were up on line of Battle at 3 A.M. and lay till daylight. Laid in Camp all day resting ourselves as we were much in need of rest from the fatigue of the last few days. The weather warm.

WEDNESDAY, MAY 18, 1864:

About midnight our pickets were attacked by the Rebels and the 39th was soon at its post along the Fortifications. The Rebs were repulsed by the pickets. They made frequent attacks on the pickets all today and were as often repulsed. We lay quiet all day along the Fortifications.

THURSDAY 19:

The Rebels did not trouble us last night but made a dash or so on our outposts through the day. We lay as usual supporting the Artillery and wishing the Rebs would come up on us.

FRIDAY 20:

The outposts were attacked 2 or 3 times last night & 5 times today but were as often repulsed. The 39th drove them the 5th time and captured Maj. Gen. Walker of the Rebel army. The Regt. lost 35 killed and about 50 wounded. Co. E had 8 wounded.

> *Beauregard began attacking the Union position on May 18, with the major assault launched on May 20. The Confederates had set fire to dry brush in front of General Quincy Gillmore's corps, on the right of the Union line, to create a smoke screen for their attack. The Southerners were successful in capturing several lines of rifle pits on the right of the Union line, but these were recaptured by the end of the day and the battle proved to be indecisive. For the time being, Beauregard concluded to end his attacks against Butler.[33]*

SATURDAY, MAY 21, 1864:

Supporting Battery on James River, Va. The Rebels came on the pickets once last night but were soon driven back. Our Batteries on the left were engaged part of the day, shelling the Rebel Forts that they were erecting. Regt. on fatigue tonight.

SUNDAY 22:

The Enemy made an attaack all along our lines about 11½ last night. The pickets, aided by the Artillery, drove them back as usual. The 29th went on picket this evening. Got on the Reserve. All quiet this evening.

MONDAY 23:

All quiet along the lines of the 39th today. Some musketry off on our left. Flag of Truce sent to Rebels this evening and they brought one to us afterwards. We were relieved at sunset this evening and came to Camp. Weather pleasant.

TUESDAY, MAY 24, 1864:

Some firing in front all night. We went to Fortifications about midnight & lay till daylight and returned to Camp and lay quiet all day, feeling much refreshed at night from our days rest.

WEDNESDAY 25:

By some mistake we were allowed to sleep all night in Camp. We rose this morning much surprised at our luck. Soon orders came to us to prepare for fatigue at 6 A.M. We worked on Rifle pits near the River till 6 P.M. News received that Grant is driving the Rebels & has driven them across the N.[orth] Anna River.

THURSDAY 26:

We were routed out to the Entrenchments about 10 P.M. last night and lay till sunrise. I returned to Camp feeling rather unwell. We moved Camp about 10 A.M. up nearer the Entrenchments. Went on picket at 6 P.M. 2nd Lt. J. Burke, Co. A, was shot through the neck last night while getting out his Company. 2 or 3 others wounded. Heavy shower this evening.

FRIDAY, MAY 27, 1864:

Camp Prince George Co., Va. on James River — We lay on picket all day in Rifle pits, the Rebels about 30 rods in front on us, digging Breastworks. No firing along the line of the 39th. We enjoyed ourselves better than when in Camp. We got to camp about 8½ P.M., got supper and went to the Entrenchments for the night.

SATURDAY 28:

We came to Camp at sunrise this morning leaving our guns— went for them at noon and fired the loads out and lay in Camp till night. Everything quiet. I was detailed for Guard tonight and posted with 3 men in front of Regt. to arouse Camp in case of alarm.

SUNDAY 29:

Relieved of Guard at daylight. We lay in Camp till evening today. Regimental Inspection at 12 M.[idday]by Capts. Baker & Whipple, Commanders of Regt. We went on picket at 6 P.M. Relieved the 85 Pa. Vols. We lay within 20 rods of the Rebel works, friendly to us this evening.

MONDAY, MAY 30, 1864:

Heavy firing North of James River all day. We lay quiet all day, watching the Enemy at work on their Batteries. About 5½ P.M. they gave us a warning to get in our pits and opened on us with 8 or 10 guns. No one hurt in Regt. Relieved at 6 P.M.

TUESDAY 31:

We lay along the Breastworks all night, came to Camp at sunrise. The Rebels opened about 2 P.M. with Artillery. Our Batteries soon silenced them. One or two men in Regt. wounded slightly. Heavy firing on our left. Various Rumors concerning it. Firing toward Richmond.

WEDNESDAY, JUNE 1:

June comes in very warm. We were aroused about 3 A.M. by the roar of cannon and the whistling of shells around our heads. Firing continued an hour or so. Good news still from Grant. Went on picket at 5½ P.M., took our old Rifle pits.

THURSDAY, JUNE 2, 1864:

The Enemy threw a few shells in our works about 11 P.M., did no harm. They charged on the 7th Conn[ecticut] on our left at daylight, drove them back, flanked our regt. We gave way, over powered, firing all day. We dug Rifle pits in field in rear. Rained some this evening. Relieved at 6½ P.M. by 67th Ohio. Picket line changed to Rear.

On June 2, Beauregard made his greatest effort to dislodge Butler's troops from their position. He had received intelligence that General Smith's corps and two of General Gilmore's divisions had been transferred away from Butler and felt that the remaining Union force would be too weakened to oppose his attack. The Confederate assault was concentrated on the right of the Union line, that portion being held by General Terry's First Division, Tenth Corps, of which the Thirty-ninth Illinois was a part. The Southerners broke the Federal line in two places and captured a large number of men from both the Third New Hampshire and Sixth Connecticut Regiments, but the attack was finally broken and the Confederates sent back to their own lines with heavy losses.[34]

FRIDAY 3:

Firing all last night. Rained all night. The 39th laid along the works, came to Camp this morning. All quiet today except an occassional shot from the pickets. It is very pleasant to get to lay in Camp. Quiet all day. Heavy firing this evening heard North of the James.

After Beauregard's failed assault, Butler's troops enjoyed a twelve-day period of relative inactivity. Although the line was constantly harassed by Rebel sharpshooters, there was little other activity and no threat of a large-scale assault. The men of the Thirty-ninth "holed up" during this period, but not to escape Rebel bullets. Instead, they were trying to hide from the extreme heat wave that was then present on the Peninsula, with temperatures ranging between 103 and 105 degrees.[35]

SATURDAY 4:

Firing along the picket line at intervals all night. We lay at the Breastworks from midnight till daylight. Went on picket this Evening. Commenced

raining about 3 P.M. and continued till night. Rather unpleasant for pick-
eting.

SUNDAY, JUNE 5, 1864:

It rained all night and continued till noon today. Our Batteries threw
a few shots this Evening and the Rebs threw a few shots in reply. About
6½ P.M. the Rebs opened again and [firing] kept up by both sides for an
hour or so.

MONDAY 6:

All quiet last night and I slept quietly in Quarters. Rather warm today.
Our Co. Records arrived today from Cincinnati, Ohio. We commenced
throwing up Entrenchments in Camp this Evening for our protection.

TUESDAY 7:

We worked all day on our works and got up two lines in Co. E and
got up our tents. The Rebs threw a few shells at our working parties today.
We went on picket this Evening. Co. E split up again.

WEDNESDAY, JUNE 8, 1864:

We had a pleasant night and day for picket. The Rebs threw a few shells
to annoy our fatigue parties. The Enemy are holding back for a while and
will open in earnest no doubt in a few days. Relieved of picket at 6 P.M.

THURSDAY 9:

Shelling on both sides commenced about 10 A.M. today an[d] kept up
an hour. About noon there was some musketry on the picket line. The
P[etersburg] & R[ichmond] R.R. cut today. Bridge destroyed across the
Appomattox River. News cheering from Grants army.

> Grant and the Army of the Potomac were on the scene at Richmond and
> Petersburg. Lee's army of Northern Virginia had been forced to assume a
> defensive posture around the two cities. Over the next few days, Grant
> would test the Confederate positions through a series of probes and assaults.
> In the end, both sides would settle in for a siege that would last till the
> final days of the war in the east.

FRIDAY 10:

All quiet last night. The Enemy are getting tired making attacks on
our works and are taking the defensive. On picket at 5 P.M., detached with
4 men to Co. F for 24 hours. Picket line drawn back tonight.

SATURDAY, JUNE 11, 1864:

Nothing but an occasional musket shot along the picket line disturbed the quiet of the Camp today. We lay at our posts all day. Relieved at 6 P.M. The sky cloudy with a pleasant Breeze.

SUNDAY 12:

Laid quiet all day, had a short sermon this afternoon at 2 P.M. On Brigade Guard this Evening, in charge 6 men. Cannonading this 7 P.M. heard in the direction of Grants army.

MONDAY 13:

Relieved as Brigade Guard at daybreak this morning and returned to Camp. Not very well today. Regt. went on picket at 5 P.M. Escaped the draft this time. 133 O[hio] V.[olunteers], 100 days men attached to 1st Brigade. Firing on James River this Evening. Rebel Ram coming down to see us.

TUESDAY, JUNE 14, 1864:

Bermuda Hundred, Va.—We were called out at 12 last night and reports that the Enemy are massing his forces for attack on us, laid at Breastworks a short time, then came to my Bunk & lay down & went to sleep. Went on picket this Evening, posted on left of our Brigade line, Lt. Savage, Com[manding].

WEDNESDAY 15:

The Rebels were expected to make an assault on us last [night] or this morning and a sharp lookout was kept up for them but no "Johnnies" came. They are very shy today & do not show themselves. Relieved at 6 P.M. Very warm today, dry & dusty.

THURSDAY 16:

Early this morning it was ascertained by the pickets that the Enemy had abandoned their works in front and reconnaissance [was] made. 39th ahead skirmishing. Large number of prisoners taken, 1 killed, 5 or 6 wounded in Regt., Capt. Rudd included sup[posed] mortal. Sergt. Harris, Co. A, mortally. Returned to Camp. On picket. Very tired of the trip. Rebs in works again tonight.

By June 16, Smith's corps and the two divisions of Gilmore's corps that had gone to reinforce Grant's army were returned to Butler and were once more manning the defenses at Bermuda Hundred. Union command had received news that the Confederates had abandoned their works in front of Bermuda Hundred, and a reconnaissance was pushed forward to ascertain the validity of the reports. The Thirty-ninth Illinois was in the advance, acting as skirmishers. The troops found the Confederate entrenchments to indeed be

Union troops in the trenches at Petersburg, Virginia. The failure of Ben Butler to prevent the Confederates from occupying and fortifying the Richmond-Petersburg corridor occasioned the longest period of siege warfare ever seen in America (U.S. Army War College).

empty, and they pushed on until they reached Ware Bottom Church, at which place they encountered a large force of the enemy. General Lee, with his entire army, was now on the scene, and the Confederates that opposed the Thirty-ninth Illinois were General George Pickett's Division of the Army of Northern Virginia. The Thirty-ninth suffered heavy casualties in the fighting, which was reported to have taken place under the observation of Confederate Generals Lee, Longstreet, and Beauregard.[36]

FRIDAY, JUNE 17, 1864:

The Enemy made an attack on us early this Morning—Repulsed. Picket firing continued, shelled us some this Evening—attacked left about 3 P.M., drove them back—flanked us—we fell back to reserves, went to works after dark by flank. Rebs on flank, drove us to reserve, deployed as skirmishers in front of reserves. Our loss slight. No Officers to command us.

SATURDAY 18:

Skirmish line advanced a few Rods, picket firing all forenoon. Shelling commenced about 3 P.M. Cos. E & F very much exposed. Wounded in left shoulder and fell to the rear. Surgeon, 67 Ohio, extracted the ball, Surgeon

Clark, 39th, dressed wound. The Rebs charged again on right and repulsed. W.F. Hertsog, Co. E mortally wounded. 39th on reserve tonight. C. Mayhew, Co. E, flesh wound in hip.

> *There had been heavy skirmishing all along the Richmond and Petersburg lines for several days preceding Kelly's wounding. On August 16, General Beauregard had withdrawn the majority of his command from Bermuda Hundred in order to reinforce the Petersburg line. On the 17, General Lee had become convinced that Grant was intent not only on capturing Richmond but Petersburg as well, and he sent the portions of the Army of Northern Virginia that were not already occupying the trenches around Richmond to reinforce Beauregard.[37]*

SUNDAY 19:

All quiet in front last night and indications are that we will have the pleasant Sabbath to rest at least from fighting. But the fighting at Petersburg still continues this morning. Heavy fighting this last few days in that direction, various rumors as to the results.

MONDAY, JUNE 20, 1864:

All quiet this morning. The picket from the Regt. were relieved at noon and came to Camp and at 5 P.M., pursuant to orders, the Regt. left Camp with 2 days Rations. Crossed the James. Went to work on fort. Wound in my shoulder not painful but still not as easy as one could wish. Weather warm.

TUESDAY 21:

I went to Maj. Clarks office and got my wound dressed this morning, feels somewhat easier afterwards. Gunboats fire on Rebel Batteries about noon & Rebels reply briskly. Firing kept up for 3 or 4 hours. M.W. Haddaway accidentally shot in foot by J. Casey, both Co. E. They were with the Regt. Very warm and sultry today.

WEDNESDAY 22:

President Lincoln passed Camp today, the boys cheering him as he passed, his two sons with him. Report that Regiment had skirmished yesterday and five wounded. All quiet today. Weather warm as usual. I lay in Camp all day, my shoulder somewhat painful.

> *Lincoln had come to Bermuda Hundred to meet with General Butler and to review the troops. In May, when the campaign began, Petersburg was not thought to be an important objective. Richmond was to have been Butler's focal point in his operations, and Petersburg only held importance*

as being a transportation hub through which men and supplies could be sent to the capital. Butler might easily have captured Petersburg if he had moved against it with his entire force in May before Beauregard had the opportunity to organize his command and mount a defense, but no one at that time was paying much attention to the strategic value of the city. But-ler's activities around Petersburg had been confined to the destruction of rail and communication lines to prevent men and supplies from being sent to Lee's army, then fighting in the Wilderness. In June, with Confederate forces firmly entrenched in a continuous line from Richmond to Peters-burg, the latter city had assumed a measure of great importance, and that is why Lincoln had come.[38]

THURSDAY, JUNE 23, 1864:

All quiet today till towards Evening when the Enemy opened on our works with their Artillery and kept up for some time when our guns replied and soon silenced the Rebels. Very warm. Had arm dressed.

FRIDAY 24:

The weather continues to get hotter. Laid quiet in Camp all day. Rebels commenced shelling about 11 A.M. and continued for 2 or 3 hours. Musketry in the afternoon. No harm done in Camp to my knowledge.

SATURDAY 25:

The Regt. came to Camp about 12½ this morning and were called up at 4 to march again. Left camp soon after. Marched to Point of Rocks, took transports and destination not known at present. Returned at 8 P.M., had been at Wilcox landing, N[orth] of J[ames] River to support Sheridan.

SUNDAY, JUNE 26, 1864:

Bermuda Hundred, Va.— The Regt. laid in Camp all day. A detail went on picket tonight. Thunder shower this Evening and prospects of cooler weather for some time. Heavy firing in direction of Petersburg. All quiet along our lines today. Shoulder healing fast.

MONDAY 27:

Regimental Inspection at 9 A.M. today. Very warm again today. Rained some this Evening and after dark. The Regt. went on picket this Evening. Can-nonading heard in the West toward Petersburg. Shoulder somewhat painful.

TUESDAY 28:

I went to Dr. Clark this morning, got some medicine for cough & cold. Laid in Camp the remainder of the day. The weather warm. The flies very troublesome. I am getting tired lying here in Camp but no relief.

WEDNESDAY, JUNE 29, 1864:

Laid in Camp till 4 P.M., then went to [Dr.] Clarks, got my shoulder dressed. Heavy cannonading at Petersburg. Great light in that direction tonight. Rumor says the City is on fire. Not credited here.

THURSDAY 30:

Mustered this morning at 8 A.M. for pay by Maj. Abrams, 85 Pa. Very heavy artillery firing at Petersburg this afternoon. I went to Dr. Clarks Qrs., got my wound dressed and some salve put on for healing it. Very warm today.

FRIDAY, JULY 1:

Pleasant day but rather warm. Nothing to destroy the tranquility & quietness of Camp but the roaring of Artillery at Petersburg which continued today. Regt. on picket today. Lonesome in Camp.

SATURDAY, JULY 2, 1864:

Bermuda Hundred, Va.— Bombardment of Petersburg continued today at intervals and I think it will be continued till that City is in our possession which time cannot be long. Pleasant Breeze today but the sun shines hot.

SUNDAY 3:

All quiet along the entire line of this Army all day. Both sides appear to be taking the Sabbath as a day of rest. All operations on both sides ceased. I lay in Quarters through the day.

MONDAY 4:

Heavy Detail from Regt. on picket today. Salute fired at noon. Bands playing. Otherwise the day passed as usual. The Enemy very quiet. 3 or 4 deserters came to our lines today. 4 of us got up a supper costing $6.85 at [the] sutlers.

TUESDAY, JULY 5, 1864:

A Co. of Rebels gave themselves up to our men early this morning. There were from 50 to 70 of them. Report that Sherman is at Atlanta, Ga. today. No news from Grant today. Regt. went on picket tonight. Pleasant Breeze today.

WEDNESDAY 6:

Nothing of importance transpired today in Camp. The Enemy continued to come into our lines, 4 came in today. Grants heavy guns can still be heard from Petersburg. Dry and sultry today.

THURSDAY 7:

Eleven deserters came to our lines today. 12 started but were fired on by the Enemy and one did not get over. The Regt. on picket tonight, every other night now. Some rain this Evening which cooled the air some.

FRIDAY, JULY 8, 1864:

Bermuda Hundred, Va. — Quiet as usual this day. A few Rebel deserters came this morning. The Enemy still remain very friendly to our pickets. The 57 Va. is doing picket in front of our lines at present. Detail on picket from Regt. tonight. Very warm.

SATURDAY 9:

Cloudy and pleasant today. A shell exploded by accident in 85 P.V., killing one man, wounding 5, one mortally. It was exploded through carelessness of one of the men. An alarm was made this Evening by some movements of the Enemy. Proved false.

SUNDAY 10:

Very hot and sultry today. Heavy firing at Petersburg continued today. Regt. went on picket this evening. Went out in front of Battery No. 6 near the Appomattox River. Went to Doctor this morning.

MONDAY, JULY 11, 1864:

Several deserters came in from the Rebel lines last night and some today. The Pirate Alabama sunk by the U.S. Gunboat Kearsage. They say is a great loss to them. Went to Dr. Clarks Qrs. this morning, got my wound dressed.

Kelly's comment refers to the CSS Alabama, one of the South's most famous commerce raiders of the war.

TUESDAY 12:

I got a blank furlough filled this morning and took it to Dr. Clark. He examined my shoulder. Very warm today. No firing heard today and no News in Camp. Detail from Regt. went to front on picket and detail went to the Appomattox R[iver] on picket. Some rain this Evening and wind.

WEDNESDAY 13:

The Detail from the River came in at noon today. Flag of Truce to the Enemy yesterday and one today. Object not known. Cloudy this Evening and more pleasant. Rained some this Evening here but the heaviest shower passed around.

THURSDAY, JULY 14, 1864:

Bermuda Hundred, Va. — General Inspection of the Regt. by Capt. R.W. Dawson, Brigade Inspector, at 9 A.M. Heavy detail for picket tonight. Went to Dr. Clark and got wound dressed this morning. Cool & pleasant.

FRIDAY 15:

Cloudy, cool and pleasant this day. All quiet here and at Petersburg. The Enemy in Md. Have done considerable damage to railroads, telegraphs and property. Detail for picket this Evening.

In an effort to relieve the pressure on his lines, General Lee had sent a portion of his army, under the command of General Jubal Early, on a raid through Maryland, with the object of threatening Washington. He was hoping that it would have the same effect as "Stonewall" Jackson's operations during the Valley Campaign of 1862. Although Early's movements did cause a measure of alarm and panic in the Northern capitol, his army was not strong enough to capture the city and there were not enough men drawn away from the Army of the Potomac to make any appreciable difference in Lee's situation.

SATURDAY 16:

We signed the Payrolls this morning and were paid off just after Dinner. Went to Clarks this morning. Heavy firing on the North side of the James River and report that the Enemy made an attack on Foster there and was repulsed.

SUNDAY, JULY 17, 1864:

This pleasant Sabbath was spent settling up with the boys and got most of my money matters settled up. The Regt. went on picket to the front of Camp this evening. Most of the Company are Expressing their money home today for fear of losing it.

MONDAY 18:

All the men able to bear arms were called out at midnight last night in expectation of an attack but up to 2 P.M. no attack made. Fighting last night and today at Petersburg. The result is unknown here. Newspaper accounts say the Rebels have left Md. & are retreating as fast as possible, our men in pursuit. Regt. came in from picket at 5 P.M.

TUESDAY 19:

The right wing of the Regt. was called out this morning at 3 A.M. and went to Batteries 4,5,& 6. Cos. E, F & G came in at daylight but were ordered back at 7 A.M. Relieved again at 10 A.M. Rained all last night and today. Heavy Artillery and Musketry heard at Petersburg tonight.

WEDNESDAY, JULY 20, 1864:

Bermuda Hundred, Va.—I went to Dr. Clark and got my shoulder dressed this morning, bought $8.50 worth of papers of L.R. Brooks For the Company. Company all on picket tonight. commenced raining about 6 P.M. Artillery firing heard at Grants army. I sent $911.17 cts. home in a letter today.

Considering that the monthly pay for a private in the ranks was but $13.00, the $911.17 that Kelly sent home was a huge sum. It doubtless included a great deal of bounty money that he had been paid for reenlisting. In all, it would amount to several years of salary for the average man.

THURSDAY 21:
All quiet today here. An occasional gun is fired at Petersburg. Newspapers say the Rebels have all left Md. and are South of Leesburg moving toward Stanton, Va. Regt. came off picket this Evening. Warm through the day but cool at night. Sherman had crossed the Chattahoochee River and still moving on Atlanta, Georgia.

FRIDAY 22:
Cool and pleasant today. All quiet here today. regt. all on picket tonight. Gen. Crook attacked the Raiders at Snickers Gap, Va. on the 18th inst. Took 400 prisoners and 300 wagons loaded with provisions stolen from Md.

SATURDAY, JULY 23, 1864:
Nothing of importance transpired here today. Dispatch from Sherman states the Enemy attacked him on the 15th & 16th and was repulsed with heavy loss. Averill whipped the Rebels at Winchester, Va. on the 19th inst. Hunters forces still in pursuit of the Raiders.

SUNDAY 24:
Heavy Artillery and Musketry at Petersburg at 10½ last night. Company Inspection at 10 A.M. Went to Clarks and got shoulder dressed, proud flesh in it, heals very slowly. 26 men from Co. E on picket tonight. Commenced raining about 6 P.M. Peace Commission at Niagra, closed on the 21st.

This was a failed effort on the part of the Confederate government to secure a negotiated peace with the North. The Lincoln administration remained adamant that there could be no peace so long as the country remained divided. The recent successes of the Union's armies put Washington in a position of power in the talks.

MONDAY 25:
Rained all last night, the wind blowing at the same time. Cleared up this morning but the wind still continues. Detail went out for 3 days picket

at 2 P.M. Pickets of last night came in at 6 P.M. Went to Clarks today again. No news from Sherman or Grant today.

TUESDAY, JULY 26, 1864:

Bermuda Hundred, Va.— Rec'd a letter from J.L. Ripple this morning from Petersburg Prison. The letter dated May 17th, the day he was captured. Sergt. Hanson, Pri. H.R. Snee, G.W. Morgan, D. Lee with him. Went to Dr. Croker this morning, had my shoulder examined. Right wing of Regt. on picket tonight. Cool and pleasant today. News of Maj. Gen. McPherson being killed at Atlanta rec'd today.

Ripple was a prisoner of war held in Richmond.

WEDNESDAY 27:

Report in camp that Grant has crossed th N[orth] side of James. Heavy cannonading in that direction today. Clear & warm all day. Indications of rain this Evening. The news from Sherman is still cheering and fall of Atlanta is expected soon. Also Petersburg & Richmond.

THURSDAY 28:

It rained some last night but pleasant today. Heavy firing this Evening at Petersburg. Some firing in Fosters Department. Very lonesome in Camp. A young show actor came to Camp this Evening and amused the Regt. for an hour or so.

FRIDAY, JULY 29, 1864:

News reached us this morning that Corporal A. Merrill, Co. E, died July 23rd at Point Lookout, Md. Report that Sheridan had captured a large number of prisoners on the Peninsula near Richmond. News that Sherman was fighting on Sts. of Atlanta at last account.

The Thirty-ninth experienced a change in command on July 29. Major General David Birney assumed command of the Tenth Corps on that date. It was the second change of command in a little more than a month. On June 17, General Gilmore had been replaced by Major General William Brooks, and it was that officer whom Birney replaced.[39]

SATURDAY 30:

Very warm today. Atlanta not yet taken as reported. Order for two days Rations to march. Regt. on picket today relieved as usual. No march today. The day is the hottest of the season here. Rumor that Burnside has blown up a Rebel fort near Petersburg, Va.

SUNDAY 31:

A very warm and lonesome Sabbath. Clouded up this Evening and we expected a refreshing shower but it passed around us to the North. Day passed reading, writing etc. News cheering from Sherman.

MONDAY, AUGUST 1, 1864:

Bermuda Hundred, Va.—Very warm today. Went to Dr. Clark this morning, got my shoulder dressed. Ames Division, 10th Corps, came to this place from Petersburg last night. Part of 19th Corps left here last night. Report of Burnside blowing up a Rebel fort confirmed today. Regt., 3 Cos. of on picket.

TUESDAY 2:

This day came in cool and pleasant but the sun soon appeared from behind the clouds making it as warm as usual. News reached us this Evening that the Rebels are in Pa. and have burned Chambersburg, Pa. & turned 3000 people out of house & home. Burned July 30 by McCauslands Cavalry.

Brigadier General "Tiger" John McCausland ordered the burning of Chambersburg in retaliation for the burning of Lexington, Virginia, by the Union Army.

WEDNESDAY 3:

Still thundering away at Petersburg today. News of Grants repulse at Petersburg July 30 reached us today. His loss is from 4000 to 7000 men. One Rebel fort blown up, 250 men captured. Burnsides Corps only engaged. Major Harry Gilmore, Rebel, killed at Chambersburg July 30 by the Citizens. Some rain this P.M., since contradicted. [that Gilmore had been killed]

THURSDAY, AUGUST 4, 1864:

Order for Drills etc. today. Squad Drill at 9 A.M. & Co. Drill at 4 P.M. and Dress parade at Retreat. I went to Dr. Clarks again this morning. My shoulder heals slow, proud flesh in it again today. Clear & pleasant day. Our loss at Petersburg not so heavy as reported. Gen. Meade & Staff & Gen. Butler passed the lines today.

FRIDAY 5:

We tore down our Breastworks today, all except the front line, by order of Capt. Baker, Com[manding] Regt. Great indignation against him by the men for the order. We got our tent up in good time this Evening. Lt. Kingsbury, wounded May 16, returned to Regt. today looking well.

Heavy firing at Petersburg this Evening. Gun boats & Horletts [?] Battery exchanged a few shots. Bat[tery] No. 1 fired a shot or so.

SATURDAY 6:
We put up a shade over our tents this morning. Estimate of loss in both armies at Atlanta, Ga. July 20, Union loss 1733, Rebels 8000. July 22, Union loss 3000, 10 pieces Artillery, Rebel loss, 3000, 18 stand Colors, 5000 small arms. July 27, Union loss 600, Rebel loss 4000. the Co. went on picket this evening. Very warm today.

Actual losses in the battles in and around Atlanta were approximately 6,051 for the Union and 17,928 for the Confederates. General John Bell Hood, the Confederate commander, all but destroyed his army by throwing it in futile frontal assaults against General William T. Sherman's strong positions. By the conclusion of the fighting around Atlanta, Hood had lost so many men that his army no longer had the numbers to contend with Sherman's forces.[40]

Hood retreated with his army toward Macon, and on September 2, Major General Henry W. Slocum's corps entered Atlanta unopposed. The great industrial center of Georgia had fallen.[41]

SUNDAY, AUGUST 7, 1864:
Bermuda Hundred, Va.—Cloudy and more pleasant today. Order came for Volunteers for some fatigue purpose, to work 7½ hours per day and receive 8 cts. per hour extra pay. Large No. in Regt. volunteering, 17 from Co. E. Paid a visit to the picket line this Evening with orderly. Spent most of day writing & reading. No news from abroad.

MONDAY 8:
Exceedingly warm today. No news today from armies abroad. All quiet here. Report this Evening that miners [Rebel] can be heard under a Redoubt in front of Battery No. 3. Some excitement caused by the report. I spent my time reading Waverly Magazine etc.

TUESDAY 9:
Still warm today. Ration of wine issued to sick & wounded this morning. Spent the day as usual reading etc. Co E went on picket this Evening. Lt. Warner returned to the Company today. Lt. Hoffman now Q[uarter] M[aster]. The Detail for fatigue called for 7th is played out. Very warm this Evening.

WEDNESDAY, AUGUST 10, 1864:
Cloudy, windy & thunder & lightning the fore part of last night. Clear

and warm again today. The Election in Pa. for the Amendment allowing soldiers to vote resulted in Victory for the Soldiers. Election August 2nd. Co. relieved at sunset this Evening from picket. Windy this P.M.

THURSDAY 11:

The sun is shining hot today but a cool breeze is stirring constantly making it pleasant. The news from the Potomac is cheering. Sheridan in command there. Averill captured 300 prisoners, 4 pieces Artillery from McCausland at Moorefield, Va. News of Birneys victory in Fla. and exchange of prisoners at Charleston reached us today. Sherman bombarding Atlanta.

Averill's action at Moorefield was the culmination of General John McCausland's raid into Pennsylvania, in which Chambersburg was burned. Averrill had been pursuing McCausland since the Confederates left Chambersburg but did not catch up to him until he had reached the relative safety of Moorefield, West Virginia.

FRIDAY 12:

Cool breeze today, sky clear, sun shines hot. Day passed quietly here. Some firing at Petersburg this P.M. Squad Drill at 7 to 8 P.M. Co Drill from 3½ to 5 P.M. Dress parade at 6½ P.M. I took the cloth from my shoulder today. It is healed over but very tender yet.

SATURDAY, AUGUST 13, 1864:

Bermuda Hundred, Va.— Considerable firing this morning between our Gun boats and Rebel Batteries along James River. Orders for 3 days Rations and preparations to march came this forenoon. Rebels still retreating from Md. Our fleet threatening Mobile, Ala.

This is the final entry in Kelly's diary. He was involved in the battle at Deep Bottom, Virginia, on August 16, in which engagement he was wounded in the leg and side. Kelly died as a result of his wounds in a Federal hospital at Fortress Monroe, Virginia, on October 31, 1864.[42]

Although Kelly's last entry mentions preparing three day's rations prior to starting the campaign, he did not get the opportunity to include his observations of the battle of Deep Bottom in his diary. A comrade in the regiment, Homer Plimpton, did leave an account of the fighting that cost Kelly his life. "When we broke up camp on the 13th of August, we concluded from the nature of the orders, that we were to embark on transports and proceed to some point which, according to various surmises, was supposed to be somewhere between Washington and Mobile. When, however, we reached the river where we naturally expected to find the transports with steam up and everything in readiness for our reception, we beheld not the above, but a long line of pontoons stretched across the river. Over these we went 'marching on' and did not stop until we found ourselves massed in a piece of woods near the enemy's line of advanced works not far from Deep Run. When morning dawned, skirmishing commenced, and it was not long before our brigade was in motion and in readiness for a charge. We charged the rebels and drove them from their first line to a second, more formidable.

"During the balance of the day we moved about from one place to another, and at night went on picket. At one o'clock, however, we were quickly withdrawn and moved back to the pontoon bridge, crossed over, and moved down the stream about a half mile and recrossed on another pontoon, and found ourselves with the Second Corps, General Hancock commanding. Both corps commenced moving toward Richmond. We advanced to within almost eight miles of the city, when we came in contact with the enemy intrenched. Our regiment supported a battery all day and the next night. No general engagement took place that day. "On the morning of the 16th, the day following, our brigade received orders to move to the right of the rebel works in support of regiments thrown out as skirmishers. We were soon brought under fire, and were not long in ascertaining that the force before us was by no means small. We found that the enemy had been driven from their rifle-pits, and were now inside their main works. We soon moved forward over the line of skirmishers to within two hundred yards of the rebel intrenchments, screened, however, from view by dense woods. We here received notice from our Division General A.H. Terry, that our brigade had been selected to charge those works. Between us and 'those works' was a strip of slashing about one hundred yards wide, and it was no easy matter to cross such obstacles under a galling fire. We formed just inside of the woods, out of sight, but near enough to the rebels for them to hear our commands.*

"The brigade was formed in double column on the center at half distance by regiments, the Thirty-Ninth being on the extreme left. When all was ready, the command 'Forward!' was given, and we moved off on common time, with arms at a 'right shoulder shift'; but as soon as we reached the edge of the slashing we received a deadly volley from the enemy which brought the guns down to a 'trail,' and our colors to the ground. These were immediately picked up by an officer [Lieutenant Norman C. Warner, Company E], and away we went with a regular Western yell, on the full jump, over logs, tree-tops and stumps thrown about in inextricable confusion.*

"The scene that now presented itself to my view I shall never forget—whole divisions of the advancing column swept down in the twinkling of an eye. On every hand could be seen the dead and dying men—our own comrades, who but a short time before were buoyant and hopeful, with no thought of death to make them sad.

"But notwithstanding this terrible slaughter, the old Western brigade did not stop, but made directly for the rebel breastworks bristling with bayonets and alive with men; nor did the enemy give way, but fought us hand-to-hand as we attempted to mount the works. Our colors were again shot down, Lieutenant Warner, who was carrying them, losing a leg. Another officer snatched them up and sprang upon the parapets, followed by scores of others, who leaped over right among the 'Johnnies,' and commenced using the bayonet and clubbed musket. Soon a break was made and then began the capturing of prisoners. After we got over the works, we immediately swung to the left and moved down the trenches, hauling out the 'graybacks,' who begged lustily for mercy. In a short time we had possession of the line and nearly eight hundred prisoners and five stands of colors."[43]

Upon Kelly's death, the surgeon in charge of the hospital at Fortress Monroe, sent his company commander a detailed listing of his personal effects. Included, along with his uniform and military accoutrements, were a photo album, a pocket book, $29.09 in cash, a gold pen with a silver holder, and two diaries. Kelly's father approved to have one of his son's comrades receive his effects and mail them home. His son's body was to be buried in a military cemetery in Virginia. Kelly was also due a sizeable amount of money, which the family would now receive. There was still $240 outstanding on his bounty payment, and he had not received his pay from the army since June.[44]

Capsule History of the Thirty-ninth Illinois Infantry

The Thirty-ninth Illinois Infantry was organized in Chicago, where it was mustered for service on October 11, 1861. The regiment was ordered to St. Louis, Missouri, on October 13 and then to Williamsport, Maryland, on October 29, where it was assigned to railroad guard duty in the Department of West Virginia. The Thirty-ninth continued to guard the rails until January of 1862, when a portion of the regiment took part in the engagement at Bath, West Virginia, on January 3. Another portion of the regiment was, on that same day, engaged at Great Cacapon Bridge, while a third saw action at Alpine Station. The entire regiment then took part in the retreat to Cumberland, Maryland, on January 5, 1862. The regiment saw service in the New Creek (Keyser) and Patterson Creek areas of West

Virginia until March, when it took part in the advance against Winchester, Virginia, from March 7–15. It fought in the battle of Kernstown on March 22 and in the battle of Winchester on March 23. For the next three weeks, the Thirty-ninth Illinois was in almost continual contact with the enemy, encountering the Confederates at Mt. Jackson, Strasburg, Woodstock, and Edinburg by April 2. It then saw service in the occupation of Mt. Jackson and in guarding bridges over the Shenandoah River in the Luray Valley until May of 1862.

On May 12, the regiment was ordered east to join Major General George B. McClellan's Army of the Potomac on the Peninsula. It was at Harrison's Landing from June 29 to July 2 and at Chickahominy Swamp from July 3 to July 4, before returning to Harrison's Landing to do service until August 16. The regiment moved to Fortress Monroe on August 16 and performed duty there until September 1. It was then sent to Suffolk, Virginia, where it remained until January of 1863. During this time, the regiment took part in the skirmishes at Blackwater on October 9–25 and 29–30 and in the action near Franklin on December 2, 1862. On January 23, 1863, it was moved to New Bern, North Carolina, and from there it was sent to Port Royal, South Carolina, on January 28.

The Thirty-ninth Illinois went into camp on St. Helena Island, South Carolina, where it remained until April 7, 1863, when it took part in the expedition against Charleston. From April 13 to July 10, it participated in the occupation of Folly Island. From July 10 to September 7, it took part in all of the operations against Forts Sumter, Wagner, and Gregg, which resulted in the capture of Forts Wagner and Gregg on September 7, 1863. The regiment continued to see service in the siege operations against Fort Sumter until October and on Folly Island until December. On January 7, 1864, the veterans of the regiment who had reenlisted were sent home on furlough till February 3. The returning veterans rejoined the regiment at Washington. The regiment was attached to Major General Benjamin Butler's Army of the James and transferred to the south side of the James River at City Point, Virginia, on May 5, 1864. It took part in the engagements at Swift Creek, Arrowhead Church, Proctor's Creek, and Palmer's Creek before fighting in the battle of Drewry's Bluff on May 12–16. The Thirty-ninth fought at Ware Bottom Church on May 20, 1864, and at Bermuda Hundred on June 2 and 14.

From June of 1864 to April of 1865, the regiment took part in the siege operations against Richmond and Petersburg. In the course of these operations, the regiment fought in the following battles and skirmishes, in whole, or in part: Strawberry Plains and Deep Bottom, August 14–18; Deep Run, August 16; Chaffin's Farm and New Market Heights, September

28–30; Darbytown Road, October 13; Fair Oaks, October 27–28; and Hatcher's Run, March 29–31, 1865. The Thirty-ninth took part in the assault on Fort Gregg and the fall of Petersburg on April 2, 1865, and in the pursuit of Lee's army, which ended in the surrender at Appomattox Court House on April 9, 1865.

After the surrender, the regiment did garrison duty at Richmond and Norfolk until December of 1865. On December 6, the men were mustered out, and they returned to Chicago to be discharged on December 16, 1865.

The Thirty-ninth Illinois lost 141 men killed and mortally wounded in the war and 132 who died of disease.[45]

Muster Roll of Company E, Thirty-ninth Illinois Infantry

Captain James H. Hooker (Rochester, N.Y. Resigned May 26, 1862)

Captain Lewis T. Whipple (Kankakee, Il. Resigned October 25, 1864)

Captain Minor W. Milliman (Promoted to major June 6, 1865)

1st Lieutenant John L. Ripple (Orbisonia, Pa. Promoted to captain June 6, 1865)

1st Lieutenant Norman C. Warner (Rockford, Il. Wounded at Deep Bottom, Va. August 16, 1864. Discharged for disability December 15, 1864)

1st Lieutenant William Baxter Wounded and taken prisoner at Drewry's Bluff, Va., May 16, 1864. Exchanged August 13, 1864.)

2nd Lieutenant John Conley (Wilmington, Il. Resigned August 8, 1862)

2nd Lieutenant George A. Clark

Sergeants

William E. Steele (Chicago, Il. Killed at Darbytown Road, Va., October 13, 1864)

David M. Hanson (Wilmington, Il. Taken prisoner at Drewry's Bluff, Va., May 16, 1864. Died in prison.)

Corporals

T.D. Gronigal (Wilmington, Il. Wounded and taken prisoner at Drewry's Bluff, Va., May 16, 1864. Died June 9, 1864, at Petersburg from his wounds.)

William Brown (Chicago, Il.)

John W. Whitman (Concord, Il. Mustered out September 27, 1864)

William Baxter (Wilmington, Il. Promoted to sergeant November 1, 1864. Killed at Fort Gregg, Va., April 2, 1865.)

George W. Burton (Wilmington, Il. Wounded at Deep Run, Va., August 16, 1864. Killed at Fort Gregg, Va., April 2, 1865.)

Privates

William Andreas (Wesley, Il. Wounded at Fort Wagner, S.C., October 3, 1863. Discharged May 16, 1864, for disability.)

Alex Anderson (Killed at Fort Gregg, Va., April 2, 1865)

Theodore F. Axtell (Wesley, Il. Wounded at Deep Run, Va., August 16, 1864, and at Darbytown Road, Va., October 13, 1864.)

Samuel C. Blakesley (Durham, Il. Deserted.)

Lawrence Baker (Wounded and taken prisoner at Drewry's Bluff, Va., May 16, 1864. Died in Richmond June 9, 1864.)

Walter Bogart (Wilmington, Il. Killed at Fort Gregg, S.C., October 12, 1863.)

Lorenz Button (Wilmington, Il. Discharged for disability in 1862.)

Silas Benton (Wilmington, Il. Killed at Drewry's Bluff, Va., May 14, 1864.)

Samuel A. Barton (Bloomington, Il. Discharged for disability July 4, 1863.)

Ralph Babcock (Chicago, Il. Wounded at Chapin's Farm, Va., October 7, 1864. Killed at Fort Gregg, Va., April 2, 1865.)

Samuel C. Batchelder (Wilmington, Il. Discharged June 3, 1865.)

William Bohmler (Chicago, Il. Discharged June 20, 1865.)

Charles W. Beam (Gaines, Il. Enlisted on April 13, 1865, at the age of fifteen.)

Charles Baldwin (Chicago, Il. Discharged for disability September 18, 1862.)

William A. Brown (Mustered out December 6, 1865.)

Levi Baker (Mustered out December 6, 1865.)

John Cannon (Wilmington, Il. Discharged for disability November 20, 1865.)

James Conley (Deserted.)

John Casey (Mustered out December 6, 1865.)

James Clark (Channahon, Il. Killed at Deep Bottom, Va., August 16, 1864.)

Frank M. Corbett (Wounded at Ware Bottom Church, Va., May 20, 1864.)

William C. Cubberly (Mustered out May 27, 1865.)

Patrick Dagan (Wilmington, Il. Wounded and missing at Darbytown Road, Va., October 13, 1864.)

Michael Dugan (Wilmington, Il. Deserted October 1861.)

John Daily (Deserted October 1861.)

George H. Dunn (Rockville, Il. Wounded at Ware Bottom Church, Va., May 20, 1864. Deserted.)

William J. Dannable (Wesley, Il. Wounded at Deep Run, Va., August 16, 1864. Deserted.)

Gideon Dunham (Mustered out December 6, 1865)

William W. Ely (Concord, Il. Wounded at Bermuda Hundred, Va.)

Joseph S. Evans (Wesley, Il. Wounded at Deep Run, Va., August 16, 1864.)

Joseph Elick (Mustered out December 6, 1865.)

William Flynn (Chicago, Il. Died of illness at Beaufort, S.C., January 10, 1864.)

Andrew J. Flowers (Sheldon, Il. Deserted October 1861.)

Lewis Flowers (Discharged October 18, 1865.)

William J. Finley (Jefferson County, Il. Discharged May 27, 1865.)

Henry Gillett (Wesley, Il. Died in hospital February, 1862.)

James Gillett (Wesley, Il. Wounded at Drewry's Bluff, Va., May 16, 1864. Died of wounds August 17, 1864.)

Daniel Grice

Alexander Gray (Wilmington, Il. Wounded at Deep Run, Va., August 16, 1864.)

Charles W. Hertzog (Rockville, Il. Transferred to Veteran Reserve Corps November 16, 1864.)

J.O. Harsh (Rockville, Il. Mustered out September 27, 1864.)

Charles C. Hudson (Wilmington, Il. Mustered out December 6, 1865.)

William F. Hertzog (Rockville, Il. Wounded May 20, 1864. Killed at Ware Bottom Church, Va., June 18, 1864.)

Daniel Howell (Wilmington, Il. Discharged.)

John Hawath (Chicago, Il. Deserted February 1862.)

Calvin H. Howe (St. Louis, Mo. Deserted January 30, 1862.)

Hermann H. Howe (St. Louis, Mo. Deserted January 30, 1862.)

M.V. Hademan (Wilmington, Il.

Wounded at Ware Bottom Church, Va., June 2, 1864, and at Appomattox Court House, Va. on April 9, 1865. One of the last men to be wounded in the war.)

George Hartman (Discharged May 3, 1865.)

George Hayworth (Taken prisoner at Appomattox Court House, Va. April 9, 1865, and released the same day.)

George Howell (Wesley, Il. Wounded October 13, 1864. Discharged for disability March 30, 1865.)

Samuel F. Hull (Chicago, Il.)

Monroe Hazzard (Chicago, Il.)

William O.O. Jewett (Wesley, Il. On recruiting service.)

Charles A. Jackson (Florence, Il. Wounded August 16, 1864. Discharged for disability November 7, 1864.)

James M. Johnson (Chicago, Il. Detailed to regimental band.)

Howard Johnston (Channahon, Il. Wounded at Drewry's Bluff, Va., May 16, 1864. Discharged for disability November 21, 1864.)

Thomas Kinney (Wilmington, Il. Wounded at Deep Run, Va., August 16, 1864. Discharged for disability June 20, 1865.)

Elisha Karr (Iroquois County, Il. Killed at Drewry's Bluff, Va., May 14, 1864.)

William T. Kelley (Wesley, Il. Mustered out December 6, 1865.)

John Kelly (Orbisonia, Pa. Wounded June 17, 1864. Wounded at Deep Bottom, Va., August 16, 1864. Died of wounds October 31, 1864.)

Lloyd W. Kahler (Mustered out December 6, 1865.)

William Kelly (Mustered out December 6, 1865.)

Albert Kelsey (Mustered out December 6, 1865.)

Chapman Kichens (Mustered out December 6, 1865.)

John Laughlin (Huntington, Pa. Died of typhoid fever February 11, 1862.)

Sydney Lyons (Florence, Il. Wounded at Darbytown Road, Va., October 13, 1864.)

Ditson Lee (Essex, Il. Captured at Drewry's Bluff, Va., May 16, 1864. Paroled at Savannah, Ga., November 19, 1864.)

Charles T. Levally (Chicago, Il. Wounded at Petersburg, Va., September 10, 1864.)

John Lansing (Deserted August 5, 1865.)

M.W. Milliman (Wesley, Il. Promoted to sergeant January 1, 1863.)

Herman Milks (Gardner, Il. Promoted to corporal March 1, 1865.)

Almon Merrill (Florence, Il. Wounded at Drewry's Bluff, Va., May 16, 1864. Died of wounds July 16, 1864.)

James Monroe (Florence, Il. Wounded at Drewry's Bluff, Va., May 16, 1864.)

Alex McCollum (Gardner, Il. Transferred to Company A.)

Moses Mayer (Florence, Il. Wounded at Ware Bottom Church, Va.)

George M. Morgan (Sheldon, Il. Wounded and taken prisoner at Drewry's Bluff, Va., May 16, 1864.)

James McMaster (Wilmington, Il. Died December 9, 1861, at Williamsport, Md.)

Ephraim Musselman (Pittsburgh, Pa. Died October 16, 1864, of typhoid fever.)

John Mahan (Pittsburgh, Pa. Deserted April 20, 1862.)

Oscar R. Morey (Florence, Il. Mustered out December 5, 1865.)

Caleb Meyher (Wounded at Ware Bottom Church, Va., June 18, 1864.)

William Martin (Chicago, Il. Mustered out December 6, 1865.)

John Monroe (Florence, Il. Wounded at Ware Bottom Church, Va., May 20, 1864. Taken prisoner at Appomattox Court House, Va. April 9, 1865, and released the same day.)

Cyran Mallett (Chicago, Il. Wounded at Darbytown Road, Va., October 13, 1864. Deserted October 3, 1865.)

William Miller (Mustered out December 6, 1865.)

Andrew P. Mills (Mustered out December 6, 1865.)

James W. Nelson (Wilmington, Il. Mustered out December 6, 1865.)

James R. Nobles (Wilmington, Il. Mustered out December 6, 1865.)

Henry O'Harra (Wesley, Il. Mustered out December 6, 1865.)

Henry Ohlhues (Florence, Il. Wounded at Ware Bottom Church, Va., May 20, 1864. Killed at Fort Gregg, Va., April 2, 1865.)

William H. Pennington (Evanston, Il. Mustered out December 6, 1865.)

A.C. Porter (Mustered out December 6, 1865.)

John J. Perry (Mustered out December 6, 1865.)

Alpheus W. Rogers (Wesley, Il. Wounded at Drewry's Bluff, Va., May 14, 1864. Discharged for disability October 20, 1864.)

William H. Robinson (Wilmington, Il. Deserted.)

William B. Ripple (Orbisonia, Pa. Died of brain fever August 18, 1862.)

Thomas Raleigh (Wilmington, Il. Accidentally wounded September 17, 1861.)

Abraham Shade (Deserted September 1862.)

Edward A. Sackett (Chicago, Il. Detailed to regimental band.)

F.L. Stearns (Taken prisoner at Strasburg, Va., May 26, 1862.)

M.F. Sheffler (Rockville, Il. Wounded at Fort Wagner, S.C., August 16, 1863.)

Hugh R. Snee (Rockville, Il. Wounded and taken prisoner at Drewry's Bluff, Va., May 16, 1864. Escaped from Andersonville September 22, 1864.)

Thomas Stewart (Wilmington, Il. Wounded and taken prisoner at Darbytown Road, Va., October 13, 1864. Paroled and died in hospital in Annapolis, Md.)

Charles M. Smith (Wilmington, Il. Discharged for disability February 14, 1863.)

Henry E. Sartell (Wilmington, Il. Wounded at Deep Bottom, Va., August 16, 1864.)

Reuben Slayton (Chicago, Il. Wounded May 20, 1864.)

William Stanton (Detailed as Commissary of Subsistence.)

Randolph Sailor (Rockville, Il. Mustered out December 6, 1865.)

Eden Stoval (Wounded at Appomattox Court House, Va., April 9, 1865.)

Samuel Smith (Mustered out December 6, 1865.)

George Thayer (Wilmington, Il. Captured at Manassas, Va., September 2, 1862.)

James Vandebogart (Florence, Il. Mustered out December 6, 1865.)

Thomas Wayne (Chicago, Il. Mustered out December 6, 1865.)

George A. Webber (Chicago, Il. Wounded October 7, 1864.)

William Walrath (Mustered out December 6, 1865.)

John T. Wilson (Mustered out December 6, 1865.)

Charles W. Ware (Promoted to corporal November 20, 1865.)

John Weiner (Wilmington, Il. Discharged for disability November 20, 1865.)

John W. Whiteman (Discharged for disability September 27, 1864.)[46]

FOUR

Private George Schmittle
Thirteenth Pennsylvania Cavalry

George Schmittle served in the 110th Pennsylvania Volunteer Infantry, raised in October of 1861. Born on May 9, 1846, in Huntingdon County Pennsylvania, he was only fifteen years of age when he went away to war. Schmittle was the son of Valantine Schmittle, a Prussian immigrant, and Mary Wagner Schmittle of Pennsylvania. The 110th Pennsylvania saw action in the Valley Campaign of 1862, fighting at both Kernstown and Port Republic. It also saw combat at Cedar Mountain, Thoroughfare Gap, Second Manassas, Fredericksburg, Chancellorsville, and Gettysburg before its term of enlistment expired. The regiment had enough men reenlist to make it a veteran regiment, and it received a thirty-day furlough in January of 1864 as a result of that veteran status. The 110th went on to fight at the Wilderness, Spotsylvania Court House, Chickahiominy, Petersburg, Fort Steadman, and Amelia Springs before the end of the war.[1]

George Schmittle did not reenlist with his comrades in the 110th Infantry. He was discharged from the 110th in December of 1862 for reasons of disability. The reason given on his discharge was "for frequent attacks of epilepsy." The attending physician noted that the "attacks had become quite severe & frequent of late" and the "cause obscure."[2]

Instead of marching, Schmittle chose to ride to war in his second hitch and enlisted in the Thirteenth Pennsylvania Cavalry on July 24, 1863. The unit was mustered into Federal service in September of 1863, just one month before it saw its first major action at Sulphur Springs, Virginia. Schmittle was captured in this engagement, his first as a cavalry trooper, and was eventually sent to Andersonville Prison in Georgia.[3]

On the 12th day of October, 1863, five hundred and sixty-four comrades, myself included, were taken prisoner near Jefferson, Virginia. For three days we were hustled back and forth to suit the movements of the

Confederate army. During this time we received no rations. On the evening of the third day after our capture each one was given three hardtack and a small piece of flitch or side meat. Then we were crowded into box cars (almost as tight as sardines packed in a box) seventy to eighty men to a car, and railroaded to Richmond, where we were confined in Smith's cotton factory and robbed of everything we had such as money, watches, jewelry, etc. Here each received a pint of bean soup and a small half brick-shaped corndoger once in twenty-four hours. It soon dawned upon our minds that, if we were not speedily paroled or given a change of food and more of it, we were doomed to starvation. The boys soon became so hungry that they got to trading their clothing for food. After spending thirty days in this den of pollution we were removed to Pemberton's tocacco factory — Libby No. 2. From 300 to 400 of us were placed on each floor. We had neither fire nor heat, and we were kept there until the 12th day of January, 1864.

The fighting at Sulphur Springs began at 4:00 A.M. on the morning of October 12. Colonel John Gregg's Second Brigade, Second Division, Cavalry Corps held its ground against the Confederate troopers for several hours until the Union horsemen began to run out of ammunition. Gregg's command had been encircled by the Confederates and were fighting the engagement dismounted. With no more cartridges to fire, the line began to break and the Rebel troopers rushed in, taking approximately 400 prisoners from the brigade, 127 of those belonging to the Thirteenth Pennsylvania Cavalry and a large portion of these came from Company E, Schmittle's company. After their capture, the prisoners were moved to Warrenton and on October 15, they were moved to Culpeper. Upon arriving at the latter place, they received the first food they had been given since being captured, some biscuits and rotten bacon. They were loaded on rail cars at Culpeper and sent to Gordonsville, where they spent the night before being sent on to Richmond on October 16.[4]

We were then taken to Belle Island, which included about six acres of ground. The one side was closed by a trench, the embankment of which formed the sentinel beat. The James River, forming a semi-circle, completed the boundary opposite. It was within this enclosure that 10,000 of us poor mortals were confined, not knowing what moment we might be called upon to give up our lives because we loved the Grand Old Flag that proclaimed Liberty to all the world and guarantees homes of peace and tranquility to all who rests within her portals.

It was here we for the first time had an opportunity to taste for ourselves the awful experiences of war.

On the river boundary of this prison there was an opening between the guards through which we were permitted to pass to obtain water and attend to the demands of nature. You can imagine the condition of the water and surroundings when the James River supplied our drinking water and at the same time was the receptacle for the sewage of this prison.

As for shelter, we had nothing except some old weather beaten tents almost torn to shreds. We were nearly naked and starving. Our allowance of wood was about fifteen cordwood sticks to each one hundred men; our rations varied from cornbread crackers and beans to raw turnips and cabbage. A medium sized head of cabbage would make from four to six rations. Men were in such starving condition that they would wander around the sink ground and pick up and eat undigested beans. On one occasion a lieutenant's dog was caught and killed and the greater portion of it cooked and eaten, but the officer found it out, and on learning who the hungry fellow was that killed his dog he was so enraged that as a punishment, he made him eat a piece of the dog raw.

Photograph of George Schmittle, probably taken at the time or just before he enlisted in the 100th Pennsylvania Infantry for his first term of enlistment in the army.

I cannot describe the awful suffering here from starvation and cold. The river froze over twice so solid that the Rebels crossed back and forth on the ice. The amount of wood apportioned us was insufficient for warmth and would be consumed before midnight. The men would huddle close together like so many chickens, trying to keep warm; some would lay prone on the frozen ground, draw their knees up and get as close together as possible, forming a long line. They would remain in this position — which they called spooning — until the upper sides of their bodies would get so cold they could stand it no longer, when someone would call out "Spoon over" and, beginning at the rear end, each one would follow suit. Many died, the direct cause being attributable to cold and starvation.

On the 6th of March we were again packed in box cars like so many cattle, and sleep had to be caught either standing or sitting; this situation for three days and nights, when we were unloaded at Charlotte, N.C., remaining there for two days and one night, re-loaded and sent to Andersonville.

There were a total of eighty-nine men from the Thirteenth Pennsylvania Cavalry who were confined as prisoners at Andersonville. The vast majority of these were captured during the engagement at Sulphur Springs, Virginia, when Schmittle was captured. It is odd that Schmittle, in his memoir, does not refer to any of these comrades from his own regiment.[5]

Andersonville is located in Sumpter County, Georgia, is 60 miles below Macon, on the Southwestern railroad, and 50 miles from the Alabama state line. It was a little station on the line and before the war consisted only of a few dwelling houses, one church and a post office. The hamlet received its name from the superintendent of the Southwestern, who was a personal friend of Major Anderson, and who, it is thought, sought to perpetuate the latter's name, for looking back to the commencement of our civil strife we find Major Anderson a prominent hero before the minds of men.

It is indeed ironic that the site that would become infamous for inhumanity to Northern prisoners should bear the name of the North's first hero of the war, Major Robert Anderson, the defender of Fort Sumter.

It would seem that the place with which was linked the name of such a man would be a bright spot in our land. But it is doubted if there can be a name in history which has the power to stir to its remotest depths the fountains of indignation and grief more effectually than that of Andersonville. As it stands, the name Andersonville is suggestive of everything that is inhuman, infamous and wicked. With it are associated the most revolting things it were possible to conceive. Imagination in her wildest flights could scarce paint such a picture of cruelty and injustice. Thirteen thousand seven hundred and six Union dead lie there — silent sentinels to the dark and malicious shading. And no curtain can be drawn that can shut out from the mind and vision of those now living the dreadful scenes they witnessed at accursed Andersonville Prison.

A solitary man may make a place notorious for all time; he may become so identified with it that the mention of the one will readily suggest the other. So it was in the case before us; therefore, henceforth Wertz and Andersonville will stand inseperable — and he who rehearses the tale of prison life at the lone and wretched Georgia station will also tell the story of the inhuman Commandant Wertz.

The Confederate government, through the agency of Howell Cobb and John H. Winder, designed and built the Andersonville stockade where it would not be subject to raids by the Union Army forces, and evidently coupled with the design of destroying their captives by use of natural, but frightful and loathsome agencies, viz; Slow starvation, exposing them unsheltered, and uncared for to the burning sun, the rains, fogs and deadly miasma from the slimy quagmire which occupied over three acres through the central part of the prison.

The island was covered with a dense forest of pine. The trees were cleared away and cut in lengths of 25 feet and then hewn in squares; a trench 5 feet deep was dug around 17 acres of ground, the logs were then set on end in the trench, close together, forming a wall 20 feet high and each stock spiked to a horizontal piece of timber 8 feet long, below the top of the wall on the outside. The pen was longest north and south, sloping from either end to the quagmire or swamp, through which ran the little creek, 1 foot wide and about 5 inches deep, which served as the water supply for the prisoners. At intervals were the guard posts, forty-four in all, and placed near the top of the wall, from whence the guards could overlook all parts of the prison. There were but two gates, both on the west side, about 10 rods from either end of the "pen" and called the North and South gates. Inside the wall and 25 feet from it was the "dead line," marked out by strips of pine boards supported on stakes 3 feet high. This no prisoner dared touch or go beyond, under pain of death. Around the stockade and at a suitable distance were a number of earthworks or forts, built up sufficiently high so the artillery could sweep the pen with shell and grape shot if necessity arose.

Makeshift tents showing the crowded conditions inside the prisoner compound in Andersonville Prison (U.S. Army War College).

About 20 rods southwest of the South gate, on high ground overlooking the prison, was a large log house wherein was quartered the Rebel officers, the Confederate flag floating from a pole in front. Near the pole were two cannon, or signal guns, used to warn the entire Rebel force in command there in case the prisoners attempted to break out. At various places between the officer's quarters and the South gate were located the different instruments of torture, viz: The stocks, thumb screws, barbed iron collar, shackles, ball and chain, etc. There were three kinds of stocks, one requiring the offending prisoner to stand on tip toe, his hands fastened

Andersonville Prison, showing the "dead line," the rail and post fence stretching from the middle bottom of the picture to the upper right. To cross the "dead line" was forbidden, and any soldier who attempted to do so would be summarily shot by the guards (U.S. Army War College).

over a piece of timber under which his head is crowded forward and another timber forcing the small of his back forward; in the second stock the prisoner was made sit on the ground, his hands and feet elevated and fastened in a frame work in front of him; the third stock, a horizontal frame, the prisoner on his back with hands and feet fastened, the head fixed in an extending head-board, which is drawn outward until the body and limbs undergo a painful tension.

About half a mile northwest of the prison was a large sandy field to which the dead comrade prisoners were carted, packed in trenches without box, coffin or shroud of any kind and strewed over them but a scant covering of earth.

On the road to this potter's field was a log house, where the dogs and bloodhounds were kept — some 30 or 40 in number — and used to scour the surrounding woods and hunt down escaped prisoners who may have in some way managed to evade the vigil of the guards. But it would seem impossible for anyone to escape, as the guards were placed so close together on top of the wall, each one calling out the number of his post from 9 o'clock in the evening till 9 o'clock in the morning; also name the hour or half hour of the night, for instance: "Post No. 1; 9 o'clock, and all is well 1." This was passed around the entire stockade from Post No. 1 to Post no. 44. In addition to this precaution, there was a guard line outside, the guards patrolling a beat, back and forth, meeting at the guard stands. Attached to all this was a most cruel order which invested every guard with power to shoot down a prisoner for the slightest offense; and had the sentinels enforced the law, then I should remain silent, but permit me to say that in many instances they reached beyond the order limit and shot down scores of poor, helpless captives without the least provocation. I can to this day testify to their inhumanity and murder.

At the sound of the musket fired by the guard on the palisade I have walked out to learn what next horror was in store for us, and to my consternation witnessed scenes to frightful to relate; but as it is in keeping with all the surroundings, I will instance the following: I have seen new prisoners just brought into the pen, who being thirsty after being confined for several days in box cars, hurry to the little creek and stoop down to get a drink, not knowing the "rules," when over they would go with a ball through their skull. I have seen men with their brains oozing out and their blood reddening the water of the stream from which they expected to quench their thirst. Often a guard would miss his mark, and the ball passing on would kill one or more prisoners quite distanced from the dead line, inside the prison.

There is no spot on the face of the earth where man's inhumanity to man was more fully demonstrated than in this hell on earth; and Andersonville will be a dark spot on American soil for centuries to come. Wertz and Andersonville are the two reprehensible wings that will bear the memory of the Southern Confederacy into eternal infamy.

On Washington's Birthday, 1864, the first groups of Union prisoners were placed in Andersonville — the nucleus of a great army of martyrs who were destined to yield up their lives to the fury and malice of a conscienceless mob.

On the 12th day of March, 1864, a large number of prisoners, including myself, who had been at Belle Island, and who from starvation and cold had been reduced to mere skeletons, entered this hellish spot. Andersonville — this place from which was dealt out to the graveyard only one-half mile away 13,706 Patriot dead.

When Andersonville was constructed, it was intended to be used for the confinement of only 6,000 men. However, when the Federal government refused to negotiate for the exchange of prisoners, the numbers continued to climb, and the Confederates were forced to cram more and more men into their existing prison facilities. By the time Andersonville reached its peak, there would be more than 30,000 prisoners confined there.[6]

Before entering this place we met the imp before referred to — who became accessory in a great measure to this fiendish scheme — Henry Wertz. Military Commandant of Andersonville prison. He was a being of fiery and ungovernable temper; profane, cruel and heartless to the last degree; one who in nowise hesitated to uphold and further the murderous plots of his superior and designing officers.

Were it possible to offer anything in extenuation of the atrocious conduct which Wertz exhibited to the Union prisoners, it could be only that he was not a native but simply an adopted citizen of the United States. This, however, would be a poor apology for the utter abscence of all those principles of virtue and compassion which are the prime glory of manhood in any land. He brought-upon himself universal execration; his name stands in history only to awake unmitigated contempt in every loyal and true heart.

This Captain Wertz was a native of the place known as the paradise of the world; and I might just say it is reputed that Satan was a refugee from Paradise — so we who knew Captain Wertz feel like giving him the original appellation and say that he was the Devil in human form.

Captain Wertz was born in Zurick, Switzerland, in November, 1823, and at this period of his noble existance was about 40 years old. Tongue cannot relate nor can language be commanded to picture that beast of a man as he should be, in order that all might know how those wretched and unfortunate prisoners were abused — unmercifully abused at the instance of this abominable hell-hound wretch.

My friends, you may think these are strong terms, but had you been there and experienced what myself and comrades did you would justify them, and I doubt not you would make the language a great deal more explicit.

The deamon, Captain Wertz, was seen more than once trample under foot poor, starving, dying wrecks of humanity for the most trivial offense. Wertz was a slave-driver before the war, when he became famous for his brutality to the down-trodden negro slaves who were unfortunate enough to be placed in his charge. His conscience was clouded, his heart closed, and his cruel and impetuous nature thirsted for participation in this unhallowed work.

And well the Rebels knew where to find a man upon whom they could depend to carry out their hellish designs. He was first placed in command of Libby prison, early in July, 1862, and held the rank of sergeant-major for a time. Severe and terrible were the cruelties he practiced upon the prisoners there. The more severe he became, the more he excited the admiration of the Rebel masters. As a reward for his unwonton barbarity, he was commissioned second lieutenant. In the spring of 1864 he was crowned with captain's honor, and chosen for the deathly work at Andersonville. He was at once sent to the little, obscure village in the very center of Georgia, where he commenced the series of crimes that cost him his life. The system he adopted there in the prison began and ended in heartless cruelty. It was a work of death and his calloused nature gloried in it, as may be inferred by the remark made when he saw hundreds of the poor starved prisoners who had been in his power hurried to untimely graves, thus: "We give them the land they came to fight for." And again he boasted of doing better service than twenty of Lee's best regiments. He usually rode a white horse — I might appropriately apply the word "Death." On the 10th day of November, 1865, this man Wertz, who dealt out misery and death to those helpless captives, paid the penalty of his crime on the gallows in the old U.S. capital prison yard, Washington, D.C. When he was informed that he was to be hung, he replied that after his death he would come back and haunt his executioners— a promise he never fulfilled.

Henry Wertz [or Wirz] was the only person to be tried for war crimes at the end of the Civil War. Whether his actions were deserving of the punishment received has been debated ever since that time. Many Northern prisons were hardly better than Andersonville, and that was not even the worst of the Southern prisons. The stockade at Salisbury, North Carolina, had a higher mortality rate than did Andersonville. The truth is that neither side was prepared for the huge numbers of prisoners that came into their hands and that apathy, resentment, and cruelty were to be seen on both sides. In past wars and in the first years of the Civil War, it was common practice to exchange or parole prisoners captured in battle. Those who were paroled took an oath not to again bear arms against the enemy until they had been properly exchanged. A paroled soldier was not exchanged until a paroled enemy soldier was swapped for him on the rolls.[7]

As before stated, we entered this place of death on the 12th day of March, 1864, and remained until the 12th of September. Upon our first entering the prison it looked as though our change would be for the better. The ground was clean and unoccupied, and there was plenty of wood, the most of this waste from the trees which had been cut for the stockade being left on the ground. This we used freely as the nights were very cold and no shelter, and none had sufficient clothing to keep them warm. Every one had traded every thing left him, when robbed in Richmond, for something to eat, in order to sustain life. The prisoners placed here were mostly brought from other prisons, had endured the hardships of winter and were reduced to mere skeletons, and were now fixed in this pen like cattle, to remain until the inhumane treatment to be meted out, further on, by our cruel captors, would prepare us for the potter's field — the martyr's graveyard — the last resting place of the patriot dead.

On arrival we were at once numbered in squads of 100 each. A Rebel sergeant came in every morning and counted each squad. Each squad had two men to draw the rations and divide them into five parts, each dividing ration for twenty men, which in turn was divided, giving each man his portion. At first our rations were issued raw—consisting of one pint of cornmeal and about three spoonsful of peas or beans, occassionally about two ounces of meat and that unfit to eat. We seldom ever got salt, and when we did it was but a teaspoonful, received in the hand and partaken of on the spot. The rations were brought into the prison enclosure by a four-mule team. The cornmeal—cobs chopped in—was shoveled into improvised bags made of old pants and drawers, borrowed from prisoners who had that much scant clothing to spare, and then distributed by the squad men. In consideration for the loan of the "bags" each fellow would be given an extra spoonful of meal. Unless a man was sick, he would eat his entire ration as soon as issued and not be half satisfied. Some had managed to procure a tin cup, can or plate in which the cornmeal would be mixed with water, placed on a joggle of wood and leaned up in front of the fire to bake "dodgers." Some would eat the mixture raw, being too hungry to bide the formality of a "bake."

I speak from knowledge when I say that during my one year and thirty-seven days of prison life the Rebs never furnished us with any clothing or a single cooking utensil. Some few, at the time of capture, had each a tin cup and plate, case knife, canteen, etc. These having gotten into camp were of priceless value. I paid at one time for a half-gallon pail $6 in greenbacks—equal to $42 in Confederate currency. This pail I used a long time in cooking my own rations and loaning it to comrades, who would return it with a spoonful of mush as rent.

A fellow prisoner at Andersonville and comrade from the Thirteenth Pennsylvania Cavalry, George Nailer, wrote the following, piteous letter to his family: "Dear Father, Mother, Brother and Sisters: Once more my attention is drawn toward the old homestead. I fear something has happened at home; for I have been downhearted for eight or ten days, and whenever I think of home, tears startle from my eyes. I have no rest day or night. I am unwell and failing. A letter from home is worth more to me than fifty dollars. I wrote once in April (1864), asking you to send me a box of crackers, meat, sugar, coffee, tea, dried fruit, such as cherries, peaches, apples, etc., onions, potatoes, 3 qts. salt, 2 lbs. pepper, 10 lbs. soap, one bar Castille soap, a box dried herring, pills, oil, Laudnum, golden tincture, camphor, baloney, sausage, pickles, knife, fork, spoon, plate, wheat flour and soda will not come amiss, butter, preserves, pickles, sauerkraut, liver puddings, cheese, 8 or 10 qts. beans, 5 or 6 lbs. rice, plenty sugar, paper, envelopes, pens and ink, a blank book large size for the pocket, 2 shirts, 2 pair drawers, pair pants, coat, old hat, stockings. A two quart pail made of block tin. Put everything in tin cans. James Woodburn, Joseph Rudy, D. Hoerner are here and well. John Natcher came in a few days ago. I would give all my possessions to be liberated and be permitted to meet my friends. I need a pair of Scissors. I ask an interest in your prayers. From your son, Serg't Geo. Nailer. Co. L, 13th Pa. Cav. A prisoner of War, Camp Sumpter, Andersonville, Georgia. P.S. I want a frying pan 3 inches in diameter with a handle. I would like a blanket. Serg't Lateer, 77th Pa. Vol. is here. Ed. Inhoff is pretty well acquainted with him. Good Bye. Pray for me. Your son, George." Nailer would die at Andersonville ten weeks after writing this letter.[8]

Prisoners arrived here day and night, brought principally from other prisons which were in danger of being besieged by the Union forces, and soon the enclosure was packed full and the supply of wood correspondingly decreased. As a last resort to ward off the cold and cook our meals, every stump and root employed to cover our dugouts and mud houses was used. These places of shelter were just big enough to crawl into to protect us from the scorching sun by day and the cold night air. But there were thousands who had no such protection.

One of the arrivals was Private Ira Pettit. He had been captured in June of 1864 and was sent to Andersonville in July. In a letter to his father, Pettit stated that "we have a shelter which affords a protection from storms and from heat a shade. We get a plenty to eat and I have been in good health and spirits until after the fourth of July; since I have had the diarrhoea which makes me very weak." Pettit was obviously trying to prevent his family from worrying by describing his conditions as being far better than they were. In November of that same year, his father received a letter from a comrade of his son's. The letter informed Mr. Pettit that "About the beginning of August Ira got the Scurvy in his mouth, and at the end of the month in his legs. In the middle of Sept. he also got the Diarhea, which I think was more the cause of his death than the Scurvy.... Your Son never despaired and was willing to lay down his life for his country if necessary, which declaration he very often made." Pettit had died on October 18 as a result of sickness and disease brought on by malnutrition.[9]

The little creek, previously referred to, flowed through the prison from west to east and had its source from numerous small springs outside the prison walls. Along these were the tented camps of the Rebels and a large number of slaves. A large cookhouse was erected there and what with the slops from it and sewage from the camp flowing into the creek the water was made as unfit for use as the refuse from a slaughter house.

But not only that: We could see numbers of Rebels and negro slaves sitting along the stream washing their dirty, lousy clothes in it — and from this we had to drink.

Prisoners continued to come until there were 35,000 to be fed and cared for. The rations were all prepared at this cookhouse. The doughtray consisted of a very large box, tainted with sour corn dough, around about and inside, which swarmed thousands of flies. A wagon load of cornmeal would be scooped into this bow, flies along, and water dipped from the filthy stream to mix the dough, which was stirred up with long poles and then shoveled into pans and marked in half-brick sizes ready for baking. They were never able to supply the entire prison with bread the same day, so the one side would get bread today, and the other side meal, or mush or beans, one pint of either being a ration for twenty-four hours: The next day the opposite side would get the bread. The beans served were sour and unfit to eat — pods, stalks, sand etc., being cooked along, and we were often led to believe sometimes that rats and mice were plenty somewhere.

I will not pretend to give you a correct picture of how those rations were served, for when I have done my best I will fall far short; some received them in old army caps, an old shoe, filthy rags, and even a cow's horn came in use. Some could be seen wandering around calling out: "Who wants to trade cooked rations for raw?" carrying their cornmeal rolled in a dirty filthy rag.

Time rolled slowly on, and we began to feel entirely forsaken and beyond the limit of civilization. Each one tried to occupy the time as best he could. By this time the older prisoners had either traded off all their clothing for something to eat, or they had become so badly worn that they would no longer cover their decaying frames. You could see men with only a shirt, others a pair of pants, some an old army blouse or pair of drawers. There in this prison hell could be seen, men going about as nude as the day they were born except having an old army cap for headgear and which they used to draw their rations.

By this time the lice got so numerous that every prisoner was compelled to employ a portion of his time killing them. As soon as the sun would rise of mornings thousands of men could be seen sitting around in groups with their filthy rags off, all busily engaged in the same business— cracking lice. This task had to be repeated day after day and then it was impossible to get rid of them. Along with these tormentors came fleas, which polluted the ground and helped to add to our misery.

When the sun would reach the meridian it would blister any portion of the body exposed to its burning rays. In the month of June we had rain for twenty-one successive days and the prison was in a horrible condition, mud ankle deep and not a dry spot to be found. The men would huddle together both day and night; like unto so many chickens on a rainy day.

There were no sinks in the prison at all, and to repair to the swamp, which was in such a bad condition that it was impossible for anybody to stay near it any length of time. This was called "Death's Acre." The pen was so crowded that hundreds were compelled to stay within a few feet of this place; it was here that more deaths occurred then elsewhere in the prison. It was here could be seen at any time comrades who were healthy, active and young and middle-aged men when they left their dear northern homes, clinging to the last spark of life wallowing in their own filth; men reduced to idiocy, some unable to speak. The miasma arising from the swamp, mingled with the stench of the dead bodies decaying in the sun, was suffocating. Passing around you would come across comrades lying on the ground who would reach out their poor scrawny hands and implore, either by word or sign, our help, which we were powerless to extend; the glassy stare in their eyes told, however, that they would soon be "exchanged" and out of suffering.

Slow starvation, sameness of food, over-crowding, and filth formed the principal cause of so much sickness and death. There seemed to be no relief; we must rot in this living tomb. Over half the old prisoners were now dead, and the most of those living were prostrated with some disease. The dead carts were now hauling on an average of one hundred bodies a day to the trenches in the sandy field.

When we first arrived there our dead was carried to the graveyard by our own men. A stretcher was formed out of an old blanket attached to two poles and on this the body was lain and carried by two living skeletons to its last resting place. It would seem to be a very unpleasant task, but there would be those who profited by it. As the Rebels were always ready to trade for anything the "Yanks" had, we could bring a load of wood that could bring two dollars, and a good armful of greens, herbs, leaves, brush and even ragweed — all would sell at good prices.

Those who were physically able to do this kind of work would buy the dead men from their comrades who were not able to carry them out for burial, $1 being the price for a corps[e]. I well remember of three comrades who lay ill near us, two of whom were brothers, and all doomed to sucumb. Eventually the one died and my messmates and myself bought the body from the brothers and buried it. When we returned we contracted with the one brother for the body of the other at his decease and sealed the bargain on a payment of $1.

The mortality increased until it touched 150 a day the first six days in August and to over 3,000 during the month. The Rebels now built a sort of morgue near the South gate, to which the dead were carried daily. Then, with the very same wagons that were used for hauling our rations, the dead would be hauled to the trench. Two men would throw the corps[e] upon corps[e] in the front of the wagon until filled and then the rear and packed full — arms, legs and heads dangling out as the conveyances were driven to that horrifying graveyard.

The prison was full of disease, diarrhea, scurvy, dropsy, gangreen and typhiod fever hourly claiming their victims. The effects of these various diseases beggars discription. The whole prison was a hell of horrors and insanity. You could hear praying, groaning, the laugh of the maniac, and the curse of the dying which is the farewell of hope.

The sun grew hotter, raiders bolder, guards more murderous, stocks more terrible, the chain gangs full of victims, the ground swarming with lice, and the long, scorching day closes and the air grows cooler, we lay us down unsheltered on the filthy ground, trying to shut out with sleep the surrounding horrors. Sleep I how? With the millions of mosquitoes from the swamp feeding upon our emaciated bodies, their buzzing only adding to the bedlam of the prison; the hoot of the owl; the mournful notes of the whipperwill; the crack of the musket of the murderous guards and the sound of their voices as they call out the hour of the night from their palisades; the moanings of the dying, could one expect sleep to come?

In addition to all the inhuman treatment received at the hands of our cruel keepers, we were further plagued by a class of ruffians known as Mosby's Raiders, who lived by plundering their fellow prisoners. It was a common thing to find in the morning men robbed and sometimes murdered. These raiders eventually got so bold that bands of them would go about in daylight robbing. And if a man tried to protect his goods, he was knocked down, and in some cases killed on the spot. The outrage became unbearable; something must be done. A "regulator's force" was organized, and with the assistance of the Rebels, one hundred and one of these outlaw-raiders were arrested and taken outside the prison. Six ringleaders were identified and seperated from them, and the balance were turned back into the prison. They were each obliged to run the gauntlet, receiveing kicks and blows from every one that could reach them; one of them was beaten and trampled to death. In searching the tent of the raiders a dead man's body was found buried with their plunder in the ground. They had been sleeping over the grave of the man whom they had murdered.

The names of the six ring leaders were Cary Sullivan, William Collins, Patrick Delaney, Charles Curtis, John Sarsfield, and A. Munn. A number of the remaining Raiders were sentenced to be placed in the stocks, wear balls and chains, or be hung up by their thumbs.[10]

A court was arranged by our men for the trial of the six ringleaders; they were found guilty of murder and sentenced to be hung. The proceedings of the trial were sent to Macon, where the Union officers were held prisoners, whose signatures were signed to the death sentences.

In addition to the approval of the Federal officers in Macon, the order for execution also had to be approved by Confederate General John Winder, who was in charge of Confederate prison camps. This approval was given, and the prisoners were then free to carry out the sentences.[11]

On the 12th day of July, 1864, a scaffold was erected, and in the afternoon the six condemned murderers were handed over to the police force by Captain Wertz, who said: "Do with them as your reason, justice and mercy dictates."

The condemned thought it was only a plan to frighten them, and clung to that idea until marched up to the scaffold. When near it, one of the sextette, Curtis by name, broke loose from the men holding him, dashed through the immense throng and crossed the swamp to the hillside opposite. He was speedily captured and brought back to the doom he had thought to escape, with such forlorn wretchedness and miserable hopelessness depicted on his countenance as is impossible to describe.

Everything now being in readiness, they were stood in a row on the scaffold, meal sacks were drawn over their heads, the ropes adjusted, the drop fell. The rope around the neck of the chief reingleader, Mosby-Collins, his right name, broke, and he fell with a thud, blood gushing from his ears, nose and mouth. He was taken back, a new rope adjusted and he was pushed off the platform to his doom. It was sad, but just — only another illustration of the truth that the way of transgression is hard. The entire prison thereafter was kept under police control.

The bodies were allowed to hang on the scaffold for fifteen minutes after the life had gone out of the condemned men. They were then cut down, and the crowd that had gathered to witness the execution began to melt away. Although there were still instances of petty theft in the camp following the executions, the Regulators took up the task of acting as a prison police force, and a reasonable degree of discipline was maintained in the camp.[12]

Many prisoners were grateful to Commandant Wertz for his handling of the Raiders. One captive soldier wrote: "Captain Wurtz deserves great credit for his prompt action in the matter, and will probably be successful in checking the operations of these theiving scoundrels.... It is an act of justice on the part of the Confederate authorities which the men have not expected, they supposing that no notice would be taken of their complaints; but the reverse has been the case, and we can now feel secure from the attacks of daylight assassins or midnight murderers; the issuing of rations was promptly commenced as soon as the men known as the ringleaders were captured."[13]

We had to have pure water, and in order to get it the prisoners went to work and dug wells, some 70 feet deep. These we dug with caseknives, canteens broken in half and tin plates. The legs of old pants and drawers tied shut at the bottom and improvised ropes made from all sorts of old clothes were used to haul the loose earth to the surface. In most cases we struck good water, but it was only a question of time until it would be contaminated.

As the number of sick had increased to thousands, and many were unable to crawl to "Death's Acre," they would dig a hole as deep as the arm could reach and use it for nature's requirements. In fact, the whole prison was honeycombed with them, and when rain fell they would overflow and run into wells and destroy their usefulness. It was then the prison was in a most fearful condition and it was prophisied that within sixty days there would not be one prisoner alive.

A fellow prisoner, John Ransom, described in a diary his condition and surroundings during this time: "Have been trying to into the hospital ... Geo. W. Hutchins, brother of Charlie Hutchins of Jackson, Mich., died today — from our mess. Jimmy Devers is dead ... Rowe getting very bad. Sanders ditto. Am myself much worse, and cannot walk, and with difficulty stand up. Legs drawn up like a triangle, mouth in terrible shape, and dropsy worse than all. A few more days. At my earnest solicitation was carried to the gate this morning, to be admitted to the hospital. Lay in the sun for some hours to be examined, and finally my turn came and I tried to stand up, but was so excited I fainted away. When I came to myself I lay along with the row of dead on the outside. Raised up and asked a rebel for a drink of water, and he said: 'Here, you Yank, if you ain't dead, get inside there!' And with his help was put inside again."[14]

Eventually a terrific storm arose and rain descended in mighty torrents, drenching the entire prison and washing filth in its strong current to the swamp in the center of the prison, and so increased the volume of the creek that it forced its way through the prison walls, leaving large openings where it entered and passed out. After this we were furnished some lumber with which we built a sluice for the little creek to pass through.

Another incident, claimed by many Providential, was the bursting forth of a natural flow of water inside the deadline, on the north side of the prison. It was pure and readily arranged so as to supply a large portion of the prisoners. So great became the rush for water that a police force had to be stationed there, and each applicant for water had to fall in line and take his turn; as many as 1,000 men could be seen at one time. This was thenceforth known as "Providence Spring."

Just prior to the appearance of "Providence Spring" a number of prisoners had begun holding regular Bible and prayer meetings, and a spirit of religious revival swept over the camp and was responsible for converting many of the inmates to Christianity. The spring that appeared as a result of the heavy rains was seen by the prisoners to be an answer to their prayers, leading it to be given the name by which it is still called.[15]

Owing to the strong bulwark and the many guards placed around the prison, it was impossible to escape from this place of hell and death, except under ground. This the boys attempted on different occasions, but in most cases failed. When a tunnel would be about completed, some traitor would reveal not only the plan to escape but the place, to the Rebels. And if those engaged in the plan of escape were found out they would be taken to the stocks or placed in the chain gang and punished in the most horrible manner.

In exceptional cases when some prisoners succeeded in tunneling out, they would be pursued and caught by blood hounds, and it is believed many when caught were torn to pieces and left to be feed for wild beasts of the forest. In one case I well remember, after we had finished a tunnel and arranged to get out after the midnight guard was placed on post duty. Just when we were about to begin our perilous attempt to gain freedom we were startled by the report of guns on the outside of the prison. A prisoner had escaped from the hospital, and it was but a short while until we heard the deep baying of the hounds break the midnight stillness coupled with distressing cries for mercy from the sick and starved prisoner, who had been overtaken; his loud cries shortly ended in low groans, leading us to believe that he was being torn to pieces by the hounds.

As all the sentinels were now on the alert, we concluded to postpone our attempt at escape for the time being. And we never did get through that tunnel. Some traitor spied and reported it and it was closed up. Nearly all our plans at escape failed from this element.

Although escape from Andersonville was very difficult, it was not impossible. During the time that Andersonville was in operation, 329 Union prisoners managed to escape from the prison and elude recapture. A far greater number made it out of the stockade, only to be caught again by the guards, and sometimes by the hounds.[16]

As the dreary days dragged along the men began to despair; some became demented; hundreds could be seen wandering about in a state indescribable. Men would voluntarily step over the dead line and appeal to the guards to shoot them; and in their sane moments, too. Indeed, death was considered a welcome visitor. Some of the men earnestly prayed for death to come and release them from the torments they were subjected to. And is it any wonder when we think of this death-like life, month after month. Think of men of delicate organization accustomed to ease and luxury, of fine tastes and a passionate love for the beautiful, without one word of sympathy or whisper of hope, wearing their days out amid such scenes. Not a pleasant sound, a fragrant odor or a vision of fairness ever reached them. They were buried from the world as completely as if they lay beneath the ruins of Pompei or Herculaneum; they breathed mechanically, but were shut out from everything that renders existence endurable. Every sense was shocked continuously, and yet the heart, by a strange inconsistency, kept up its throbs and persevered the physical being of a portion of those wretched captives who often prayed to die.

Another prisoner, John Urban, described the mental state of many of the captives: "The ravings, prayers and curses of these men added much to the horrors of the prison. Some of them wandered around the prison in the most helpless manner, and begged piteously for something to eat. Some of the poor wretches imagined themselves animals, and moved around on their hands and knees, hunting for something to eat. Some of them gathered the undigested beans lying around on the ground, and ate them. The number of these poor unfortunates who were becoming idiotic was fearfully on the increase, and this had now become the worst feature of our prison-life."[17]

Take into consideration the scant and miserable rations which no one except he be half famished could eat; the necessity of going cold and hungry through the wet, wintry weather; the constant torture of vermin, from which all care and precaution could not free one; the dreaded monotony; the continual turning inward of the mind upon itself; the self-devouring of the heart week after week and month after month — this would seem to be an awful test of patriotism.

There were thousands who endured the most terrible pangs of starvation. Men with shrunken frames almost naked, shivering from cold and dampness, their faces pinched with pain, I have seen offered food and comfort if they would consent to join the Rebels. Gathering their scanty, filthy rags close about their shivering bodies, they scornfully replied: "No! Do your worst. We will never go back on the Old Flag!" Did these men join the Union Army through patriotism? Or did they join it for the $13 per month, as has been asserted by some renegade editors, who sanction or justify the pension veto and the returning of the Rebel flags?

Schmittle is making reference to the attempt to have the captured Confederate battle flags returned to their respective states a few decades after the war. The government initially adopted this course of action, but had to reconsider due to vehement opposition by Union veteran groups.

With pride we to day look back to those 60,000 graves and say, those comrades chose the most cruel death rather than dishonor their flag and country, and under the most trying circumstances—naked, starving, racked with pain and disease, and certain torture and death staring them in the face, they refused the oft-repeated offers of relief.

These 60,000 men consisted of kind fathers, loving husbands and affectionate sons, who gave up all their bright hopes, prospects, cherished homes and pursuits of happiness and submitted even to death, rather than have one act of wrong doing rest upon their consciences.

The Confederate records show that they captured 188,145 prisoners; that they paroled or exchanged 94,073, leaving a balance of 94,972 to be accounted for. Now give them a credit of 10,000 which may have escaped or joined the Rebel army, what became of the remaining 84,972? They perished at Andersonville and other prison hells, and in attempting to escape fell victims to bloodhounds or deamons in human form, and their mangled remains left to carion birds.

Schmittle's calculations here are highly exaggerated. Statisticians estimate that some 24,866 Union soldiers died during the war in Southern prison camps. The numbers given in official statements, although excessive, are far below those stated by Schmittle.[18]

Any of my fellow prisoners can bear testimony to numbers of prisoners who escaped and never returned; and those who were caught and brought back, unless they were too fearfully mangled by the hounds, would be taken to the stocks and tortured from twelve to twenty hours, sometimes fastened in such a way they could not move, their wounds uncared for, the blow-flies depositing their eggs therein, the hot sun beating down upon them. In this fearful condition they would be put back into the prison. Some would be so badly torn by the fangs of the hounds they could not walk. They would be brought to the gate, pushed inside, and left to crawl around on their hands and knees. Their sores would soon become a mass of living vermin. Men would live for several days in this condition, their eyes, ears and nose full of maggots; sometimes they were carried out before they were dead and left to spend the last moments of their lives in the deadhouse.

On the 12th of September we were called out and told we were going to be paroled. We were again packed in cars and taken to Savannah, where we were imprisoned in the "bull pen."

Rumors had been rampant that the prisoners were being taken to Savannah to be paroled, but when they arrived at that place, they were herded into the stockade known as the "Bull Pen" and any hopes of being exchanged soon disappeared. By comparison, the Bull Pen was a small prison, holding only a few thousand men. Conditions there were an improvement over what had existed at Andersonville, with the food ration being larger and more wholesome. The prisoners were also given soap and allowed to take the first real bath many of them had had in months.[19]

I and some others managed to get some Rebel clothes on our way, intending to make our escape as soon as possible. We put up our blanket tent close to the dead-line and began work the first night, closing the hole during the day. By one o'clock the second night we had the tunnel completed 20 feet, and succeeded to getting out. A comrade by the name of Tredo and myself started together. We did not travel far until we found ourselves in a swamp, lost, where we had to stay until daylight — and still lost. We spent four days wandering about in that swamp. On the evening of the fourth day we met a negro, who gave us a large crab and a quart of peanuts, and who piloted us to Thunderbolt river. I gave him my shoes for getting me a plank so that I could take my comrade across the river, as he could not swim. We reached an island and remained on it for five days. We could see our gunboats and hear the drums beat every day, but could not get to the boats. We lived on the bean of honey locust and a mussel we found along the beach, for five days, when we were re-captured by a party of Rebels who were scouting on the island. We were so reduced in flesh and weakened that we could scarcely walk. We were blindfolded and taken back and replaced in the bull pen. The next day we were placed in a dungeon under the "pen" where we were kept for several days. Another comrade was confined herein. One corn dodger and a quart bottle of water, for three of us, constituted our rations each day. From this dungeon we were taken and placed in seperate cells, where I remained until I was carried out on a stretcher to the hospital at Milin, where all the prisoners who were not fit to be moved further were taken.

Gradually my health recruited and I determined to try another escape as soon as I felt able to travel. In the course of a month a little drummer boy, of Tennessee, and myself succeeded in getting out. We were kept concealed by negroes two days and two nights in a wood hut of theirs and for three subsequent days in the back of the 12th provost marshal's house and four days more in another place, all this time expecting to reach the Union gunboats.

Our negro protectors learning that we were to be paroled and sent to our lines, we followed their advice and returned to the prison. On Wednesday, November 18, 1864, all the Union prisoners there were paroled and sent to Hilton head and taken on the Union boats. There were 175 in all, seventeen of whom died on the way to Parol[e] Camp, at Annapolis, Md. Thus, my friends, ends a partial recital descriptive of one who took part in that living drama of horror which will never be fully described until the earth and sea give up their all.

Schmittle's time of incarceration did not end with his release from Andersonville. From there, he was sent to Camp Parole, Maryland, to await his being exchanged, and on December 4, 1864, he was granted a one-month furlough. During this period, the army made a clerical error and Schmittle was listed on the rolls as being absent without leave, and desertion, and was brought up on court martial charges. These were found to be erroneous and the case was dismissed. He received a second thirty-day furlough on January 17, 1865. Before the expiration of this furlough, Schmittle became involved in a sham in an effort to try to falsely secure a bounty payment for enlistment. On February 16, 1865, he was arrested at the Draft Rendezvouz at Carlisle, Pennsylvania, for fraudulently attempting to enlist his brother for a bounty payment. He was held there as a prisoner by the Provost Marshall's Department until he was finally allowed to rejoin his regiment in April of 1865. By that time, the regiment had been transferred to Major General William T. Sherman's western army and had taken part in his march through the Carolinas and in the battle of Bentonville. By the time Schmittle rejoined his regiment, the war was all but over. General Joseph E. Johnston would surrender the Army of the South on April 21, 1865, at Bennett's Place, North Carolina, effectively eliminating any major Confederate military presence east of the Mississippi.

Schmittle was mustered out with the regiment at New Bern, North Carolina, on July 14, 1865. During his second term of service, he had had the rare opportunity to find himself a prisoner of both armies.[20]

The end of the Civil War did not signal the end of Schmittle's military service or the end of his incarceration. George enlisted in the First United States Cavalry in February of 1866 and was assigned to Troop D, joining the troop in April of 1866. The troops of the First Cavalry had been scattered from Washington State to California to the Indian Territory, with Troop D serving in Idaho. Trooper Schmittle deserted in July of 1866, just a few months after joining his unit, and was not apprehended by the authorities until February of 1867. After a short period of incarceration, he was returned to duty without a court martial, and the time he had been absent was added to the expiration date of his enlistment. Trooper Schmittle was discharged from his third and final tour of duty in October of 1869. In his request for an Invalid Pension, dated 1894, Schmittle states that the reason for his absence from the First Cavalry was an injury to his spinal column, sustained when a pile of coal he was unloading fell on him.[21] George married Rachael Briggett in Pittsburgh in February of 1870. The marriage produced ten children: five boys and five girls. In civilian life, Schmittle supported himself and his large ever-increasing family by working as a merchant.[22] George Schmittle died in 1922 at the age of 76, at his home in Altoona, Pennsylvania. He is buried in the Rose Hill Cemetery in Altoona. His memoir of his imprisonment at Andersonville was written in 1914, several years before his death, and was distributed as a broadside, free to the public, by a local representative of the state assembly.[23]

Capsule History of the Thirteenth Pennsylvania Cavalry

The Thirteenth Pennsylvania Cavalry bore the official state designation of the 117th Regiment, Thirteenth Cavalry being the 117th regiment to muster for state service, overall, and the Thirteenth of cavalry. The regiment had its roots in the Irish Dragoons, a squadron of cavalry raised predominantly in the Philadelphia area and intended to be attached to the Irish Brigade, which was then being raised by Francis Meagher in New York. In July of 1862, the squadron was given permission to recruit to regimental status, and five more companies were added to its number. Although the unit was still short of the twelve companies that normally constituted a full regiment of cavalry, it was assigned to perform various guard and patrol duties around Camp Carroll in Baltimore, Maryland. In

March of 1863, the twelfth and final company was added to the roster, and the regiment was ordered to report to Brigadier General Robert Milroy at Winchester, Virginia, where it was assigned to Brigadier General Washington Elliott's brigade of cavalry. The regiment was continually engaged in picket, patrol, and escort duties until the battle of Winchester during the Gettysburg Campaign.

The Thirteenth Cavalry was actively engaged in the battle of Winchester, and it covered the rear of Milroy's army during the retreat on June 15, 1863. The regiment, much battered, rode into the town of Harper's Ferry, West Virginia, that same day. Of the 643 men that were on the rolls prior to the battle of Winchester, only 321 were with the regiment in Harper's Ferry on June 16. During the four days of fighting in and around Winchester, more than half their number were killed, wounded, or missing. The Thirteenth Pennsylvania remained in Harper's Ferry until June 30, when they were evacuated to Frederick, Maryland. On July 8, the regiment was ordered to Boonsboro, Maryland, where it was incorporated into the Army of the Potomac and took part in the pursuit of General Robert E. Lee's army into Virginia.

After being posted for some time at Amissville and Jefferson, Virginia, the regiment took part in the engagement at Culpepper, Virginia, on September 11, 1863. It was then detached for duty at Catlett's Station, Virginia, before rejoining the brigade at Culpepper on October 10.

On October 12, while the regiment was in the neighborhood of Culpepper, the Union forces in the area were compelled to fall back because of an assault on their right flank and rear. On October 12, the Thirteenth Pennsylvania was performing picket duty at Jefferson, on the south side of the Rappahannock River opposite Sulphur Springs, Virginia, when it was attacked by an overwhelming force of the enemy. It was reinforced by the Fourth Pennsylvania Cavalry, and the two regiments made a determined stand until the afternoon, when force of numbers and a lack of ammunition caused the Union troopers to give way. The Thirteenth Pennsylvania lost 163 men in the engagement, most of them captured. For the next three days, the regiment was almost constantly engaged with the enemy, covering the rear and flank of the army during its retreat to Centreville, Virginia.

On October 24, the regiment was given the honor of performing guard duty at Army Headquarters. During the winter, it was assigned to guard duty along the Orange and Alexandria Railroad, with headquarters at Bristoe, Virginia.

On May 3, 1864, the Thirteenth was transferred to the Ninth Corps and covered the rear of the army during the Wilderness Campaign. The regiment had a hand in the severe fighting that took place between May 5 and 11 and in the flank movement of the army past Spotsylvania Court House.

On May 26, the regiment rejoined its brigade and took part in General Phil Sheridan's raid toward Richmond. The Thirteenth took part in the fighting at Beaver Dam Station, in which four hundred Union prisoners were released, and at Haw's Shop on May 28.

The regiment also took part in Sheridan's raid toward Lynchburg, Virginia, designed to break up the Confederate's supply route from that city. It fought in the battle of Trevillan Station, where Sheridan's troopers were turned back by a superior force of Confederate infantry.

On June 22, the cavalry corps crossed the Chickahominy River at Jone's Bridge and made its way for the James. On June 24, the cavalry encountered the enemy in a strong position at St. Mary's Church, and a brisk encounter ensued. The Union cavalry held its position until the afternoon, when it was forced back by superior numbers.

The regiment performed various service and participated in numerous small engagements in the vicinity of Richmond through the months of July and August. On September 29, it was hotly engaged at Wyatt's Farm. On October 22, it took part in the fighting at Boydton Plank Road, and on December 8, it saw action in the battle of Hatcher's Run.

On February 6, 1865, the Thirteenth Pennsylvania attacked the enemy at Dabney's Mills, where its division commander, Major General David M. Gregg, was wounded. This was to be the last service the regiment would see with the Army of the Potomac.

In the middle of February, the regiment was ordered to Wilmington, North Carolina, where it reported to Major General John Schofield. Schofield had been charged with the mission of marching inland from Wilmington to establish communication with major General William T. Sherman's army, which was then marching north from its successful capture of Savannah, Georgia. The regiment made contact with Sherman's main body on March 13 at Fayetteville, North Carolina. On March 19, it was assigned to Major General Judson Kilpatrick's cavalry division. After the surrender of General Joseph E. Johnston and his army, the regiment was assigned to garrison duty at Fayetteville and, except for some action against irregular bands of enemy operating in the area, it served out the rest of its enlistment in this city. The Thirteenth Pennsylvania was mustered out of the service on July 14, 1865, and was discharged on July 27 at Camp Cadwallader in Philadelphia. During its term of enlistment, the regiment lost seventy men killed or mortally wounded and 220 who died of disease.[24]

Muster Roll of Company B, Thirteenth Pennsylvania Cavalry

Captain Michael Kerwin (Promoted to major October 22, 1862.) Captain Daniel B. Meaney (Mustered out July 14, 1865.) Captain Henry Gregg (Captured at Sulphur Springs, Va., October 12, 1864.) 1st Lieutenant Jesse J. Bowers (Mustered out with company July 14, 1865.) 1st Lieutenant George F. McCabe (Promoted to major October 15, 1863.) 2nd Lieutenant Edward J. Parker (Discharged July 27, 1864.) 2nd Lieutenant Joseph A. Green (Captured at Sulphur Springs, Va., October 12, 1864. Discharged November 21, 1864.) 2nd Lieutenant Curtis H. Eldridge (Mustered out with company July 14, 1865.)

Sergeants

George McLane (Promoted to lieutenant April 29, 1865.)
William O'Conner (Promoted to sergeant major.)
Walter Webb (Transferred to Company A September 15, 1863.)
Henry H. Brunner (Promoted to 2nd lieutenant April 20, 1865.)
Joseph D. Gallway (Prisoner from October 12, 1863, to November 17, 1864.)
John McElhenny (Mustered out with company July 14, 1865.)
Samuel W. Taylor (Mustered out with company July 14, 1865.)
Francis A. Leavy (Captured at Sulphur Springs, Va., October 12, 1863. Died at Andersonville, Ga., May 26, 1864.)
Joseph R. Myers (Captured at Sulphur Springs, Va., October 12, 1863. Died at Andersonville, Ga., May 26, 1864.)
James R. Johnson (Killed at St. Mary's Church, Va., June 24, 1864.)

Jeremiah Mahoney (Transferred to Company M.)
Phillip Rowland
Edward Shea
Joseph Bailey

Corporals

Samuel Edmiston (Prisoner from October 12, 1863, to November 17, 1864.)
John Morris (Prisoner from October 12, 1863, to March 16, 1864.)
Charles Mills (Prisoner from October 12, 1863, to November 17, 1864.)
Charles E. Wolf (Mustered out with company July 14, 1865.)
David Leitz (Mustered out with company July 14, 1865.)
Martin Beck (Mustered out with company July 14, 1865.)
John Henry (Prisoner from October 12, 1863, to March 16, 1864.)
Aaron P. Benson (Died at Camp Stoneman, Va., October 20, 1863.)
Abednego Stevens (Captured. Died at Andersonville, Ga., June 5, 1864.)
John Seebock (Killed at Coggin's Point, Va., September 16, 1864.)
John Mangen
David P. Thomas
Charles S. Harris (Transferred to Company E.)
Thomas Clearey
James McGrann
John Cubbison (Transferred to Company A September 15, 1863.)
Matthew McGeny
William Kitchennian

Bugler

Landis Eichoitz (Prisoner from September 16 to September 24, 1864. Discharged June 21, 1865.)
James Clayton (Mustered out with company July 14, 1865.)

Daniel McLeer
Matthew Brady

Blacksmith

Conrad Orth (Mustered out with company July 14, 1865.)
Cornel McMonagal

Farrier

John Collins

Privates

M.S. Ammerman (Captured at Sulphur Springs, Va., October 12, 1863. Died at Richmond February 19, 1864.)
Thomas Arbie (Captured at Sulphur Springs, Va., October 12, 1863. Died at Andersonville, Ga., May 26, 1864.)
William Andrews
Andrew C. Baker (Mustered out with company July 14, 1865.)
Lewis Briggs (Prisoner from October 12, 1863, to August 22, 1864.)
George W. Brindle (Captured at Sulphur Springs, Va., October 12, 1863.)
James Brooks (Mustered out with company July 14, 1865.)
John Buckley (Mustered out with Company July 14, 1865.)
John Lee Burns (Captured at Sulphur Springs, Va., October 12, 1863. Died at Andersonville, Ga., April 2, 1864.)
Andrew Briggs (Captured at Sulphur Springs, Va., October 12, 1863. Died at Andersonville, Ga., April 2, 1864.)
Isaac Burns (Deserted September 10, 1863.)
Paul Bernheardt (Deserted August 20, 1863.)
Robert Bernheardt (Deserted August 20, 1863.)
Theophilus Baird (Deserted September 1, 1863.)
Benjamin Butler (Deserted August 12, 1863.)

Daniel Brunig (Transferred to Company M.)
Charles Bettinger
Edward Burns
Samuel Carpenter (Mustered out with company July 14, 1865.)
Thomas Calderwood (Mustered out with company July 14, 1865.)
William Clean (Mustered out with company July 14, 1865.)
Robert Campbell (Mustered out with company July 14, 1865.)
George W. Cromlich (Deserted September 10, 1863.)
Michael Connor
Samuel Colgan
John Connor
Alfred Cooper
Jacob Diffenbaucher (Captured at Wyatt's Farm, Va., September 29, 1864. Died at Salisbury, N.C., January 2, 1865.)
Miles G. Davis (Mustered out with company July 14, 1865.)
John W. Davis (Mustered out with company July 14, 1865.)
Hugh Degert (Captured at Sulphur Springs, Va., October 12, 1863.)
Jeremiah Dougherty (Captured at St. Mary's Church, Va., June 24, 1864.)
Christian Devenney
John Donahue
John Duffy
Riley A. Davis
John Dwyer
Connell Dugin
Isaac H. Edwards (Absent without leave.)
Francis Elters (Captured at Sulphur Springs, Va., October 12, 1863.)
Henry Elters (Captured at Sulphur Springs, Va., October 12, 1863. Died at Andersonville, Ga., May 9,1864.)
John Edwards (Prisoner from October 12, 1863, to April 6, 1865.)
William Earheart (Deserted August 18, 1863.)
Thomas Ennis
Henry Fuller (Captured at Sulphur

Springs, Va., October 12, 1863. Died at Andersonville, Ga., May 10, 1864.)

Reuben J. Fox (Mustered out with company July 14, 1865.)

John Fahy (Captured. Died at Andersonville, Ga., September 2, 1864.)

Francis A. Fowler

Elzgar Fowler

Patrick Fitzpatrick

Reuben Gordon (Captured at Catlett's Station, Va., April 16, 1864.)

Isaac F. Gray (Mustered out with company July 14, 1865.)

Israel Grazier (Mustered out with company July 14, 1865.)

Robert Goodman (Captured at Sulphur Springs, Va., October 12, 1863. Died at Andersonville, Ga., March 19, 1864.)

James Galloway (Deserted September 1, 1863.)

Fanigle Gallagher (Transferred to Company M.)

John Gingheart

John Green

Squire Howe (Prisoner from October 12, 1863, to November 17, 1864.)

Albert Hilton (Captured at Sulphur Springs, Va., October 12, 1863. Died at Richmond, Va., February 12, 1864.)

James Houseman (Prisoner from October 12, 1863, to September 16, 1864.)

Joseph Hassenplug (Mustered out with company July 14, 1865.)

Samuel Hetrick (Mustered out with company July 14, 1865.)

John Hooleman (Prisoner from October 12, 1863, to April 16, 1864.)

Martin Horning (Captured at Sulphur Springs, Va., October 12, 1863.)

Alfred Hall (Died at Washington, D.C., November 14, 1864.)

Henry Heale (Deserted August 1, 1863.)

George Hamilton

Samuel H. Harris

Levi Halderman (Transferred to Company A.)

Abner Hilt

William Johnson

John C. Keller (Captured at Sulphur Springs, Va., October 12, 1863.)

F.P. Kunzman (Mustered out with company July 14, 1865.)

Calvin Keatley (Mustered out with company July 14, 1865.)

Jacob Kitchenman

Luther Kessler

Christopher Killmung

John Kelly

William King

Patrick Kennedy

Peter H. Lightel (Mustered out with company July 14, 1865.)

Naum Locke (Mustered out with company July 14, 1865.)

George Lundy (Mustered out with company July 14, 1865.)

George T. Lane (Mustered out with company July 14, 1865.)

James Lee (Captured at Sulphur Springs, Va., October 12, 1863. Died at Andersonville, Ga., July 18, 1864.)

Samuel Logan (Died at Camp Curtis, Pa., September 12, 1863.)

John F. Landig (Transferred to Company A.)

Richard Laughlin

Richard Luch

George Miller (Prisoner from October 12, 1863, to March 3, 1864.)

John Mason (Prisoner from October 12, 1863, to November 17, 1864.)

Albert Miles (Mustered out with company July 14, 1865.)

Matthew Morrow (Mustered out with company July 14, 1865.)

James Moore (Captured. Died at Andersonville, Ga., October 25, 1864.)

John Mullin

John Moore

John Meoser (Captured. Died at Andersonville, Ga., May 18, 1864.)

Clement P. McCall (Mustered out with company July 14, 1865.)

Rud. C. McConnell (Mustered out with company July 14, 1865.)

Wlliam McConnell (Died May 1864.)

Thomas H. McAdams

Michael McGuire

Alexander McNeil

Peter McCallin (Transferred to Company M.)

Edward O'Shea (Transferred to Company A.)

William O'Kefe

Charles Perkins (Mustered out with company July 14, 1865.)

Robert Purdy (Mustered out with company July 14, 1865.)

William Patsekke (Mustered out with company July 14, 1865.)

Peter Philips

Charles Quinn

Andrew P. Rager (Mustered out with company July 14, 1865.)

George B. Renninger (Mustered out with company July 14, 1865.)

G.W. Richardson (Captured at Sulphur Springs, Va., October 12, 1863.)

Marion T. Ruth (Mustered out with company July 14, 1865.)

John Rhodenizer (Mustered out with company July 14, 1865.)

Eminger S. Rudy (Wounded October 14, 1863.)

George Schmittel (Prisoner from October 12, 1863, to November 18, 1864.)

Joseph Schmittel (Mustered out with company July 14, 1865.)

John Sellers (Mustered out with company July 14, 1865.)

Jacob Sipes (Captured at Sulphur Springs, Va., October 12, 1863.)

Benjamin F. Sloan (Mustered out with company July 14, 1865.)

Henry Schall (Mustered out with company July 14, 1865.)

John Schubert (Mustered out with company July 14, 1865.)

Isaac Slusher (Mustered out with company July 14, 1865.)

John Saunders (Captured at Sulphur Springs, Va., October 12, 1863.)

William A. Stewart (Mustered out with company July 14, 1865.)

Henry Sturtzman (Absent.)

Martin Sharlock (Mustered out with company July 14, 1865.)

Hugh Speer (Mustered out with company July 14, 1865.)

James Shaffer (Mustered out with company July 14, 1865.)

Henry J. Scroop (Discharged July 14, 1865.)

John A. Skinner (Captured. Died at Andersonville, Ga., July 3, 1864.)

Jacob H. Stine (Deserted August 1, 1863.)

John Stewart (Deserted August 12, 1863.)

James Seymour (Deserted August 31, 1863.)

Franklin Smith (Deserted August 1, 1863.)

Charles Stevens

Vincent Smith

Michael Sullivan

Michael Sullivan Jr.

Joseph Seither

James L. Shea (Transferred to Company A.)

Patrick Shannon

William Smith

John C. Stanton

James Sheridan

Robert Stephens

William Turner (Died at Philadelphia, Pa., April 14, 1864.)

James Thompson (Transferred to Company A.)

James S. Vaughn (Mustered out with company July 14, 1865.)

Samuel Valentine (Transferred to Company L.)

Thomas Valentine (Deserted September 13, 1863.)

Adam Wisman (Mustered out with company July 14, 1865.)

Martin Winterhalter (Absent.)

John Wolford (Mustered out with company July 14, 1865.)

Thomas Wonderly (Mustered out with company July 14, 1865.)

Robert H. Ward (Transferred to Company L.)

Samuel A. Walker (Mustered out with company July 14, 1865.)

Benjamin B. White (Mustered out with company July 14, 1865.)

Peter White (Accidentally killed September 16, 1863.)

Nathaniel Watkins (Deserted August 10, 1863.)

John Welsh

William Yester (Died at Washington, D.C., January 22, 1864.)

Leander K. Zuck (Captured at Sulphur Springs, Va., October 12, 1863.) [25]

Epilogue

The four brave men whose war experiences have just been presented vastly contrasted with one another. In fact, about the only things they had in common were that they were all in the Union Army and all suffered hardships and privations of various sorts. Hunger seems to be a common thread, as each man, at some point in his story, talks of being short of rations and of scrounging for food to stave off the pangs of hunger. All of them faced the spectre of death on a daily basis. For George Schmittle, the deaths around him come through starvation and exposure in the cramped and unsanitary conditions of Andersonville, a place where even drinking the water could be fatal. For John Kelly and William Glisan, death most frequently appeared before them as battlefield casualties, as friends and comrades fell in combat with the foe. Will Duncan and his comrades battled against death from disease, which claimed more lives in the war than were sustained in battle.

With the exception of the Trans-Mississippi Department, these four men saw the war in its geographical breadth: the Eastern Theater, Western Theater, and the Deep South. Between them, they fought and served in twelve states. From Gettysburg to Chickamauga, from Antietam to Fort Sumter, they took part in the most desperate struggles of the war. Some marched, some rode on horseback, and some reached their destination aboard ships, but once they arrived at the scene of war, all undertook the business of being a soldier.

Each of these men initially joined the service from a sense of patriotism, with three of the four enlisting in 1861 during the frenzy that swept the entire nation to join up before the great adventure was over. Will Duncan did not enlist until 1863, but he then did so during the emergency of the invasion of Pennsylvania, out of a desire to protect his native state. He then, despite his advanced age, signed up for another short term of duty with the 206th Pennsylvania Infantry. Truly, Duncan's patriotism was akin to that of another elder statesman of Pennsylvania: John Burns of Gettysburg, the famed citizen-soldier who took up his War of 1812 musket and marched out with the troops to fight against Lee's army. Kelly and Schmittle also both opted to sign up for a second tour of duty; Glisan was the only one of the four who had seen all the war he wanted and declined to re-enlist. In Glisan's case, he had already seen more than enough death and misery to last a life time. While some men reenlisted from a desire to see the conflict to its conclusion, it would appear that both Kelly and Schmittle did so for the bounty money that was then being paid. This was a prime motivator for many young men in the North. In my own family history, one of my great-great-grandfathers enlisted in the Ninety-third Pennsylvania to collect the three hundred dollar bounty that was then being paid. With this money, a huge sum by 1864 standards, he was able to pay off the family farm.

One of the many things that struck me while I was compiling this work was the apparent freedom afforded these men. When not on active campaign or detailed to picket or fatigue duty, it seems that they were fairly free to come and go. Glisan, Duncan, and Kelly all make numerous references to excursions they took away from camp in search of food, to visit friends, and to just see the sights. It is obvious that the officers were quite lenient in allowing them time for themselves when conditions permitted.

In reading these diaries and memoirs, one can readily ascertain that none of these men had an easy time during their terms of enlistment. John Kelly was the only member of the group to sacrifice his life in the performance of his duty. George Schmittle must be recognized as perhaps suffering the most of the surviving members of the group because of the horrors and privations that were Andersonville. Will Duncan possibly suffered the least, serving on garrison and guard duty, but even Duncan had to battle against the sickness and disease that claimed the lives of many of his comrades, and he did so at an advanced age, more than twice that of the average man in the ranks.

I hope that through the lives of these four Union soldiers, the reader has gained an insight into the differing experiences that make up but a glimpse of the complete story of the war. It was a conflict that was waged in thousands of places across this land, and every soldier's reminiscence of his service will be slightly different from those of other comrades-in-arms in the service. In the end, the highest praise that can be said for all of them is that they did their duty, manfully faced the dangers and hardships of army life, and contributed to the overall victory. A comrade of John Kelly's wrote the following: "As for bravery, I can't say that I have ever done anything to brag on. I always did my duty when called on, and was always with the regiment."[1] The four patriotic men whose reminiscences this book contains all did their duty and, in the end, no higher praise can be afforded them. They are but four stories out of the millions, North and South, who took an active part in the war.

Union Corps and Theaters of Operation

As can be seen from the accounts reproduced in this book, the theaters of operation for the various units of the Union Army took them to many and varied places in this country. The following is a listing of the Army Corps that existed in the Federal Army, along with a brief history of where each one saw service during the war:

FIRST CORPS

The First Corps was created on March 13, 1862, but was disbanded when its troops were sent to General John Pope's Army of Virginia on April 4, forming the Third Corps of that army. It was reformed on September 12, 1862, upon its return from that army. The First Corps was disbanded on March 24, 1864, when its surviving members were merged with the Fifth Corps. During the war, the First Corps served in all the major engagements of the Army of the Potomac, including Antietam, Fredericksburg, and Gettysburg.

SECOND CORPS

The Second Corps was created on March 3, 1862, and saw continuous service with the Army of the Potomac until it was disbanded on June 28, 1865. During that time, it took part in every major battle of the Army of the Potomac, including Antietam, Fredericksburg, Chancellorsville, Gettysburg, the Wilderness Campaign, and the siege of Richmond and Petersburg.

THIRD CORPS

The Third Corps was created in March of 1862 and fought in every major engagement of the Army of the Potomac until it was merged with the Second Corps on March 24, 1864.

FOURTH CORPS (ARMY OF THE POTOMAC)

The Fourth Corps was created on March 3, 1862, and participated in the Peninsula Campaign with the Army of the Potomac. Following that campaign, the Fourth Corps remained on the peninsula after the rest of the army was withdrawn. Troops were gradually transferred to North Carolina, Washington, and other places until the Fourth Corps was finally discontinued on August 1, 1863.

FOURTH CORPS (ARMY OF THE CUMBERLAND)

The Fourth Corps was created on September 28, 1863, by the merger of the Twentieth and Twenty-first Corps. It was assigned this numeric designation because of the fact that the Fourth Corps in the Army of the Potomac had already gone out of existence. The Fourth Corps fought with the Army of the Cumberland through all its engagements, including Chickamauga, Chattanooga, the Atlanta Campaign, Franklin, and Nashville. It was disbanded April 1, 1865.

FIFTH CORPS

The Fifth Corps was created on March 3, 1862. On April 4, it was detached and temporarily became the Second Corps in John Pope's Army of Virginia, but on May 28, it officially resumed its designation as the Fifth Corps. The Fifth Corps fought in every major engagement of the Army of the Potomac until it was disbanded at the end of the war.

SIXTH CORPS

The Sixth Corps was created on May 18, 1862. It participated in every major engagement of the Army of the Potomac and took part in General Phil Sheridan's Valley Campaign of 1864, fighting at Fisher's Hill and Cedar Creek. The Sixth Corps was disbanded on June 28, 1865.

SEVENTH CORPS (DEPARTMENT OF VIRGINIA)

The Seventh Corps was organized on July 22, 1862. It served in the coastal Virginia region and was based at Fortress Monroe. The Seventh Corps participated in the defense of Suffolk in 1863 and in the engagement at Deserted House, Virginia. It was discontinued on August 1, 1863.

SEVENTH CORPS (DEPARTMENT OF ARKANSAS)

The Seventh Corps was organized on January 6, 1864, as part of the Military Division of West Mississippi. It took part in General Steele's Arkansas Campaign and served in the Trans-Mississippi region until it was discontinued on August 1, 1865.

EIGHTH CORPS

The Eighth Corps was created on July 22, 1862, and was stationed at various places in Maryland and West Virginia. It mainly saw small-scale action in West Virginia, but it did take part in the battle of Monocacy on July 9, 1864. The Eighth Corps was disbanded on August 1, 1865.

NINTH CORPS

The Ninth Corps was created on July 22, 1862. It had previously seen service as Burnside's Expeditionary Corps and had taken part in the capture of Roanoke Island and New Bern. The Ninth Corps fought at Second Manassas, Chantilly, South Mountain, Antietam, and Fredericksburg before being transferred to the Department of the Ohio in March of 1863. It then took part in the campaign against Vicksburg and the siege of Knoxville before being transferred back to the Army of the Potomac in May of 1864. From that point to the end of the war, it took part in all of the campaigns of that army. The Ninth Corps was discontinued on August 1, 1865.

TENTH CORPS

The Tenth Corps was created on September 3, 1863, as a part of the Department of the South. It primarily saw service in the campaigns against Charleston, South Carolina; however, one division was sent to Florida and took part in the battle of Olustee in February of 1864. In April of 1864, it was transferred to the Army of the James in Virginia and took part in the battle of Drewry's Bluff and the operations against Petersburg and Richmond. The Tenth Corps was disbanded on August 1, 1865.

ELEVENTH CORPS

The Eleventh Corps was created on September 12, 1862. It had previously seen service as the First Corps of the Mountain Department under Generals William S. Rosecrans and John Fremont. It saw service in every major engagement of the Army of the Potomac through the Gettysburg Campaign. The Eleventh Corps was then sent to Chattanooga to relieve General Rosecrans's Army that was besieged there. It took part in the battles for Chattanooga, the relief of Knoxville, the campaign for Atlanta, the March to the Sea, and the Carolinas Campaign. In April of 1864, it was merged with the Twelfth Corps to form the new Twentieth Corps.

TWELFTH CORPS

The Twelfth Corps was created on September 12, 1862, from the Second Corps, Army of Virginia, under General Nathaniel Banks. It served in every major engagement of the Army of the Potomac through the Gettysburg Campaign, after which it was transferred west to Chattanooga to help raise the siege of that place. The Twelfth Corps took part in the battles at Chattanooga, the Atlanta Campaign, the March to the Sea, and the Carolinas Campaign. It was merged with the Eleventh Corps in April of 1864 to form the new Twentieth Corps.

THIRTEENTH CORPS

The Thirteenth Corps was created on October 24, 1862, in the Department of the Tennessee. The Thirteenth Corps saw service in the Yazoo Expedition, Chickasaw Bluffs, Arkansas Post, Vicksburg, Helena, Port Gibson, and Jackson before being transferred to the Army of the Gulf on August 7, 1863. With that army, it saw action in the Red River Campaign and the capture of Mobile. The Thirteenth Corps was disbanded on July 20, 1865.

FOURTEENTH CORPS

The Fourteenth Corps was created on January 9, 1863, when the Army of the Ohio was redesignated the Army of the Cumberland. The Fourteenth Corps saw service at Stones River, Chickamauga, the Chattanooga Campaign, the Atlanta Campaign, the March to the Sea, and the Carolinas Campaign. It was disbanded on August 1, 1865.

FIFTEENTH CORPS

The Fifteenth Corps was created on December 18, 1862, in the Army of the Tennessee. The Fifteenth Corps participated in the Yazoo Expedition, the Vicksburg Campaign, the Chattanooga Campaign, the relief of Knoxville, the Atlanta Campaign, the March to the Sea, and the Carolinas Campaign. It was disbanded on August 1, 1865.

SIXTEENTH CORPS

The Sixteenth Corps was created on December 18, 1862. During the war, the Sixteenth Corps or portions thereof saw service at Vicksburg, Chattanooga, the Atlanta Campaign, and the Red River Campaign. The Sixteenth Corps was disbanded on November 1, 1864, but a portion of it was sent to Nashville to assist General Thomas's army and participated in the battle at that place.

SEVENTEENTH CORPS

The Seventeenth Corps was created on December 18, 1862. It took part in whole or by detachments in the Vicksburg Campaign, Sherman's Meridian Campaign, the Atlanta Campaign, the March to the Sea, the Carolinas Campaign, the Red River Campaign, and the battle of Nashville. The Seventeenth Corps was disbanded on August 1, 1865.

EIGHTEENTH CORPS

The Eighteenth Corps was created on December 24, 1862, from troops in the Department of North Carolina. It took part in the operations in and around Charleston harbor until it was transferred to the Army of the James in Virginia in April of 1864. It then fought at Drewry's Bluff, Cold Harbor,

Bermuda Hundred, and the campaigns against Petersburg and Richmond until it was disbanded at the end of the war.

NINETEENTH CORPS

The Nineteenth Corps was created on January 5, 1863, from troops in the Department of the Gulf. In whole or by detachments it took part in the Port Hudson Campaign, the Red River Campaign, the battle of Sabine Crossroads, the battle of Fisher's Hill, the battle of Cedar Creek, the occupation of Savannah, and the capture of Mobile. The Nineteenth Corps was disbanded on March 20, 1865.

TWENTIETH CORPS

The Twentieth Corps was created on April 4, 1864, by the merger of the Eleventh and Twelfth Corps. It served in the Atlanta Campaign, the March to the Sea, and the Carolinas Campaign. The Twentieth Corps was disbanded on June 1, 1865.

TWENTY-FIRST CORPS

The Twenty-first Corps was created on January 9, 1863, from troops from the Army of the Cumberland. The only battle the Twenty-first Corps took part in was Chickamauga. On October 9, 1864, it was merged with the Twentieth Corps to form the new Fourth Corps.

TWENTY-SECOND CORPS

The Twenty-second Corps was created on February 2, 1863, from troops occupying the defenses of Washington. This Corps's only action occurred when General Jubal Early's Confederate Army attacked Washington on July 12, 1864.

TWENTY-THIRD CORPS

The Twenty-third Corps was created on April 27, 1863, from troops from the Department of the Ohio. The Twenty-third Corps fought in the Knoxville Campaign, the Atlanta Campaign, at Franklin, and at Nashville before being transferred to North Carolina to take part in the capture of Fort Fisher. The Twenty-third Corps was disbanded on August 1, 1865.

TWENTY-FOURTH CORPS

The Twenty-fourth Corps was created on December 3, 1864, from troops of the Tenth and Eighteenth Corps, Army of the James. In whole or in part it took part in the capture of Fort Fisher, North Carolina, and the operations around Petersburg. The Twenty-fourth Corps was disbanded on August 1, 1865.

TWENTY-FIFTH CORPS

The Twenty-fifth Corps was created on December 3, 1864. It bears the distinction of being the only all-black corps in American military history. In whole or in part it participated in the capture of Fort Fisher, North Carolina; the operations around Petersburg; and the postwar occupation of Texas. The Twenty-fifth Corps was disbanded on January 8, 1866.

FIRST CORPS (ARMY OF THE OHIO)

The First Corps was created on September 29, 1862. It took part in the Perryville Campaign before being merged into the Fourteenth Corps on October 24, 1862.

SECOND CORPS (ARMY OF THE OHIO)

The Second Corps was created in September of 1862. It fought at Bardstown and in the Perryville Campaign before being merged into the Fourteenth Corps on October 24, 1862.

THIRD CORPS (ARMY OF THE OHIO)

The Third Corps was created in September of 1862. It took part in the Perryville Campaign before being merged into the Fourteenth Corps on October 24, 1862.

CAVALRY CORPS (MILITARY DIVISION OF MISSISSIPPI)

The Cavalry Corps was created in October 1864. In whole or in part it participated in the battle of Nashville, the battle of Columbus, the Carolinas Campaign, and the battle of Bentonville.

RESERVE CORPS (ARMY OF THE CUMBERLAND)

The Reserve Corps was created on June 8, 1863. It served through the Tullahoma Campaign and at Chickamauga before being portioned out to the Fourth and Fourteenth Corps on October 9, 1863.

RESERVE CORPS (ARMY OF THE GULF)

The Reserve Corps was created on December 5, 1864. It was merged into the Thirteenth Corps on February 18, 1865.

SOUTH CAROLINA EXPEDITIONAL CORPS

The South Carolina Corps was created in September of 1861. It took part in the capture of Port Royal. Thereafter, it formed the nucleus from which the Tenth Corps was formed.

FIRST CORPS (ARMY OF VIRGINIA)

The First Corps was created on June 26, 1862, from troops of the Mountain Department under General John Fremont. It took part in General Pope's Virginia Campaign and the battle of Second Manassas before being merged into the Eleventh Corps on September 12, 1862.

SECOND CORPS (ARMY OF VIRGINIA)

The Second Corps was created on June 26, 1863, from troops from the Department of the Shenandoah. It participated in Pope's Virginia Campaign and in the battle of Second Manassas before being merged into the Twelfth Corps in September of 1862.

THIRD CORPS (ARMY OF VIRGINIA)

The Third Corps was created on June 26, 1863, from troops in the Department of the Rappahannock (the original First Corps). It participated in Pope's Virginia Campaign and in the battle of Second Manassas before once more being designated the First Corps, following that campaign.

CAVALRY CORPS (ARMY OF THE POTOMAC)

The Cavalry Corps was created in July of 1862. It fought in every major engagement of the Army of the Potomac until it was disbanded in May of 1865.[1]

"The Blue and the Gray"

By the flow of inland river,
Whence the fleets of iron have fled,
Where the blades of the grave-grass
    quiver,
Asleep are the ranks of the dead:
Under the sod and the dew,
Waiting the judgment-day;
Under the one, the Blue,
Under the other, the Gray.

These in the robings of glory,
Those in the gloom of defeat,
All with the battle-blood gory,
In the dusk of eternity meet:
Under the sod and the dew,
Waiting the judgment-day;
Under the laurel, the Blue,
Under the willow, the Gray.

From the silence of sorrowful hours
The desolate mourners go,
Lovingly laden with flowers
Alike for the friend and the foe:
Under the sod and the dew,
Waiting the judgment-day;
Under the roses, the Blue,
Under the lilies, the Gray.

So with an equal splendor,
The morning sun-rays fall,
With a touch impartially tender,
On the blossoms blooming for all:
Under the sod and the dew,

Waiting the judgment-day;
Broidered with gold, the Blue,
Mellowed with gold, the Gray.

So, when the summer calleth,
On forrest and field of grain,
With an equal mummur falleth
The cooling drip of the rain:
Under the sod and the dew,
Waiting the judgment-day;
Wet with the rain, the Blue,
Wet with the rain, the Gray.

Sadly, but not with upbraiding,
The generous deed was done,
In the storm of the years that are fad-
    ing
No braver battle was won:
Under the sod and the dew,
Waiting the judgment-day;
Under the blossoms, the Blue,
Under the garlands, the Gray.

No more shall the war cry sever,
Or the winding rivers be red;
They banish our anger forever
When they laurel the graves of our
    dead!
Under the sod and the dew,
Waiting the judgment-day;
Love and tears for the Blue,
Tears and love for the Gray.
Francis Finch[1]

Chapter Notes

Chapter One

1. Muster and Descriptive Cards, William Glisan Service Record, National Archives, Washington, D.C.

2. E. Hannaford, *The Story of a Regiment: A History of the Campaigns, and Associations in the Field, of The Sixth Regiment Ohio Volunteer Infantry* (Cincinnati, Oh.: E. Hannaford, 1868), 36.

3. J.T. Headley, "The Great Rebellion: A History of the Civil War in the United States," *The National Tribune*, Washington, D.C., 1898, 255.

4. Hannaford, *The Sixth Ohio*, 422.

5. *Ibid.*, 442–443.

6. *Ibid.*, 443–444.

7. *Ibid.*, 445–446.

8. *Ibid.*, 450.

9. Peter J. Parish, *The American Civil War* (New York: 1975), Holmes & Meier, 296.

10. Glenn Tucker, *Chickamauga: Bloody Battle in the West* (Dayton, Oh.: Morningside Bookshop, 1976), 113–114.

11. Samuel M. Schmucker, *The History of the Civil War in the United States: Its Cause, Origin, Progress and Conclusion* (Philadelphia, Pa.: Jones Brothers, 1865), 597, Robert Underwood Johnson and Clarence Clough Buel, *Battles and Leaders of the Civil War*, Vol. 3, (New York: Castle Books, 1956), 670–672.

12. Johnson and Buel, *Battles and Leaders*, Vol. 3 73; and William H. Price, *The Civil War Centennial Handbook* (Arlington, Va.: Prince Lithography, 1961), 68; Hannaford, *The Sixth Ohio*, 458.

13. C.R. Graham, *Under Both Flags: A Panorama of the Great Civil War* (Chicago, Il.: W.S. Reeve, 1896), 477.

14. Tucker, *Chickamauga: Bloody Battle in the West*, 380–381.

15. Hannaford, *The Sixth Ohio*, 477.

16. *Ibid.*, 480–481.

17. *Ibid.*, 480.

18. Ezra J. Warner, *Generals in Blue: Lives of the Union Commanders* (Baton Rouge: Louisiana State University Press, 1964), 100.

19. Hannaford, *The Sixth Ohio*, 483–484.

20. Howard N. Meyer, *Let Us Have Peace: The Story of Ulysses S. Grant* (New York: Collier Books, 1966), 111–112.

21. Robert E. Denny, *The Civil War Years: A Day-by-Day Chronicle* (New York: Gramercy Books, 1992), 334.

22. Hannaford, *The Sixth Ohio*, 487.

23. Bob Young, and Jean Young, *Reluctant Warrior: Ulysses S. Grant* (New York: Julian Messner, 1971), 110.

24. Johnson and Buel, *Battles and Leaders*, Vol. 3, 684–688.

25. *Ibid.*, 690.

26. Hannaford, *The Sixth Ohio*, 497–498.

27. *Ibid.*, 498–499.

28. Johnson and Buel, *Battles and Leaders*, Vol. 3, 703–704.

29. Clement A. Evans, *Confederate Military History: Tennessee* (New York: Blue & Grey Press, 1956), 118–119.

30. Maury Klein, "The Knoxville Campaign," *Civil War Times Illustrated*, (November 1971, 6–8, 40–42.

31. Henry Davenport, Northrup, *Life and Deeds of General Sherman Including the Story of His Great March to the Sea* (Harrisburg: Pennsylvania, 1891), 379–380.

32. Klein, "The Knoxville Campaign," 42; Jeffery D. Wert, *General James Longstreet: The Confederacy's Most Controversial Soldier* (New York: Touchstone Books, 1993), 355–356.

33. Johnson and Buel, *Battles and Leaders*, Vol. 3, 750–751.

34. *Ibid.*, 673.

35. Hannaford, *The Sixth Ohio*, 522–523.

36. *Ibid.*, 523.

37. *Ibid.*

38. Wert, *General James Longstreet*, 355.

39. Hannaford, *The Sixth Ohio*, 524.

40. *Ibid.*, 524.

41. William T. Sherman, *Memoirs of General William T. Sherman*, Vol. 1, D (New York: Appleton, 1865), 386.

42. Hannaford, *The Sixth Ohio*, 521.

43. Frederick H. Dyer, *A Compendium of the War of Rebellion* (Des Moines, Ia.: F.H. Dyer, 1908), 1499; Pension Papers, William Glisan Pension Records, National Archives, Washington, D.C.

44. Pension Papers, William Glisan Pension records, National Archives, Washington, D.C.

45. Dyer, *Compendium of the War*, 1498–1499.

46. Hannaford, *The Sixth Ohio*, 616–617.

Chapter Two

1. Floyd G. Hoenstine, *Military Services and Geneological Records of Soldiers of Blair County Pennsylvania* (Hollidaysburg, Pa.: Blair County Historical Society, 1940), 131–132.

2. Muster and Descriptive Cards, Duncan Military Service Records, National Archives, Washington, D.C.

3. W. Wayne Smith, *The Price of Patriotism: Indiana County, Pennsylvania and the Civil War* (Shippensburg, Pa.: Burd Street Press, 1998), 60.

4. Daniel Carroll Toomey, *The Civil War in Maryland* (Baltimore, Md.: Toomey Press), 75; Stephen Schlosnagle, *Garrett County: A History of Maryland's Tableland* (Parsons, W. Va.: McClain Printing, 1978), 253; Harry I. Stegmaier, *Allegheny County: A History* (Parsons, W. Va.: McClain Printing, 1976), 184.

5. Boyd B. Stutler, *West Virginia in the Civil War* (Charleston, W. Va.: Education Foundation, 1966), 231–236.

6. Stegmaier, *Alleghany County: A History*, 184–185.

7. *Ibid.*, 187.

8. Schlosnagle, *Garrett County*, 235.

9. Phil Conley, *Beacon Lights of West Virginia History* (Charleston: West Virginia, 1939), 253.

10. Frederick H. Dyer, *A Compendium of the War of Rebellion* (Des Moines, Ia.: F.H. Dyer, 1908), 1592.

11. John D. Billings, *Hardtack & Coffee: The Unwritten Story of Army Life* (Lincoln: University of Nebraska Press, 1993), 147–155.

12. Toomey, *The Civil War in Maryland*, 95.

13. Smith, *The Price of Patriotism*, 84.

14. Dyer, *Compendium of the War*, 1625.

15. Graves Registration Book; Indiana County Historical Society; Indiana, Pennsylvania.

16. Samuel P. Bates, *History of Pennsylvania Volunteers, 1861–1865* (Harrisburg: State of Pennsylvania, 1866–1873), 1319; Dyer, *Compendium of the War*, 1578.

Chapter Three

1. Frederick H. Dyer, *Compendium of the War of Rebellion* (Des Moines, Ia.: F.H. Dyer, 1908), 1063.

2. Muster and Descriptive Roll, John M. Kelly Service Records, National Archives, Washington, D.C.

3. Dyer, *Compendium of the War*, 1528.

4. Charles M. Clark, *The History of the Thirty-Ninth Regiment Illinois Volunteer Veteran Infantry (Yates Phalanx) in the War of the Rebellion 1861–1865* (Chicago, Il.: Veteran Association of the Regiment, 1889).

5. *Ibid.*, 109–110.

6. Ezra J. Warner, *Generals in Blue: Lives of the Union Commanders* (Baton Rouge: Louisiana State University Press, 1964), 274–275.

7. Clark, *Yates Phalanx*, 111–112.

8. *Ibid.*, 112.

9. *Ibid.*, 112–113.

10. Clark, *Yates Phalanx*, 115; Robert Underwood Johnson, and Clarence Clough Buel, *Battles and Leaders of the Civil War*, Vol. 4 (New York: Castle Books, 1956), 54; J.T. Headley, "The Great Rebellion: A History of the Civil War in the United States," *The National Tribune*, Washington, D.C., 1898, 182.

11. Clark, *Yates Phalanx*, 120.

12. *Ibid.*, 124–125.

13. *Ibid.*, 126.

14. Hamilton Cochran, *Blockade Runners of the Confederacy* (New York: Bobbs-Merrill, 1958), 281–283.

15. Clark, *Yates Phalanx*, 132.

16. *Ibid.*, 133.

17. *Ibid.*, 134–135.

18. *Ibid.*, 136–137.

19. Russell Duncan, *Blue-Eyed Child of Fortune: The Civil War Letters of Col. Robert Gould Shaw* (New York: Avon Books, 1994), 387.

20. Clark, *Yates Phalanx*, 142.

21. *Ibid.*, 150.

22. *Ibid.*, 143.

23. *Ibid.*, 144.

24. *Ibid.*, 145–148.

25. *Ibid.*, 153–155.

26. Dyer, *Compendium of the War*, 1063; Johnson and Buel, *Battles and Leaders*, Vol. 4, 103.

27. Johnson and Buel, *Battles and Leaders*, Vol. 4, 355–357.

28. W.E. Woodward, *Meet General Grant* (New York: Literary Guild of America, 1928), 320–321.

29. Johnson and Buel, *Battles and Leaders*, Vol. 4, 206.

30. Frederic S. Klein, "Bottling Up Ben Butler at Bermuda Hundred," *Civil War Times Illustrated*, November 1967, 5–6, 11.

31. *Ibid.*, 11, 45.

32. Clark, *Yates Phalanx*, 187.

33. Klein, "Bottling Up Ben Butler," 45–45.

34. Clark, *Yates Phalanx*, 200–201.

35. *Ibid.*, 202–203.

36. *Ibid.*, 204.

37. Robert E. Denney, *The Civil War Years: A Day-by-Day Chronicle* (New York: Gramercy Books, 1998), 427.

38. Klein, "Bottling Up Ben Butler," 47.

39. Clark, *Yates Phalanx*, 205–206.

40. William H. Price, *The Civil War Centennial Handbook* (Arlington, Va.: Prince Lithograph, 1961), 68.

41. James P. Boyd, *The Life of General William J. Sherman* (New York: Publisher's Union, 1891), 302.

42. Clark, *Yates Phalanx*, 459.

43. *Ibid.*, 210–211.

44. Death Report and Personal Effects Voucher, John M. Kelly Service Record, National Archives, Washington, D.C.

45. Clark, *Yates Phalanx*, 449–463.

46. Dyer, *Compendium of the War*, 1063.

Chapter Four

1. Certificate of Death, George Schmittle Pension Record, National Archives, Washington, D.C.

2. Invalid Discharge, George Schmittle Service Record, National Archives, Washington, D.C.; Floyd G. Hoenstine, *Military Services and Geneological Records of Soldiers of Blair County* (Hollidaysburg, Pa.: Blair County Historical Society, 1940), 255.

3. Hoenstine, *Soldiers of Blair County*, 126, 136.

4. Harold, Hand, Jr., *One Good Regiment: The 13th Pennsylvania Cavalry in the Civil War, 1861–1865* (Victoria, B.C. Canada: Trafford Books, 2000), 81–82, 84; Edward G. Longacre, *Lee's Cavalrymen: A History of the Mounted Forces of the Army of Northern Virginia* (Harrisburg, Pa.: Stackpole Books, 2002), 255–257.

5. Longacre, *Lee's Cavalrymen*, 242–244.

6. Ovid L. Futch, *History of Andersonville Prison* (Gainesville: 1978), 4.

7. James M. McPherson, *Battle Cry of Freedom: The Civil War Era* (New York: Ballantine Books, 1988), 797.

8. *Ibid.*, 246.

9. J.P. Ray, *The Diary of a Dead Man 1862* (New York: Eastern Acorn Press, 1981), 198, 200–201.

10. Futch, *History of Andersonville*, 71; Warren Lee Goss, *The Soldier's Story of His Captivity at Andersonville, Belle Isle, and Other Rebel Prison* (Boston, Ma.: I.N. Richardson, 1873), 156.

11. Futch, *History of Andersonville*, 71.

12. *Ibid.*, 74.

13. *Ibid.*, 70–71.

14. Bruce Catton, *John Ransom's Diary* (New York: Dell Books, 1964), 107–108.

15. Futch, *History of Andersonville*, 62.

16. *Ibid.*, 49.

17. John W. Urban, *Battlefield of Prison Pen or Through the War and Thrice a Prisoner, in Rebel Dungeons* (Philadelphia: Edgewood, 1882), 374–375.

18. Burke Davis, *The Civil War: Strange & Fascinating Facts* (New York: Fairfax Press, 1982), 220.

19. Urban, *Battlefield of Prison Pen*, 428–429.

20. Muster and descriptive cards, George Schmittle service record, National Archives, Washington, D.C.; Hand, *One Good Regiment*, 196–205.

21. Adjutant General's Report, April 18, 1894, and Invalid Pension Application, 1894, George Schmittle Pension Records, National Archives, Washington, D.C.

22. Pension Application, dated 1898, George Schmittle Pension Papers, National Archives, Washington, D.C.

23. Hoenstine, *Soldiers of Blair County*, 255.

24. Samuel P. Bates, *History of Pennsylvania Volunteers, 1861–1865* (Harrisburg: State of Pennsylvania, 1866–1873), 1267–1271; Frederick H. Dyer, *Compendium of the War of Rebellion* (Des Moines Io.: F.H. Dyer, 1908), 1566.

25. Bates, *History of Pennsylvania Volunteers*, 1272–1279.

Epilogue

1. Charles M. Clark, *The History of the Thirty-Ninth Regiment Illinois Volunteer Veteran Infantry (Yates Phalanx) in the War of the Rebellion 1861–1865* (Chicago, Il.: Veteran Association of the Regiment, 1889), 334.

Appendix I

1. Francis Trevelyan Miller, *The Photographic History of the Civil War: The Armies and Lenders* (New York: Castle Books, 1957), 186–238.

Appendix II

1. Francis Trevelyan Miller, *The Photographic History of the Civil War: Poetry and Eloquence from the Blue and the Gray* (New York: Castle Books, 1957), 270, 272.

Bibliography

"Adjutant General's Report (April 18, 1894) and Invalid Pension Application (1894), George Schmittle Pension Records." Washington, D.C.: National Archives.

Amann, William. *Personnel of the Civil War.* New York: Thomas Yoseloff, 1961.

Badeau, Adam. *Military History of Ulysses S. Grant from April 1861 to April 1865.* New York: D. Appleton, 1868.

Barnes, Frank. *Fort Sumter National Monument South Carolina.* Washington, D.C.: Government Printing Office, 1952.

Billings, John D. *Hardtack & Coffee: The Unwritten Story of Army Life.* Lincoln: University of Nebraska Press, 1993.

Boyd, James P. *The Life of General William T. Sherman.* New York: Publisher's Union, 1891.

Carse, Robert. *Blockade: The Civil War at Sea.* New York: Rinehart, 1958.

Catton, Bruce. *John Ransom's Diary.* New York: Dell Books, 1964.

"Certificate of Death, George Schmittle Pension Record." Washington, D.C.: National Archives.

Clark, Charles M. *The History of the Thirty-Ninth Regiment Illinois Volunteer Veteran Infantry.* (Yates Phalanx) Chicago, Il.: Veteran Association of the Regiment, 1889.

Cochran, Hamilton. *Blockade Runners of the Confederacy.* New York: Bobbs-Merrill, 1958.

Conley, Phil. *Beacon Lights of West Virginia History.* Charleston: West Virginia, 1939.

Davis, Burke. *The Civil War: Strange & Fascinating Facts.* New York: Fairfax Press, 1982.

"Death Report and Personal Effects Voucher, John M. Kelly Service Records." Washington, D.C.: National Archives.

Denney, Robert E. *The Civil War Years: A Day-by-Day Chronicle.* New York: Gramercy Books, 1992.

Duncan, Russell. *Blue-Eyed Child of Fortune: The Civil War Letters of Colonel Robert Gould Shaw.* New York: Avon Books, 1994.

Dyer, Frederick H. *A Compendium of the War of Rebellion.* Des Moines, F.H. Dyer, 1908.

Editors of Time Life. *A Compendium of the War of Rebellion.* New York: Time Life Books, 1996.

Evans, Gen. Clement. *Confederate Military History.* New York: Blue and Grey Press, 1956.

Futch, Ovid L. *History of Andersonville Prison.* Gainesville: University of Florida Press, 1978.

Goss, Warren Lee. *The Soldier's Story of His Captivity at Andersonville, Belle Isle, and Other Rebel Prison.* Boston, Mass.: I.N. Richardson, 1873.

Graham, C.R. *Under Both Flags: A Panorama of the Great Civil War.* Chicago, Il.: W.S. Reeve, 1896.

Grant, Ulysses. *The Personal Memoirs of U.S. Grant*, Vol. 2. New York: Charles L. Webster, 1885.

Graves Registration Book. Indiana, Pa.: Indiana County Historical Society.

Guernsey, Alfred H., and Henry M. Alden. *Harper's Pictorial History of the Civil War.* New York: Fairfax Press, 1866.

Hand, Harold, Jr. *One Good Regiment: The 13th Pennsylvania in the Civil War.* Victoria, BC, Canada: Trafford.

Hannaford, E. *The Story of a Regiment: A History of the Campaigns, and Associations in the Field, of the Sixth Regiment Ohio Volunteer Infantry.* Cincinnati, Oh.: E. Hannaford, 1868.

Headley, J.T. "The Great Rebellion: A History of the Civil War in the United States." *The National Tribune.* Washington, D.C.: 1898.

Herbert, H.A. *Official Records of the Union and Confederate Navies in the War of the Rebellion.* Washington, D.C.: Government Printing Office, 1895.

Hoenstine, Floyd G. *Military Services and Genealogical Records of Soldiers of Blair County Pennsylvania.* Hollidaysburg, Pa.: Blair Country Historical Society, 1940.

"Invalid Discharge, George Schmittle Service Record." Washington, D.C.: National Archives.

Johnson, Rossiter. *Campfires and Battlefields: The Pictorial History of the Civil War.* New York: Civil War Press, 1967.

Klein, Frederic S. "Battle Up Ben Butler at Bermuda Hundred." *Civil War Times Illustrated* (November 1967): 5–6, 11.

Klein, Maury. "The Knoxville Campaign." *Civil War Times Illustrated* (November 1971): 6–8, 40–42.

LeVan, Russell G. *The Great War of Destruction.* Raleigh, N.C.: Pentland Press, 1999.

Longacre, Edward G. *Lee's Cavalrymen: A History of the Mounted Forces of the Army of Northern Virginia.* Harrisburg, Pa.: Stackpole Books, 2002.

Lowdermilk, Will H. *History of Cumberland, Maryland from the Time of the Indian Town, Caiuctucuc in 1728, Up to the Present Day.* Baltimore, Md.: Regional, 1976.

Lykes, Richard Wayne. *Petersburg National Military Park.* Washington, D.C.: Virginia, Government Printing Office, 1951.

McPherson, James M. *Battle Cry of Freedom: The Civil War Era.* New York: Ballantine Books, 1988.

Meyer, Howard N. *Let Us Have Peace: The Story of Ulysses S. Grant.* New York: Collier Books, 1966.

Miller, Francis Trevelyan. *The Photographic History of the Civil War: Prisons and Hospitals.* New York: Castle Books, 1957.

Moody, William H., and Edward K. Rawson. *Official Records of the Union and Confederate Navies in the War of the Rebellion*, Series 1, Vol. 14, Washington, D.C.: Government Printing Office, 1902.

"Muster and Descriptive Cards, Duncan Military Service Records." Washington, D.C.: National Archives.

"Muster and Descriptive Cards, William Glisan Service Record." Washington, D.C.: National Archives.

"Muster and Descriptive Roll, John M. Kelly Service Records." Washington, D.C.: National Archives.

Northrup, Henry Davenport. *Life and Deeds of General Sherman Including the Story of His Great March to the Sea.* Harrisburg: Pennsylvania, 1891.

"Pension Application (dated 1898), George Schmittle Pension Papers." Washington, D.C.: National Archives.

"Pension Papers William Glisan Invalid Pension Records." Washington, D.C.: National Archives.

Price, William H. *The Civil War Centennial Handbook*. Arlington, Va.: Prince Lithograph Co., 1961.

Randall, J.G. *The Civil War and Reconstruction*. Lexington, Mass.: D.C. Heath, 1969.

Ray, J.P. *The Diary of a Dead Man 1862–1864*. New York: Eastern Acorn Press, 1981.

Richardson, Albert D. "The Field, Dungeon, and Escape." *The National Tribune*, Washington, D.C., 1897.

Robertson, James I., Jr. *Soldiers Blue & Gray*. New York: Warner Books, 1991.

Schlosnagle, Stephen. *Garrett County: A History of Maryland's Tableland*. Parsons, W. Va.: McClain Printing, 1978.

Scott, Robert N. *The War of the Rebellion: A Compilation of the Official Records of the Union and Confederate Armies*. Washington, D.C.: Government Printing Office, 1890.

Sherman, William T. *Memoirs of General William T. Sherman*, Vol. 1. New York: D. Appleton, 1875.

Smith, W. Wayne. *The Price of Patriotism: Indiana County, Pennsylvania and the Civil War*. Shippensburg, Pa.: Burd Street Press, 1998.

Stegmaier, Harry I. *Allegheny County: A History*. Parsons, W. Va.: McClain Printing, 1976.

Stewart, J.T. *Indiana County Pennsylvania: Her People, Past and Present*. Chicago, Il.: J.H. Beers, 1913.

Stutler, Boyd B. *West Virginia in the Civil War*. Charleston, W. Va.: Education Foundation, 1966.

Sullivan, James R. *Chickamauga and Chattanooga Battlefields*. Washington, D.C.: Government Printing Office, 1956.

Toomey, Daniel Carroll. *The Civil War in Maryland*. Baltimore, Md.: Toomey Press, 1986.

Truesdale, Captain John. *The Blue Coats and How They Lived, Fought and Died for the Union*. Philadelphia, Pa.: Jones Brothers, 1867.

Tucker, Glenn. *Chickamauga: Bloody Battle in the West*. Dayton, Oh.: Morningside Bookshop, 1976.

Urban, John W. *Battlefield and Prison Pen or Through the War and Thrice a Prisoner in Rebel Dungeons*. Philadelphia: Edgewood, 1892.

Wert, Jeffrey D. *General James Longstreet: The Confederacy's Most Controversial Soldier*. New York: Touchstone Books, 1993.

Williams, Major George F. *The Memorial War Book: As Drawn for the Historical Records and Personal Narratives of the Men Who Served in the Great Struggle*. New York: Arno Press, 1979.

Wilmer, L. Allison. *History and Roster of Maryland Volunteers, War of 1861–5*. Baltimore, Md.: Press of Guggenheimer, Weil, 1898.

Woodward, W.E. *Meet General Grant*. New York: The Literary Guild of America, 1928.

Young, Bob, and Jan Young. *Reluctant Warrior: Ulysses S. Grant*. New York: Julian Messner, 1971.

Index

Ames, Gen. Adelbert 152
Anderson, Col. Nicholas 44
Andersonville Prison 2, 3, 162, 165, 166, 167, 168, 169, 170, 171, 172, 179, 181
Army of Northern Virginia 11, 39, 45, 135, 137, 142
Army of Tennessee 30
Army of the Cumberland 30, 196, 198, 199
Army of the James 82, 137, 138, 157, 197
Army of the Potomac 135, 136, 137, 142, 149, 157, 185, 195, 196
Atlanta, Ga. 11, 150, 151, 153
Averill, Gen. William 154

Baltimore & Ohio Railroad 64, 69, 77, 80, 82
Banks, Gen. Nathaniel 134
Battery Gregg 113, 115, 157
Beauregard, Gen. P.G.T., C.S.A. 113, 138
Belle Isle Prison 163, 168
Bermuda Hundred 82, 138, 143, 145, 146, 147, 148, 149, 151, 152, 153
Birney, Gen. David 151, 154
Blacklog, Pa. 114, 124, 125, 126
Bragg, Gen. Braxton, C.S.A. 10, 11, 12, 16, 17, 19
Brooks, Gen. William 151
Brown's Ferry, Tenn. 25, 26, 28, 52
Buffington, Ohio 57
Burnside, Gen. Ambrose 32, 33, 35, 46, 52, 151, 197
Butler, Gen. Benjamin 82, 134, 136, 152, 157

Camp Buell, Ky. 51
Camp Cadwallader, Pa. 185
Camp Carroll, Md. 183
Camp Dennison, Ohio 51, 52
Camp Douglas, Ill. 127
Camp Fry, Ill. 127, 128

Camp Grant, Va. 130, 131, 132, 133
Camp Harrison, Ohio 5
Camp Lininger, Md. 78
Camp Parole, Md. 182
Camp Prince George County 140
Carlisle Barracks, Pa. 125, 182
Carnifex Ferry, Va. 5
Carrick's Ford, Va. 5, 51
Casey, Gen. Silas 132
Charleston, S.C. 1, 3, 34, 82, 83, 94, 95, 99, 108, 113, 117, 118, 153, 157
Chattanooga, Tenn. 3, 7, 10, 11, 12, 16, 17, 21, 23, 24, 26, 27, 28, 32, 33, 34, 39, 42, 48, 65
Chesapeake & Ohio Canal 59, 60, 64, 66, 77, 80
Chickamauga, Battle of 3, 15, 18, 44, 52, 68
City Point, Va. 135, 136, 157
Clarysville, Md. 62, 63
Coles Island, S.C. 105, 106
Corinth, Miss. 6
Cox, Cornelius 117
Crittenden, Gen. Thomas 20
C.S.S. *Alabama* 148
Cumberland, Md. 56, 57, 58, 62, 66, 70, 76, 86, 156
Curtin, Gov. Andrew 55

Davenport, Julia 88
Deadhouse 181
Deep Bottom, Va. 154
Drewry's Bluff, Va. 138, 157
Duncan, Will 2, 55, 65, 67, 70, 74, 77, 79, 191, 192
Du Pont, Admr. Henry 94

18th Corps 198
8th Corps 196
85th Pennsylvania Infantry 92, 93, 113, 116, 121, 147

211